IS CHRIST
DIVIDED?

by Gary Hargrave

LIVING WORD PUBLICATIONS

Is Christ Divided?
Copyright © 2014 by The Living Word

The Living Word is a California nonprofit corporation. All rights reserved. This publication may not be reproduced, in whole or in part, in any way, or by any means electronic or otherwise, including but not limited to photocopying, electronic transmission, or scanning, without written permission from the publisher and copyright holder.

Is Christ Divided? is a compilation of messages by Gary Hargrave and copyright The Living Word, *No Excuse for Division* © 1996; *The Pathway to Oneness* © 1996; *Baptized Into the Spirit of Unity* © 1997; *Stand in Your Place* © 1997; *God Has So Composed the Body* © 1997; *Am I Committed to Oneness?* © 1999; *Tabernacles: United, We Gather* © 1999; *The Call to Oneness* © 2000; *Why We Have the Church* © 2005; *That They May All Be One* © 2006; *Finding the Way Back Into Oneness* © 2008; *We Are Responsible for Oneness* © 2008; *We Are One Man* © 2008; *Oneness of Spirit Precedes Oneness of Faith* © 2008; *Our Unity Brings His Anointing* © 2009; *He Is Gathering the Nations* © 2010; *Oneness Triggers the Outpouring* © 2012; *There Is No Division in Christ's Body* © 2013; *Oneness—Our Authority to Bind Satan* © 2013; *Oneness— The Enabling to Fulfill Our Purpose* © 2013; *Our Faith for the Catholic Church* © 2013; *We Celebrate Christ's Coming in His Many-Membered Body* © 2013; *Only As One Can We Take the Kingdom* © 2013; *Making Disciples of the Nations* © 2013; *In Oneness and Filled With the Spirit* © 2013; *Remember, You Were Included* © 2013; *Immaturity Is the Direct Result of Division* © 2013; *The Ezekiel Company Prophesies Oneness* © 2013; *The Lord Our God Is One* © 2014; *The Bride of Christ* © 2014; *Our Oneness, the Measure of His Glory* © 2014.

Unless otherwise designated, all Scripture quotations are taken from the New American Standard Bible®, © 1960, 1962, 1963, 1968, 1971, 1972, 1973, 1975, 1977 by The Lockman Foundation. Used by permission.

Religious writing styles vary greatly among writers. This book follows the standards developed by Living Word Publications. Words such as Father, Son, Word, Living Word, Gospel, and Scripture are capitalized for emphasis, while the name "satan" is purposefully not capitalized. Additional style guides consulted for this book include The Chicago Manual of Style and The Associated Press.

For your convenience, Scriptures are included as footnotes on each page; if a Scripture appears more than once in a single chapter it is footnoted at its first reference.

Cover design by Laurie Beckman, Heidi Brown, and Joleen Poole.
© 2014 The Living Word. All rights reserved.

Printed in the U.S.A.
ISBN 978-1-891787-07-2
2014-1020-1R

Living Word Publications
The Living Word
P.O. Box 958 • North Hollywood, CA 91603

"The Word of God is living and powerful" logo is a registered trademark of The Living Word, a California nonprofit corporation, and may not be used without permission.

I dedicate this book to

Each and every one who has chosen to be a part of this Living Word family.

Since 1951 you have chosen to be led by a Living Word from God; you have opened your hearts not only to hear a teaching, but you have believed for God to work that Word in your own hearts and create you as the living vessels of that Word. Therefore, this book for you is not a compilation of sermons but the history of God working in the lives of a people to make these words on oneness a living reality available in the earth. Thank you!

I ask that you seek Him with all of your heart (Jeremiah 29:13); pursue always to "know Him, and the power of His resurrection" (Philippians 3:10); "do not grow weary of doing good" (2 Thessalonians 3:13); and above all, "beloved, if God so loved us, we also ought to love one another" (1 John 4:11)!

Acknowledgments

This book was made possible by the faith, intercession, and dedicated labor of many people. Diverse teams of careful "Word workers" in audio recording, cataloging, transcribing, editing, proofreading, layout, and design have devoted countless hours at Living Word Publications. Thank you to Rick Holbrook and Steve Seboldt whose hands, for many years, have been directly linked to this book and all that Living Word Publications produces.

We want to specifically acknowledge Chere Berman and Steve Alder, principal editors, and Matt Walkoe and Becky Seboldt for their final editing and evaluation, working closely with my wife Marilyn and myself. In addition, grateful recognition is given to Laurie Beckman, Heidi Brown, and Joleen Poole who comprise the art design team. We are also so thankful for the faith and energy of Rick and Lorena Holbrook, Silas and Selma Esteves, and Craig and Phyllis Haworth who helped create the atmosphere for these messages to be spoken.

Marilyn and I would like to express an extra special thanks to our grandson, Kane Kekaneakua Hargrave, who helped with the proofreading and who also enriches our lives and the life of our family with extraordinary gifts, joy, laughter, and love.

To acknowledge each individual who has been a part of producing this book would not be possible; however, acknowledging them in our hearts and prayers is something that we do every day.

"We give thanks to God always for all of you, making mention of you in our prayers; constantly bearing in mind your work of faith and labor of love" (1 Thessalonians 1:2-3).

Gary and Marilyn Hargrave

Contents

Introduction 1

CHAPTER 1   No Excuse for Division 5

CHAPTER 2   The Pathway to Oneness 15

CHAPTER 3   Baptized Into the Spirit of Unity..................... 23

CHAPTER 4   Stand in Your Place................................ 31

CHAPTER 5   God Has So Composed the Body..................... 39

CHAPTER 6   Am I Committed to Oneness? 47

CHAPTER 7   Tabernacles – The Great Ingathering................. 61

CHAPTER 8   Our Prime Directive................................ 71

CHAPTER 9   Are We the Church That Christ Spoke Of?............ 79

CHAPTER 10   That They May All Be One 83

CHAPTER 11   Finding the Way Back Into Oneness 91

CHAPTER 12   We Are Responsible for Oneness 99

CHAPTER 13   We Are One Man 107

CHAPTER 14   A Case for Unity Between Christianity and Judaism... 115

CHAPTER 15   Our Unity Brings His Anointing 127

CHAPTER 16   He Is Gathering the Nations 133

Chapter 17	Oneness Triggers the Outpouring	143
Chapter 18	There Is No Division in Christ's Body	155
Chapter 19	Oneness – Our Authority to Bind Satan	163
Chapter 20	Oneness – The Enabling to Fulfill Our Purpose	175
Chapter 21	Our Faith for the Catholic Church	185
Chapter 22	We Celebrate Christ's Coming in His Many-Membered Body	195
Chapter 23	Only As One Can We Take the Kingdom	205
Chapter 24	Making Disciples of the Nations	215
Chapter 25	In Oneness and Filled With the Spirit	221
Chapter 26	Remember, You Were Included	229
Chapter 27	Immaturity Is the Direct Result of Division	235
Chapter 28	Creating Oneness in the Body of Christ	251
Chapter 29	A Prophetic Message for the Church Today	263
Chapter 30	The Lord Our God Is One	273
Chapter 31	The Bride of Christ	287
Chapter 32	Our Oneness – The Measure of His Glory	305

Endorsements 321

Introduction

For those in The Living Word Fellowship, the subject of oneness in the Body of Christ has been an underlying theme for over sixty years. The true drive for oneness was instilled in our hearts by our spiritual father, John Robert Stevens, who began the churches of our fellowship in June of 1951 with the founding of Grace Chapel in South Gate, California. Those early days of Stevens' ministry, which created what would become The Living Word Fellowship, would find him seeking to impart oneness among Pentecostals, Lutherans, Baptists, and other denominational pastors. Then, during the mid-1960s, Stevens initiated regular weekly meetings with local pastors from several denominations. These meetings continued consistently for more than two and a half years. His heart was to help these men of God into the new day which the Lord, by revelation, had made real to him. The relationships that Stevens sought to develop with these church leaders included his ministering in their churches and allowing them to minister in his churches. He desired to teach and impart to them the vision he had of the unfolding Kingdom of God which was taking place in that generation.

These meetings were discontinued because they failed to produce the true fruit that Stevens was looking for. After seeking the Lord, it became real to him that, for this burden of oneness within the Body of Christ to be realized, he would have to first create oneness in the congregations that he was leading. Once that oneness was achieved, he would truly have the tidings necessary to run with this vision and impart it to the worldwide Body of Christ. Through the remainder of his ministry, Stevens continued to impart to people, by a Living Word from God, the ability to walk in the true oneness which Christ spoke of in John chapter 17. Stevens' faithfulness created in a body of believers the same cry that he had to see God pour out His glory in a true spiritual oneness.

Following John Stevens' death in June of 1983, my wife Marilyn and I continued his drive to see a body of people walking together in oneness. It became well-known throughout our churches that, as leaders of The Living Word Fellowship, our requirement was "you cannot be one with us and not be one with one another." God has taken many years to work oneness in us, because it is one thing to have the revelation of oneness and another thing entirely to have the manifestation of it. God has to create a pattern. That is what He did with Jesus. He created the pattern Son who was the firstborn among many brethren. It has to be done the first time before it can be duplicated. We could never be taking this step today with the global Body of Christ if we had not had this focus, and first achieved the oneness that God was looking for among ourselves. Now we can take that which God has hammered us into, and minister it to the rest of the Body of Christ.

The oneness that we experience as a fellowship is built upon the foundation created by John Robert Stevens, and I credit him for the entire revelation of oneness that is expressed in this book. All we are doing is expanding that revelation. *Is Christ Divided?* constitutes a chronology of how the Lord has led us, as a fellowship, into this experience of oneness. As you will notice by the descriptions at the start of each chapter, these messages cover almost eighteen years and came in a variety of places and to a variety of audiences. Some of the principles and Scriptures are repeated, but the application is unique depending on the location and the hearer. This book is a log of truth after truth, breakthrough after breakthrough, that came in our journey into oneness.

Now, more than ever, the world needs the Body of Christ to move in the power of God. The oneness that the early Church had must be restored. That oneness will be a witness for all the world to believe that Christ, in truth, was sent by the Father. This book will explain how it is incumbent upon us, as believers, to start moving in this oneness. We repent for the schisms in His Body, and determine to relate to our brothers, for whom Christ died. Our diversity will not be the cause of division; to the contrary, our diversity will create oneness when we see how much we need one another. The world will see the glory of God turned loose when the Body of Christ is one.

Chapter 1

No Excuse for Division

September 1, 1996
Living Word Chapel, Palmer Lake, Colorado

This message was spoken during a ministries conference that brought together pastors and other leaders of The Living Word Fellowship, as well as special guests from the Baptist community. The conference was titled "We Create Oneness."

When you look at the history of the Body of Christ, you realize that the original oneness unraveled back in the first century. What we struggle with today is not any different. We continue to fight the number one enemy of Christ's Body: the spirit of division. If you want to put it another way, it is the lack of oneness. There are really two things at work at the same time. While principalities and powers are warring against our spirits (Ephesians 6:12), there is also a tremendous need for us individually to reach into a level of oneness where we do not allow division.

We have nothing to fear from the satanic realm. Satan is like a roaring lion, but that is not the problem (1 Peter 5:8). When the

---

Ephesians 6:12 For our struggle is not against flesh and blood, but against the rulers, against the powers, against the world forces of this darkness, against the spiritual forces of wickedness in the heavenly places.

1 Peter 5:8 Be of sober spirit, be on the alert. Your adversary, the devil, prowls about like a roaring lion, seeking someone to devour.

devil came against Christ, it never stopped Him from fulfilling the will of God in His life. It never stopped Him from completing His Father's business, because His response was, "Satan has nothing in Me" (John 14:30).

Yes, there are spirits of division at work in a tremendous assault against the whole Body of Christ all over the world. But somewhere along the line, we have to put our foot down and say that there is no longer any excuse for schism or division. By the relationship of the Father and the Son, there is available in the Holy Spirit an unbroken oneness. But as long as we give ourselves an excuse for not being one, we will never reach into what is available to us. Christ said, "I and the Father are one" (John 10:30). We cannot separate them; the Father and the Son will not be separated. And somewhere, in the global Body of Christ, there has to be a place where we drive a stake into the ground and say, "This division is over!"

I am not talking about a man-made unity that suppresses individuality. We want people to move into the diversity of their ministries. If we keep people confined to an organization or an exclusive group, then we are creating our own kingdoms. We must refuse to have any barriers or boundaries. We cannot become exclusive entities hiding behind our walls of doctrine, safe and secure. That is not the truth of what we are about, and it is not what we are going to do. We should encourage others, minister the Lord to people, and reach out to young people. We should be eager to reach out in love to other cultures and other races with the Word that the Lord is giving us.

Let's look at what happened to the Church in the first century. They were scattered throughout all the earth. They took the Word of God to the whole civilized world as it existed in their time. The

---

John 14:30 "I will not speak much more with you, for the ruler of the world is coming, and he has nothing in Me."

persecution that came spread them all over the known world. It began with the stoning of Stephen (Acts 7:59—8:1). Everyone ran from the persecutions, and as a result, the Gospel was preached.

Simultaneously, however, the Church lost its power and its anointing. It began to decline until, at some point, it was not the *ekklesia*[1] that Christ spoke of. It was without the divine order and the leading of the Spirit. Now look around at the Church we have today; it is not even a semblance of what started on the Day of Pentecost. It is not what we read of in the first several chapters of the Book of Acts. It is not the same Church.

It is not good enough for us just to reach out. There has to be something greater; <u>there has to be a oneness that happens</u> with our outreach. This is the period of the end-time harvest (Revelation 14:15). You do not go out and harvest so that you can scatter the crop, do you? You gather the harvest together and bring all of it into the barn (Matthew 13:30). There is something in this hour that must happen, not just for us, but throughout the whole earth. Someone has to glue the Body of Christ back together.

Acts 7:59—8:1   And they went on stoning Stephen as he called upon the Lord and said, "Lord Jesus, receive my spirit!" [60] And falling on his knees, he cried out with a loud voice, "Lord, do not hold this sin against them!" And having said this, he fell asleep. [1] And Saul was in hearty agreement with putting him to death. And on that day great persecution arose against the church in Jerusalem; and they were all scattered throughout the regions of Judea and Samaria, except the apostles.

Revelation 14:15   And another angel came out of the temple, crying out with a loud voice to Him who sat on the cloud, "Put in your sickle and reap, because the hour to reap has come, because the harvest of the earth is ripe."

Matthew 13:30   "Allow both to grow together until the harvest; and in the time of the harvest I will say to the reapers, 'First gather up the tares and bind them in bundles to burn them up; but gather the wheat into my barn.'"

[1.] Greek word used in New Testament texts for the coming together or assembly of believers, and translated as "church" in English.

When the early apostles separated, it became a convenient excuse for the divisions that already existed. Conflict was already arising within the Church. Paul was rebuking Peter (Galatians 2:11-13). Barnabas was disagreeing with Paul about whether to take John Mark on a missionary journey (Acts 15:36-39). In another instance, one group of widows, the Hellenistic Jews, were griping about the Hebraic widows as to <u>who was getting the most soup</u> (Acts 6:1). <u>The seeds of division existed. They always have;</u> satan has made sure of that. When the apostles allowed the separation to happen, the Church did not come into a level of oneness that really reflected the relationship of Christ and the Father. In this day, however, we must come into something greater. It has to be real to us that there is only one way for the devil to stop what God started. The only way that the blood of Christ, which was spilled for us, can be averted from its fulfillment is that Christ be divided.

Remember, there is no division in the Body of Christ; He is one Body (Romans 12:5). We are Christ's Body (1 Corinthians 12:27);

Galatians 2:11-13 But when Cephas came to Antioch, I opposed him to his face, because he stood condemned. [12] For prior to the coming of certain men from James, he used to eat with the Gentiles; but when they came, he began to withdraw and hold himself aloof, fearing the party of the circumcision. [13] And the rest of the Jews joined him in hypocrisy, with the result that even Barnabas was carried away by their hypocrisy.

Acts 15:36-39 And after some days Paul said to Barnabas, "Let us return and visit the brethren in every city in which we proclaimed the word of the Lord, and see how they are." [37] And Barnabas was desirous of taking John, called Mark, along with them also. [38] But Paul kept insisting that they should not take him along who had deserted them in Pamphylia and had not gone with them to the work. [39] And there arose such a sharp disagreement that they separated from one another, and Barnabas took Mark with him and sailed away to Cyprus.

Acts 6:1 Now at this time while the disciples were increasing in number, a complaint arose on the part of the Hellenistic Jews against the native Hebrews, because their widows were being overlooked in the daily serving of food.

Romans 12:5 So we, who are many, are one body in Christ, and individually members one of another.

1 Corinthians 12:27 Now you are Christ's body, and individually members of it.

and it is deception to say, "I am Christ in the earth," but in your heart be divided from your brother who is also Christ, because Christ is not divided. Many times our diversities, our ministries, and our burdens in the Lord become convenient excuses for us not to pursue a real oneness. On the Day of Pentecost, the disciples stood up as one man (Acts 2:14). Peter may have spoken, but it did not matter who was talking; they had become one. However, that oneness began to dissipate. The power of God—the miracles and the authority that we need to see—is not here today.

Let's not fool ourselves; the Church as we know it is an emasculated version of what we read about in the Book of Acts. That emasculation process began with one thing: the dissipation of the oneness that was a reality on the Day of Pentecost when the Spirit fell upon them. Remember, it wasn't the Spirit falling on them that made them one. Acts 2:1 (KJV) records that they were already "all with one accord in one place." Because of that oneness, the Spirit fell. If we want to get the Spirit back into the Body of Christ, oneness must be released until we are in one accord again.

The Body of Christ cannot excuse itself any longer. We cannot accept schism and division, all in the name of the diversity of our ministries. As we experience a real oneness in our own midst, we will begin to experience it throughout the whole earth! The Body of Christ must become one man. Just as the apostles did in their age, we have allowed too much division to continue to exist. When problems arise, we should come together with fasting and prayer and seeking God until the division is gone, until the enemy comes and finds nothing in us (John 14:30). We must refuse to allow division

---

Acts 2:14 But Peter, taking his stand with the eleven, raised his voice and declared to them: "Men of Judea, and all you who live in Jerusalem, let this be known to you, and give heed to my words."

Acts 2:1, KJV And when the day of Pentecost was fully come, they were all with one accord in one place.

any longer by virtue of convenience. I loose us from the passivity that we have as the Body of Christ toward division. If we do not deal with it, we will allow this seed of destruction to continue to grow. Here in our hearts and throughout the Church, division must end.

We read in Ephesians the 4th chapter, "And He gave some as apostles, and some as prophets, and some as evangelists, and some as pastors and teachers, for the equipping of the saints for the work of service, to the building up of the body of Christ" (Ephesians 4:11-12). The Body of Christ, in the first century, did not continue to build itself up. It was the responsibility of those apostles, prophets, evangelists, pastors, and teachers to see that the Body of Christ not scatter, but build itself up. "Until we all attain to the unity of the faith, and of the knowledge of the Son of God, to a mature man, to the measure of the stature which belongs to the fulness of Christ. As a result, we are no longer to be children" (Ephesians 4:13-14).

This is the hour when the people of God are to come forth. We are to be fully grown, not babies. "To a mature man,…no longer to be children, tossed here and there by waves, and carried about by every wind of doctrine, by the trickery of men, by craftiness in deceitful scheming" (Ephesians 4:13-14). If I am reading this right, the Scripture does not leave us any room for division. It does not matter whether we are dealing with false prophets, trickery, deceitful scheming, or confusion over doctrine. None of these are an excuse for us to be divided—for Christ to be divided.

"But speaking the truth in love, we are to grow up in all aspects into Him, who is the head, even Christ, from whom the whole body, being fitted and held together" (Ephesians 4:15-16)—that does not sound like scattering to me. Using the imagery of a physical body, it does not make sense that the legs go and minister in one part of the world, but the head and arms separate and minister somewhere else! We cannot excuse ourselves anymore, even in the name of spreading the Gospel throughout the earth. It is a deception to say that we are really doing the Father's will if we are being scattered through division.

God may physically scatter us all over the face of the earth. But wherever He leads us physically, it cannot be an excuse for division. We are all connected to Him, "from whom the whole body, [is] fitted and held together" (Ephesians 4:16). Wherever we go, there is going to be a core of oneness created in the Body of Christ to hold us together. Then, whatever we are doing, wherever we are, however we are ministering, we will not be divided. What has God called you individually to do? There will be no power in that ministry, except through the oneness of the whole Body that brings about that power. There is no strength and anointing if there is division.

This is the time of the ingathering (Matthew 13:38-39). God is gathering His Body together. We are absolutely being bonded together into one, so that wherever we go, whatever we do, the power and the anointing of Pentecost is with us always. We should not be struggling to attain this oneness; we should be binding the strong man and plundering his house (Mark 3:27).

We do not lack many things. We lack only one thing: this oneness! It is like the rich young ruler who came to the Lord. Jesus said, "I know you have done all these things, but this one thing you lack" (Mark 10:21). That is what God is saying to us. We have fulfilled so many Words, we have walked so faithfully in so many areas, we have done so much, but this one thing we lack. Christ's

---

Matthew 13:38-39 "And the field is the world; and as for the good seed, these are the sons of the kingdom; and the tares are the sons of the evil one; ³⁹ and the enemy who sowed them is the devil, and the harvest is the end of the age; and the reapers are angels."

Mark 3:27 "But no one can enter the strong man's house and plunder his property unless he first binds the strong man, and then he will plunder his house."

Mark 10:21 And looking at him, Jesus felt a love for him, and said to him, "One thing you lack: go and sell all you possess, and give to the poor, and you shall have treasure in heaven; and come, follow Me."

Body lacks the oneness that brings about the true power and authority of His Kingdom!

"Being fitted and held together by that which every joint supplies, according to the proper working of each individual part, causes the growth of the body" (Ephesians 4:16). Christ is stunted because His Body has not grown. Each individual part causes that growth. If the Body of Christ is separated by walls, disagreements, hatreds, doctrines, and schisms, there will be no power and there will be no growth. But if there is the proper working of each individual part, it will cause the growth of the Body for the building up of itself in love. We commit ourselves to this oneness. Each of us must say, "I am responsible for oneness." Do not put this on someone else. What is the problem in every church? We think that somebody else is responsible for the oneness. Instead, we take it upon ourselves and say, "I am responsible. I am going to reach in and there is going to be oneness."

This is no small thing. This is not only the battle of the ages; it is the issue of this age. Everything is set to stop this ingathering that makes us one. We must refuse to see ourselves as local church groups with our own little problems. The issue here is the Body of Christ. Division stops the global Body of Christ from growing into a mature man. As much as we talk about moving as Christ in the earth, it is just useless doctrine if there is no oneness. We will never manifest as the sons of God until the whole Body fits together, with all the systems of the Body functioning together in oneness.

Do not see the issues that we face as churches as little personality conflicts or disagreements. This is our opportunity to participate in the battle of the ages and refuse for division to go on any longer. If we do not beat division in our own churches, let's not fool ourselves into thinking we will beat it in a larger area of ministry. We cannot end the division in the global Body of Christ if we cannot do it in our own homes, if we cannot do it in our own local churches. It would be futile for us to say, "Let's start reaching out to all these Christian groups throughout the world," only to do what the first-century apostles did—use it as a convenient excuse for division. Having fellowship is easy. But oneness is the issue, and that is **not** easy. It is dedication; it is work.

We have to plant a stake in the ground and say in our hearts by faith that division is over. Wherever we find it, we must have this reaction: "I refuse to buy into division. I refuse to be a promoter of it! I refuse to be a believer in division, an accepter of it, or a broadcaster of it. I refuse to be one who causes destruction in the Body of Christ by what I say or do."

This reality of oneness is available in God. We reach into the oneness that Christ prayed for in John 17:22-23:

> "And the glory which Thou hast given Me I have given to them; that they may be one, just as We are one; I in them, and Thou in Me, that they may be perfected into one, that the world may know that Thou didst send Me, and didst love them, even as Thou didst love Me."[2]

I am responsible for oneness, and you are responsible for oneness. We are not going to stop what we are doing; we are just going to include this element of oneness in everything we are already doing. If we believe in oneness, then, by God's grace, let us be one!

---

[2] Throughout this book, the New American Standard 1977 edition is used as the primary Bible translation. In John 17:23, the translators chose to say: "that they may be perfected in unity." "In unity" is clearly a poor choice of words as the Greek emphatically says "in one." In the New American Standard 1995 edition this error is corrected by a notation which changes the phrase to say: "that they may be perfected into one." Throughout the remainder of this book I will continue to use the New American Standard 1977 edition; however, I will quote this text as "into one" in accordance with both the original Greek and the correction found in the New American Standard Bible 1995 edition.

Chapter 2

The Pathway to Oneness

September 13, 1996
Church of the Living Word, North Hills, California

This message was spoken during an annual gathering of churches for the celebration of the Feast of Trumpets (Leviticus 23:24), a biblical feast focused on ushering in the New Year.

The 12th chapter of 1 Corinthians is always a good place to begin understanding oneness in the Body of Christ:

> But one and the same Spirit works all these things, distributing to each one individually just as He wills. For even as the body is one and yet has many members, and all the members of the body, though they are many, are one body, so also is Christ. (1 Corinthians 12:11-12)

You should take this Scripture and post it on your mirror so that you can read it when you get up every morning; not because it is something to attain, but because it is the reality that already exists. If you are a part of His Body, then you are a part of that reality, and that reality is that Christ is not divided.

"For by one Spirit we were all baptized into one body, whether Jews or Greeks, whether slaves or free, and we were all made to drink of one Spirit" (1 Corinthians 12:13). You were not baptized into an individual experience; you were baptized into one Body. I have trillions of cells in my body, but my body is one. If it is not one, it ceases to exist. It does not matter how excluded you may feel at times. It does not matter how divided you may feel, whether from others in the Body, in your homes, or within yourself. If we allow ourselves to be divided, then we exclude ourselves from the life of Christ, because Christ is not divided. Christ and His Body are one; we must accept this as our reality. We must participate in the oneness of Christ's Body.

How do we experience this reality of oneness? There are three phases, which we see expressed in this passage in 1 Corinthians 12. The first phase is **immaturity and competition**, which is described in verses 15 to 17. Look at this picture, comparing the Body of Christ to a physical body. "If the foot should say, 'Because I am not a hand, I am not a part of the body,' it is not for this reason any the less a part of the body" (1 Corinthians 12:15). The foot is being immature, isn't it? It is looking at the hand and saying, "I am not nearly as beautiful or as functional as that hand is. Therefore I am not worthy to be a part of the Body." Insecurity breeds competition. It breeds people who compare themselves with one another, and who constantly feel and express insecurity (2 Corinthians 10:12). Don't you get tired of constantly competing with one another? Nobody wants to be a deacon; everybody wants to be an elder. That is a symptom of a Body that is constantly comparing itself with itself. "I'm not good enough, so I must not be a part of the Body. I don't know why God made me a foot; I'm not worthy to be a foot." This is how we exclude ourselves. Yet the truth is, "If the foot should say, 'Because I am not a hand, I am not a part of the body,' it is not for this reason any the less a part of the body."

---

2 Corinthians 10:12   For we are not bold to class or compare ourselves with some of those who commend themselves; but when they measure themselves by themselves, and compare themselves with themselves, they are without understanding.

Voicing these insecurities becomes the number one cause of division. Immaturity and competition make it impossible to relate in oneness, because relationships do not work in an atmosphere of competition. In this first phase of immaturity and competition, you are constantly competing with the other members of the Body of Christ. You have no revelation of who you are in God, what He has made you, and how He has placed you in the Body. We all begin as immature babes in Christ. We begin to see our need of others, yet we feel insecure about our place in the Body, not knowing how to function there; we compete one with another. However, when you begin to have a revelation of God's choosing, you serve Him in that capacity, aware of your uniqueness, but flowing in oneness with the other members of the Body.

The real danger in this phase of immaturity and competition comes when we feel that we must completely detach ourselves from the oneness of the Body.

> And if the ear should say, "Because I am not an eye, I am not a part of the body," it is not for this reason any the less a part of the body. If the whole body were an eye, where would the hearing be? If the whole were hearing, where would the sense of smell be? But now God has placed the members, each one of them, in the body, just as He desired. And if they were all one member, where would the body be? (1 Corinthians 12:16-19)

It is imperative that we grow out of this phase of immaturity and competition, believing by faith that God has placed us in His Body as it is pleasing to Him.

The second phase in our progression into oneness is **independence**. This phase is expressed in 1 Corinthians 12:21: "And the eye cannot say to the hand, 'I have no need of you.'" This is the exact opposite of what is expressed in the insecurity of immaturity. Here is the eye getting such a revelation of itself that instead of saying, "I'm not worthy," it says to the other members, "If only you were an eye! I have such a revelation of my destiny, I am going to function on my own. I can't be a part of the Body."

Finding your individual destiny is absolutely necessary; it is the only road out of the first phase of immaturity. You have to get a revelation of who you are as a member of the Body of Christ. If you try to just get a revelation of the Body, it will not work. You have to understand that "God has placed the members, each one of them, in the body, just as He desired" (1 Corinthians 12:18). You have to have a revelation of who you are, what you are, and why God has brought you to the Kingdom at such a time as this (Esther 4:14, KJV). You have to know that you are called from your mother's womb to be a part of the great Body of Christ that is coming forth to usher in His Kingdom (Jeremiah 1:5). You have to know what you are doing and how to do it or you cannot really function in the Body of Christ.

Without developing this independence, we are more like a shapeless amoeba than a body. Imagine inserting yourself as a single cell somewhere in the physical body, and then trying to figure out what the body is all about. But if you understand what your function is and you are placed where you belong, then you can more clearly understand what the whole body is doing. As members of the Body of Christ, we must each begin to discover our individual destinies; it is an absolutely essential step on this road to oneness. You must have a revelation of yourself, your ministry, and your destiny. The concern in this phase, however, is that your revelation of yourself

---

Esther 4:14, KJV For if thou altogether holdest thy peace at this time, then shall there enlargement and deliverance arise to the Jews from another place; but thou and thy father's house shall be destroyed: and who knoweth whether thou art come to the kingdom for such a time as this?

Jeremiah 1:5 "Before I formed you in the womb I knew you, and before you were born I consecrated you; I have appointed you a prophet to the nations."

does not morph into an arrogance that causes you to reject the rest of the Body. This is the warning of 1 Corinthians 12:21: "And the eye cannot say to the hand, 'I have no need of you'; or again the head to the feet, 'I have no need of you.'"

Phase three is **interdependence** within the Body; it is expressed in verses 22 to 26. This is the reality of the Body of Christ: it is synergistic. One chases a thousand, and two chase ten thousand (Deuteronomy 32:30). There is a quality of multiplication that we must reach into.

> On the contrary, it is much truer that the members of the body which seem to be weaker are necessary; and those members of the body, which we deem less honorable, on these we bestow more abundant honor, and our unseemly members come to have more abundant seemliness, whereas our seemly members have no need of it. But God has so composed the body, giving more abundant honor to that member which lacked, that there should be no division in the body, but that the members should have the same care for one another. And if one member suffers, all the members suffer with it; if one member is honored, all the members rejoice with it. (1 Corinthians 12:22-26)

In the first phase, you have an immature revelation of your place as a member in the Body of Christ. In the second phase, you see the reality of your independent destiny in God as an individual. There is no way to become a functional Body unless we go through both the first and second phases of our maturity. However, if we do not get out of these phases and into the next one, it will be very destructive. Division sets in, the disconnected members begin to fly apart, and the Body of Christ ceases to exist! The Body must experience this

---

Deuteronomy 32:30 "How could one chase a thousand, and two put ten thousand to flight, unless their Rock had sold them, and the Lord had given them up?"

third phase of interdependence in order to achieve oneness and synergy. We must have a revelation of how much we honestly need one another. Without the many members, there is no Body.

If you really have a revelation of your destiny in God, the next revelation waiting for you is that you will never fulfill that destiny by yourself. There is no work of God, whether big or small, that does not require more than one individual and their unique anointing to fulfill it. It may seem like there is an impossible conflict between independence and interdependence, but there is not. In fact, it is the only way this can work. In your independence you will come to the place where you will say, "I set out to accomplish certain things, and it's just not working. I can't do it. I don't have the time, the energy, the skill, or the know-how to do this all by myself."

Once you get a revelation of your destiny in God, realize that just like Christ, you cannot fulfill it by yourself. It will not work. Christ Himself was unable to complete His destiny in God without the interdependent relationships He had with the disciples, His mother, and the others who faithfully walked with Him through His time of ministry and death on the cross. Even His greatest act—dying for us on the cross—required the help of Simon of Cyrene who carried His cross to Golgotha (Luke 23:26).

We understand that independence is absolutely a necessary step on our pathway to oneness. Even if you have been afraid of the step of getting a revelation of yourself, you must open up to it. It does not matter how little you may seem in your own eyes, you are needed. However, you can't stop there; that second phase becomes destructive when you are being repelled from one another in your independence. Finding your destiny is one thing, but realizing your need for one another is something else. We will have no fulfillment

---

Luke 23:26 And when they led Him away, they laid hold of one Simon of Cyrene, coming in from the country, and placed on him the cross to carry behind Jesus.

in a ministry without this reality of oneness, and that is where the Holy Spirit is leading us.

We have to understand the absolute depth of this revelation of oneness. Nothing is going to work beyond this point unless we are one. Christ will not be divided from our participation as members of His Body. This does not mean, of course, that Christ will enter into sin with us. He died on the cross once for all. This is a salvation experience that we must enter into. Oneness is there if we want it, but Christ will never divide Himself between us; He will never participate in our sin of division. He will not divide Himself in order to make us one. He has provided the oneness for us, and we must appropriate it. There has to be a commitment on our part to submit to it.

We submit to God by being one. This message is not just for you or for me; it is not only for us as a church; this is for the whole Body of Christ. Christ is not divided (1 Corinthians 1:13). And yet the Body of Christ is the most divided entity on the face of the earth. We have all been living in either phase one or phase two, but we have not come to this next step of moving together in the real interdependent synergy of oneness. Now we must take the initiative. We have an open door. If God is speaking this to us, it is available. This is the next step for the Body of Christ in the whole earth. I believe it is already the reality of Christ's Body. It is spoken in His Word (1 Corinthians 12:12). We enter into this truth by faith, and we walk in the reality of it with all of our hearts.

---

1 Corinthians 1:13 Has Christ been divided? Paul was not crucified for you, was he? Or were you baptized in the name of Paul?

Chapter 3

Baptized Into the Spirit of Unity

February 23, 1997
Church of the Living Word, North Hills, California

As the series on oneness continued into a new year, this message was spoken in a Sunday morning service to the local congregation.

The book *Walking Together*, by John Robert Stevens, contains a message titled "Multiplying the Power Through Unity." A great deal of that message concentrates on the 4th chapter of the Book of Acts where the Church came together and all prayed in one accord. Stevens spoke about the power and authority that comes through the unity of the Body of Christ:

> I would like to see that kind of prayer come forth, the kind of prayer that opens up everything to us. The place was shaken, literally shaken. Would you like to have that happen, that the place where the people are gathered is really shaken? Something was turned loose of which we have no concept, because there has not been such unity in the Body of Christ for almost two thousand years. Yet it is ready to come again as God brings the Body together. We must be dedicated to it, to be in one accord in one place.[3]

[3.] John Robert Stevens, "Multiplying the Power Through Unity," in *Walking Together* (North Hollywood: The Living Word, 1973), 40.

Coming into this oneness will be as challenging as it is for a camel to go through the eye of a needle (Mark 10:24-27). Ancient cities in the Middle East sometimes had gates with very small openings, called "needle's eyes."[4] When a camel was led through such a gate, all that it was carrying had to be removed from its back and the camel would have to get down on its knees to pass through the gate. The experience of coming into the oneness of the Body of Christ will be like going through the eye of the needle, because we will have to unload the sectarian conditionings and influences that have become the baggage we all carry in our walk with the Lord. This will be the greatest challenge that we as a people will face, not just in our fellowship, but in the worldwide Body of Christ.

As I was reading this message from *Walking Together*, the Lord began to show a vision, a picture of the incredible process that God is putting His people through. That picture was of a transplant operation in which someone was receiving a new donor organ, like a heart or a lung. The reason for the operation was that the person would soon die unless he or she received the transplant. Yet in the transplant process, the body receiving the new organ relates to that organ as the enemy. The reaction of the recipient's body is to reject the organ that is being given. That is the biggest problem. In fact, a person who receives a transplant organ must live the remainder of their life being medicated to keep their body from rejecting that new organ.

Mark 10:24-27 And the disciples were amazed at His words. But Jesus answered again and said to them, "Children, how hard it is to enter the kingdom of God! [25] It is easier for a camel to go through the eye of a needle than for a rich man to enter the kingdom of God." [26] And they were even more astonished and said to Him, "Then who can be saved?" [27] Looking upon them, Jesus said, "With men it is impossible, but not with God; for all things are possible with God."

[4.] James M. Freeman and Harold J. Chadwick, *Manners and Customs of the Bible* (North Brunswick, NJ: Bridge-Logos Publishers, 1998), 447.

The parallel to the Body of Christ is amazing. God is forming His Body by creating the pieces separately from one another. Instead of forming the Body as one being, as a child would be formed in a womb, God is creating the heart in one location, the kidneys in another, and the lungs somewhere else. Now He is in the process of trying to graft this great Body of His together. Every single part is transplanted. There is another picture in the Scriptures of this concept about the Body of Christ. We see that branches were broken off of Israel and the Gentiles were grafted in. So isn't it possible, if God grafted them out, that He will graft them back in again (Romans 11:19-24)?

So we see that this concept is very scriptural: God creates His Body and then He grafts it into Himself. He is grafting all of these organs that He has created into Himself to make one living organism. Christ is the head and everything else flows together to make up the Body (Ephesians 4:15). But while God is trying to graft all of these organs to Himself, those organs are constantly rejecting one another. The Body is actually in this struggle to decide whether it is going to kill itself or whether it is going to receive life!

When someone goes through a heart transplant, that person essentially lies there on the surgery table for some period of time with no heart at all. If you turn off the life-support machinery, that

---

Romans 11:19-24 You will say then, "Branches were broken off so that I might be grafted in." [20] Quite right, they were broken off for their unbelief, but you stand by your faith. Do not be conceited, but fear; [21] for if God did not spare the natural branches, neither will He spare you. [22] Behold then the kindness and severity of God; to those who fell, severity, but to you, God's kindness, if you continue in His kindness; otherwise you also will be cut off. [23] And they also, if they do not continue in their unbelief, will be grafted in; for God is able to graft them in again. [24] For if you were cut off from what is by nature a wild olive tree, and were grafted contrary to nature into a cultivated olive tree, how much more shall these who are the natural branches be grafted into their own olive tree?

Ephesians 4:15 But speaking the truth in love, we are to grow up in all aspects into Him, who is the head, even Christ.

body is literally dead. Then, after the transplant is complete, the new heart begins to pump blood through the veins providing life to the whole body. All the time, however, that body is in the process of rejecting and attempting to destroy the life-giving heart.

The Body of Christ is going through the same kind of struggle right now, virtually grappling with itself. This struggle is happening throughout the whole world. Individual members of the Body of Christ are wrestling with the decision, "Am I going to allow this seemingly innate response to rise up within me and destroy that which truly is my life?" That which is going to feed life to us, that which is going to make us whole and complete, seems to be our enemy. Our initial response is an overwhelming reaction to reject it. We have lived this. It has never been more pronounced than it is now, and I don't think that we have ever understood this like we do now. Never before have we really experienced the depth of need to lay hold of the revelation of the Body of Christ in the earth. Self-sufficiency and individual ministry have very much gone by the wayside—the life and the anointing is not in that anymore. Yet we still find something within us rising up to reject coming together in oneness.

What we need is a people who will begin to cry out with one voice. As you remember in Acts chapter 4, they were literally praying out of a Scripture. They were re-prophesying a prophecy of David (Psalm 2:1-2), all with one voice and in one accord. The place was shaken, they spoke the Word with boldness, miracles took place,

---

Psalm 2:1-2 Why are the nations in an uproar, and the peoples devising a vain thing? [2] The kings of the earth take their stand, and the rulers take counsel together against the Lord and against His Anointed.

and power was turned loose, all because of their unity (Acts 4:24-26, 31-32). We are in a time again when this same prophecy could be spoken with one heart and one voice out of the mouth of a people who are proclaiming their oneness. And the same reaction is going to take place. The authority, and the power, and the promises—all that we have contended for is going to be loosed!

No matter what we have gone through in our churches and fellowships, we are now facing the greatest challenge that we have ever faced. We are standing at the eye of the needle, and it is time to pass through. We declare an end to the reaction of rejecting our very life, rejecting our very salvation and fulfillment. We declare that is put aside and something new comes forth in the Body of Christ—an ability to come into the unity of the Spirit (Ephesians 4:3). The unity of the Spirit allows the Body to pull all of these individual, diverse, distinct parts together and see them become one. It fashions the Body into a whole being before the Lord, with no walls, with no rejection, with no destruction (1 Corinthians 12:24-27). Then it is

---

Acts 4:24-26 And when they heard this, they lifted their voices to God with one accord and said, "O Lord, it is Thou who DIDST MAKE THE HEAVEN AND THE EARTH AND THE SEA, AND ALL THAT IS IN THEM, [25] who by the Holy Spirit, through the mouth of our father David Thy servant, didst say, 'WHY DID THE GENTILES RAGE, AND THE PEOPLES DEVISE FUTILE THINGS? [26] THE KINGS OF THE EARTH TOOK THEIR STAND, AND THE RULERS WERE GATHERED TOGETHER AGAINST THE LORD, AND AGAINST HIS CHRIST.'"

Acts 4:31-32 And when they had prayed, the place where they had gathered together was shaken, and they were all filled with the Holy Spirit, and began to speak the word of God with boldness. [32] And the congregation of those who believed were of one heart and soul; and not one of them claimed that anything belonging to him was his own; but all things were common property to them.

Ephesians 4:3 Being diligent to preserve the unity of the Spirit in the bond of peace.

1 Corinthians 12:24-27 Whereas our seemly members have no need of it. But God has so composed the body, giving more abundant honor to that member which lacked, [25] that there should be no division in the body, but that the members should have the same care for one another. [26] And if one member suffers, all the members suffer with it; if one member is honored, all the members rejoice with it. [27] Now you are Christ's body, and individually members of it.

a whole man, standing in the strength, the authority, and the power of God. That is where we are. I don't care how small the opening in the eye of that needle may seem, or how impossible this may appear. We must not care how offended we have been in the past, how many walls we have had, how much we have been rejected, or how many times we have utterly failed on this point.

Today the Lord, by this Word, releases unto His people the unity of the Spirit that Ephesians 4 describes. We are baptized into that spirit of unity; we cleave to it with all of our hearts (Ephesians 4:4-5). We are going to beat our arrows over this point. We will not stop short of victory (2 Kings 13:18-19). The Body of Christ will be one, in the name of the Lord. We allow ourselves to be grafted in so that the life can flow. The Church will become one heart, one mind, and one spirit before the Lord.

Christ's Body throughout the earth is going to awaken, come together, and arise like a great sleeping giant. God's Kingdom shall stand; His Kingdom shall prevail. Jesus taught that "a house divided against itself cannot stand" (Matthew 12:25). The Kingdom of God cannot any longer be a house that is divided against itself. Our personal challenge comes when we look at each other and think that we must decide how each piece fits in. Imagine looking at a disassembled elephant and trying to put it together if you had never seen an elephant before. You would think that it was a manufacturer's defect! "How do these big stumpy legs have anything to do with this

---

Ephesians 4:4-5 There is one body and one Spirit, just as also you were called in one hope of your calling; [5] one Lord, one faith, one baptism.

2 Kings 13:18-19 Then he said, "Take the arrows," and he took them. And he said to the king of Israel, "Strike the ground," and he struck it three times and stopped. [19] So the man of God was angry with him and said, "You should have struck five or six times, then you would have struck Aram until you would have destroyed it. But now you shall strike Aram only three times."

Matthew 12:25 And knowing their thoughts He said to them, "Any kingdom divided against itself is laid waste; and any city or house divided against itself shall not stand."

gigantic wall of a belly? Who would ever guess that this trunk was the nose? And how do you end up with a little tail like that?" Having never seen an elephant, it would seem absolutely disjointed from itself. But since we have all seen an elephant before, assembling it would make much more sense because we would understand how it fits together. The same applies to the Body of Christ. The problem is that neither we nor many generations before us have ever experienced or witnessed the Body of Christ functioning in oneness, so it can seem impossible for us to imagine how to bring about the unity of the faith.

The Body of Christ is going to come together. It will begin by us opening our hearts and taking down our walls. We refuse to assume it will just happen. Whether we have ever seen it before or not, we create this spirit of unity. We create it by the Word of the Lord out of our mouths and out of our hearts. We determine that if God said it, it will happen.

Chapter 4

Stand in Your Place

March 30, 1997
Hale O Nā Kāula, Haiku, Maui, Hawaii

While in the Islands, this message was spoken to the local congregation of Hale O Nā Kāula ("House of the Prophets").

God is again working as He did in the days of the early Church. Following the resurrection of Christ, the disciples were thrown into a new reality of functioning, and it was not a functioning in religion. Nowhere in the Scriptures can you find Christ instructing the disciples about how to set up a church. There were no specific guidelines given. All they had was a relationship with Him. They reached in daily to hear His voice, so that Christ could come forth within a body of people by the Holy Spirit. Their experiences daily were based only on the miracle of His resurrection, His life within them.

Jesus said, "I am the resurrection and the life" (John 11:25). Thus Christ, as the resurrection and the life, was a reality the disciples walked in daily. From the day that He rose from the dead, they really did not know where to go or what to do. They were absolutely dependent upon Him to lead and guide them. He truly was their life; they were a church based on the miracle of the resurrection.

John 11:25 Jesus said to her, "I am the resurrection and the life; he who believes in Me shall live even if he dies."

They had no doctrines, no history. What they did have was a relationship with the Lord and a relationship with one another. It was a tremendous place to be in.

The disciples had a revelation of the Lord as the way, the truth, and the life (John 14:6), and based upon that revelation, they sought the Lord together (Acts 1:14). Yet the apostles were not alike in many ways; they were very different from one another. In the Gospels, you read about Peter, James, and John growing together through conflicts and personality differences. They were all strange misfits in terms of fitting in with each other. Still, all of them were men whom God raised up, and they dared to let God fulfill His plan and His purpose within them. After the resurrection, not only did they have a revelation of the Lord; they had a tremendous revelation of one another's gifts and anointings. Not one of them was trying to protect the area of ministry that God had given him. Peter was not afraid that Paul would come into his territory and take some of the churches away from him. The same applied to all the apostles; they had an amazing way of recognizing the distinct sphere of ministry that God had given to each one (Galatians 2:7-9). Because the apostles saw one another as who each one was in the Lord, they did not usurp each other's place, but trusted God to take care of them (Joel 2:7-8).

John 14:6 Jesus said to him, "I am the way, and the truth, and the life; no one comes to the Father, but through Me."

Acts 1:14 These all with one mind were continually devoting themselves to prayer, along with the women, and Mary the mother of Jesus, and with His brothers.

Galatians 2:7-9 But on the contrary, seeing that I had been entrusted with the gospel to the uncircumcised, just as Peter had been to the circumcised [8] (for He who effectually worked for Peter in his apostleship to the circumcised effectually worked for me also to the Gentiles), [9] and recognizing the grace that had been given to me, James and Cephas and John, who were reputed to be pillars, gave to me and Barnabas the right hand of fellowship, that we might go to the Gentiles, and they to the circumcised.

Joel 2:7-8 They run like mighty men; they climb the wall like soldiers; and they each march in line, nor do they deviate from their paths. [8] They do not crowd each other; they march everyone in his path. When they burst through the defenses, they do not break ranks.

Today, each member of the Body of Christ is in a position that no one else on this earth is anointed to fill. When Christ ascended to the Father, the Holy Spirit then descended and gave gifts to men (Ephesians 4:8). He literally distributed Himself and indwelt His Body in such a way that it is impossible for one person to replace another, nor is it necessary to compete with one another. No one else in the earth can fulfill the unique ministry that you have. Only if you walk away from your ministry would God then raise up someone else to do it (Acts 1:20). As long as you are open to do the will of God, no one else can fill the place God has called you to fill, and no one can take it away from you. As you begin to flow together, you do not need to worry about your inheritance. No man is going to covet your land (Exodus 34:24). God gave you that place and it is yours absolutely. Therefore, you can open your hearts to one another.

After Christ's resurrection, He began creating His Body coming forth within a people (Acts 2:42-47). But as the early Church progressed, that process stopped because of division. Today, Christ is creating something that we have not seen for a long time; He is coming and filling His Body. He is fitting and joining us together

---

Ephesians 4:8 Therefore it says, "When He ascended on high, He led captive a host of captives, and He gave gifts to men."

Acts 1:20 "For it is written in the book of Psalms, 'Let his homestead be made desolate, and let no man dwell in it'; and, 'His office let another man take.'"

Exodus 34:24 "For I will drive out nations before you and enlarge your borders, and no man shall covet your land when you go up three times a year to appear before the Lord your God."

Acts 2:42-47 And they were continually devoting themselves to the apostles' teaching and to fellowship, to the breaking of bread and to prayer. 43 And everyone kept feeling a sense of awe; and many wonders and signs were taking place through the apostles. 44 And all those who had believed were together, and had all things in common; 45 and they began selling their property and possessions, and were sharing them with all, as anyone might have need. 46 And day by day continuing with one mind in the temple, and breaking bread from house to house, they were taking their meals together with gladness and sincerity of heart, 47 praising God, and having favor with all the people. And the Lord was adding to their number day by day those who were being saved.

with this unique revelation and understanding that out of our diversity—even out of our differences—He is coming forth within us and is making us one (Ephesians 4:16).

On a natural plane, men are always fighting over their differences. Differences in a natural sense cause division, but God uses the differences between us so that they literally become our strength. Now, that seems impossible, and it is impossible on a natural level. But in the Body of Christ, differences actually create our oneness. Many wars today are taking place, not between different countries, but within countries. They take place between countrymen who seem much the same, yet their little differences are creating wars. It is brother against brother over minor differences within their own countries and between their own peoples. It is significant that at the very same time that people are divided over their differences, God is speaking, "I am going to take your differences and make that your oneness." The miracle is that we are going to be welded together in all of our vast diversity and in all of our uniqueness! Everything that could cause destruction is going to turn around and cause the blessing of the Lord to rest upon us.

God is creating unity, but not through conformity. We are not going to lay down rules and regulations, or laws of conduct or worship. You will never find the truth of God in rules and doctrines. You may have the best of intentions, but laws, regulations, and doctrines will never work to bring about the righteousness of God. They can only attempt to force conformity on a human level. Unity and oneness are divine attributes of God.

Christ does not make ministries by stamping them out on an assembly line. Instead, He sets everyone in the Body as it pleases Him

---

Ephesians 4:16 From whom the whole body, being fitted and held together by that which every joint supplies, according to the proper working of each individual part, causes the growth of the body for the building up of itself in love.

(1 Corinthians 12:18). There are not too many fingers or too many toes, too many legs or too many arms. Do not covet one another's place, because the Body is perfect just as it is. God is creating unity through the diversity of the ministries He has created, and that very diversity assures them of their place in the Body. No one can say to you, "I have no need of you," nor can you say to anyone in the Body, "I have no need of you" (1 Corinthians 12:21).

We are actually maturing to the place where the revelation of the Body strikes us and we say to one another, "I really need you!" That is what the physical body does. Your body cleaves together because it realizes that every part is unique and essential to keeping you alive and helping you function. It is the same way in the Body of Christ. In His resurrection, Christ dispersed Himself to us in a way that would guarantee our oneness. He did not make us all the same; we cannot replace one another or do without each other. We must flow together. That is why the focus of our hearts is on unity. Lord, bring us into the unity of the faith and the knowledge of the Son of God. We have been living together in the unity of the Spirit, but at some point God draws us together by that unity of the Spirit into the unity of the faith (Ephesians 4:3, 13).

This is going to happen throughout the whole Body of Christ everywhere. All of the walls are going to come down. All of the divisions, all of the separations due to diversity have got to fall until the Body comes together. It is going to happen in a unique way.

---

1 Corinthians 12:18 But now God has placed the members, each one of them, in the body, just as He desired.

1 Corinthians 12:21 And the eye cannot say to the hand, "I have no need of you"; or again the head to the feet, "I have no need of you."

Ephesians 4:3 Being diligent to preserve the unity of the Spirit in the bond of peace.

Ephesians 4:13 Until we all attain to the unity of the faith, and of the knowledge of the Son of God, to a mature man, to the measure of the stature which belongs to the fulness of Christ.

If you just stand and do what you are called to do, it will affect the whole earth. When Noah built the ark, his actions brought judgment. In obedience to God, he built the ark, and it judged the whole earth (Hebrews 11:7).

You say, "How do we bring about the unity of the whole Body of Christ all over the world?" As with Noah, by an act of obedience. By being one right where we are, by opening our hearts on a deeper level to each other until we are one in spirit. We must walk together in what God has called us to do. We must seek to have the depth of recognition of one another that existed in the first-century Church. This openness in our spirits will bring a revelation of one another, allowing us to come together like the Word proclaimed we would. We must give ourselves one to another, seeing one another as more important than ourselves (Philippians 2:3).

We submit ourselves one to another in the fear of Christ (Ephesians 5:21). This is how we literally can change the whole world. By determining to come together in a oneness of spirit to recognize one another, to submit one to another, and to do the will of the Lord together, we impact the entire world! Any church, no matter its size or location, can have a functional purpose within the scope of what God is doing in the entire earth. He is not just concerned about us; "the earth is the Lord's, and the fulness thereof" (Psalm 24:1, KJV).

Hebrews 11:7 By faith Noah, being warned by God about things not yet seen, in reverence prepared an ark for the salvation of his household, by which he condemned the world, and became an heir of the righteousness which is according to faith.

Philippians 2:3 Do nothing from selfishness or empty conceit, but with humility of mind let each of you regard one another as more important than himself.

Ephesians 5:21 And be subject to one another in the fear of Christ.

Psalm 24:1, KJV The earth is the Lord's, and the fulness thereof; the world, and they that dwell therein.

What God is doing, He is creating throughout the earth. Our drive is to be a part of it with Him, so we give ourselves to this oneness of heart and spirit to function together in the Lord.

We bless the Body of Christ with this. When we speak about the ministry that God has created, we are not talking about ministers; we are talking about Ephesians 4:12—each saint has a ministry "for the work of service, to the building up of the body of Christ." Every person in the Body is a ministry. God has imparted a unique ministry, a unique place to each one. Stand in your place. Determine to faithfully stand in that ministry; it is a gift and anointing from God. God places us in the Body as it pleases Him, then all we do is stand each one in our place (1 Corinthians 12:18). Once we are placed, then we stand firm (Ephesians 6:13).

There is nothing more unsettling for the Body than when somebody moves out of their place; everything just gets lopsided. It does not work. As God sets us in the Body, we stand in that unique ministry. It is like the great commandment. First of all, you must love the Lord with all of your heart, all of your mind, all of your strength. In other words, stand before Him where He has placed you. The next thing you do is love your neighbor as yourself (Matthew 22:36-39). We do not force one another to stay in place, but we strengthen one another to stand in our ministries. That is the greatest thing you can do to minister to the Body of Christ—stand in that anointing, in that ministry, in what you are. It is not a title. It is not a position. It is just you being who God created you to be. Then we bless and strengthen one another with the resolve to stand, in the name of the Lord.

Ephesians 6:13 Therefore, take up the full armor of God, that you may be able to resist in the evil day, and having done everything, to stand firm.

Matthew 22:36-39 "Teacher, which is the great commandment in the Law?" [37] And He said to him, "'YOU SHALL LOVE THE LORD YOUR GOD WITH ALL YOUR HEART, AND WITH ALL YOUR SOUL, AND WITH ALL YOUR MIND.' [38] This is the great and foremost commandment. [39] The second is like it, 'YOU SHALL LOVE YOUR NEIGHBOR AS YOURSELF.'"

Chapter 5

God Has So Composed the Body

September 12, 1997
Church of His Kingdom, San Diego, California

In this message to the local church congregation in San Diego, the Lord continued to speak about the necessity of oneness within His Body.

1 Corinthians 12:22-24 contains a description of how the members of the Body of Christ are to relate. Here we read about the seemly members and the unseemly members, and upon whom we should bestow less honor or more abundant honor. It is easy to get caught up in the details of how the Body works, but I want to focus on one simple phrase: "God has so composed the body" (1 Corinthians 12:24). We can't lose the simplicity of the idea that it is God who is composing His Body. He is bringing it together. Like a great composer, He is writing all of the parts.

When you compose, you realize that music is not just some lyrics and a melody; it is the composition of all the elements. A composer has to be trained in the sounds of all the instruments, their different

---

1 Corinthians 12:22-24 On the contrary, it is much truer that the members of the body which seem to be weaker are necessary; [23] and those members of the body, which we deem less honorable, on these we bestow more abundant honor, and our unseemly members come to have more abundant seemliness, [24] whereas our seemly members have no need of it. But God has so composed the body, giving more abundant honor to that member which lacked.

tonalities, and how these diverse tonalities blend together. God is awesome; He is the greatest composer. I am so impressed with God and how He does what He does. What He creates is so amazing that I often think, "I never could have come up with that!" Right now He is taking the Body of Christ and literally composing it. He knows all the instruments. He not only knows what each part can do; He also realizes the relevance and the importance of each part and how they all work together. He understands exactly what your unique part adds to the composition, and He understands exactly how much you lack without the rest of the parts in the composition.

We are witnessing the bringing together of God's composition in a way that has never been seen before. No man could ever make this happen. If it were not for God's working, our fellowship of churches would have blown apart into many schisms and divisions a long time ago. The truth is that our personalities never blend us together, nor do they encourage us to remain together. If it were up to us, we would separate over the many issues and viewpoints, and over the different ways of expression and manifestation.

Thankfully it is not up to us. God is composing something that will be brought together, and we are very much in the process of that. God has so composed the Body "that there should be no division" (1 Corinthians 12:25). He is bringing every aspect together with no division and no separation. He is putting together this beautiful symphony orchestra that is ready to play the composition He has been writing. No fellowship of believers is insignificant or tucked away in a corner somewhere. We are all part of this tremendous composition that God is putting together.

We need to be prepared, practiced, and placed, so that we are ready to play our part in what God is getting ready to do. Every

---

1 Corinthians 12:25 That there should be no division in the body, but that the members should have the same care for one another.

fellowship is different and unique. We encourage everybody to get prepared and to play their part, realizing what the Lord is really doing. We are nothing in ourselves, but we embrace who we are in His composition; we come to life and manifest that unique aspect of who we are. It may seem small, but the truth is, unless every part is ready to come together, there is no composition.

As part of this composition, God gives us a Word that we now are responsible for. We should think of ourselves, not so much as a church, but as a body of people with a mission, a job to do. Your destiny in God, both individually and collectively, rests upon you; you must execute that destiny. This was Paul's cry: "That I might complete the work and finish the course" (2 Timothy 4:7). In walking with God, finishing the course is everything. We are not here without a goal; we are here to run the race with endurance and finish the course (Hebrews 12:1).

You need to see that there is a purpose behind everything you are doing. When you see that your part in the composition is unique to you, then you are able to run the race. You have a clear goal of where you are going and what you are doing, and a mantle literally rests upon your spirit (1 Kings 19:19). You are not an observer. Yes, an audience comes to watch the orchestra play the composition, but you are not part of the audience! You are part of the orchestra that is to play this tremendous composition that God is putting together.

---

2 Timothy 4:7 I have fought the good fight, I have finished the course, I have kept the faith.

Hebrews 12:1 Therefore, since we have so great a cloud of witnesses surrounding us, let us also lay aside every encumbrance, and the sin which so easily entangles us, and let us run with endurance the race that is set before us.

1 Kings 19:19 So he departed from there and found Elisha the son of Shaphat, while he was plowing with twelve pairs of oxen before him, and he with the twelfth. And Elijah passed over to him and threw his mantle on him.

So the issue now is practice. Practice honing your skills until you are enabled. When you read about Paul, you get such a sense of him reaching for a destiny that he knew God had placed upon his spirit before he was ever born (Galatians 1:15-16). In the same way, you are a people of destiny. Carry that destiny like a mantle from God. Paul said, "I don't box as one who beats the air. I don't just swing aimlessly" (1 Corinthians 9:26). You are not only a part of the Body; you carry a unique anointing and destiny. Therefore, you are not just to move in any random direction. Move on a clear course toward the will of God for you.

It's imperative that we find, refine, and clarify that course for us as a people. If a connecting joint is not perfectly fashioned, how does it connect to the other joints? The workmanship of the Body is tremendous, especially where it interconnects (Ephesians 4:16). When you look at a single member of the physical body by itself, it can seem strange. But when you see how it is attached to the body as a whole, it is beautiful. This is no generalized workmanship; one joint is perfectly made to attach to the other joint. And that is what God is doing—perfecting His Body. He is making it more specific than it has ever been.

In the past, the Body of Christ has been far more generalized in its makeup and manifestation because its members have functioned in a disconnected state. The Body has had to function with all the schisms, denominations, and divisions that have existed. But God

---

Galatians 1:15-16 But when He who had set me apart, even from my mother's womb, and called me through His grace, was pleased ¹⁶ to reveal His Son in me, that I might preach Him among the Gentiles, I did not immediately consult with flesh and blood.

1 Corinthians 9:26 Therefore I run in such a way, as not without aim; I box in such a way, as not beating the air.

Ephesians 4:16 From whom the whole body, being fitted and held together by that which every joint supplies, according to the proper working of each individual part, causes the growth of the body for the building up of itself in love.

is beginning to refine and smooth off the rough edges until each member is perfected in its unique gift and it fits together with the other members. God is getting ready to connect you in to the rest of the Body of Christ.

As He does this, you may find yourself thinking, "Here's a part of me that I've been missing. I have been looking for this all of my life, and here it is!" It seems contradictory, but once you are linked together with another part of the Body, individually you may be less than what you were before, but you become more of what you are gifted to be in the Body of Christ. This joining together, part to part, is beginning to take place throughout the whole Body. It is a tremendous revelation. In this experience of becoming your part, you will find a mantle resting on you from those who fathered you. Like Elisha, you may have picked up that mantle to carry it, but it is your mantle now (2 Kings 2:13-14). You must never lose the drive of where you are going, and of the destiny that rests upon you. Here is a quote from our founder, John Robert Stevens:

> He has given you a charge. No man ever receives any speck of truth from God but what that truth becomes a stewardship. He must have a faithful heart, always to hold before him the objectives that the Word of God has stirred within him. He must be faithful to live it and faithful to speak it forth to others.[5]

A strong sense of purpose rests on you. If you cannot hear even one bit of truth and become a steward of it, then what will happen when God dumps a truckload of truth on you? The Living Word

---

2 Kings 2:13-14 He also took up the mantle of Elijah that fell from him, and returned and stood by the bank of the Jordan. [14] And he took the mantle of Elijah that fell from him, and struck the waters and said, "Where is the Lord, the God of Elijah?" And when he also had struck the waters, they were divided here and there; and Elisha crossed over.

[5.] John Robert Stevens, "Our Faithfulness," in *Sparks From the Altar* (North Hollywood, CA: The Living Word, 1977), 66.

you have heard is now your Word. It is your Word to give to the world. We are learning how much more of a stewardship we truly have. We are each in our place to sharpen our skills and to perfect that which concerns us individually as well as the stewardship that rests upon us in our local fellowships. May we have the same drive that Paul had: "That I may know Him…and the fellowship of His sufferings…but I press on in order that I may lay hold of that for which also I was laid hold of by Christ Jesus" (Philippians 3:10, 12).

God did not just speak some Word; He laid hold of your life. He laid hold of your spirit. He infused within you a destiny that is a part of this great composition that He is bringing forth. By faith, we lay hold of that for which we were laid hold of. Individually, we lay hold of it until we are no longer observers, but participators. We are driven to finish the course that was set before us, to see the composition brought forth in this tremendous orchestra that is the Body of Christ.

What a miracle we are watching as we see the Body of Christ throughout the world literally coming together. It is the greatest miracle and sign of God's presence that there has ever been, and we are observing it now. But do not stand back in awe; dive into it. This message must not become just another doctrine or teaching. The world must observe in us the manifestation of this Word becoming flesh (John 1:14). That will be the only thing that is convincing. People have had enough doctrines. Doctrines are never going to bring us to the truth or lead us to Christ.

Philippians 3:10 That I may know Him, and the power of His resurrection and the fellowship of His sufferings, being conformed to His death.

Philippians 3:12 Not that I have already obtained it, or have already become perfect, but I press on in order that I may lay hold of that for which also I was laid hold of by Christ Jesus.

John 1:14 And the Word became flesh, and dwelt among us, and we beheld His glory, glory as of the only begotten from the Father, full of grace and truth.

God is implanting His Word in the hearts of sons. That Word itself is maturing us until the Word will be made flesh again. Therefore, even the Word is nothing without you. There is no Word unless you become that Word. That is your destiny, to become a living letter that is known and read of all men (2 Corinthians 3:2). God grant us the realization that we are not just in a church; we are yoked together in a stewardship before Him to complete the course that has already been composed and laid out for us.

We cannot do this for one another, but by faith we can strengthen each other. Do not let the intensity of this drive falter or waver in your heart. This is not some glib movement. This is a stewardship of the truth that has been imparted to each one of us. May the eyes of our hearts be enlightened, both individually and as a Body, to understand what is the great hope of His calling within us (Ephesians 1:18). This tremendous calling is being manifested every day in greater ways. We are going to walk in amazing things that are written for us to fulfill, a tremendous destiny that rests upon us as God brings it forth. It is already done. He has already composed the Body and created you as a part of that composition. The vision of what God is composing in His Body must be alive and burning in our hearts, so that we are driven to finish the course.

---

2 Corinthians 3:2 You are our letter, written in our hearts, known and read by all men.

Ephesians 1:18 I pray that the eyes of your heart may be enlightened, so that you may know what is the hope of His calling, what are the riches of the glory of His inheritance in the saints.

Chapter 6

Am I Committed to Oneness?

September 26, 1999
Church of the Living Word, North Hills, California

At the annual gathering of churches for the celebration of the Feast of Tabernacles (Leviticus 23:34), this message was part of a series surrounding John 17:21: "That They May All Be One."

The issue before us today, as the Body of Christ, is our walking together in oneness. I want to read from a book that is very appropriate for us now concerning this oneness. Within it is a key for us in where we are going as a people, and as the whole Body of Christ. The book is titled *Walking Together* by John Robert Stevens. In the message titled "Operation Buddy," we read,

> God is bringing a Word that will produce unity in the Body, a standing fast with one spirit that has not been seen in two thousand years. "I pray that they all may be one, Father, as We are one, that the world may believe that Thou hast sent Me" (John 17:21-22). We are ready for the great witness of the Lord Jesus Christ to come forth in the earth.[6]

John 17:21-22 "That they may all be one; even as Thou, Father, art in Me, and I in Thee, that they also may be in Us; that the world may believe that Thou didst send Me. [22] And the glory which Thou hast given Me I have given to them; that they may be one, just as We are one."

[6.] John Robert Stevens, "Operation Buddy," in *Walking Together* (North Hollywood, CA: The Living Word, 1973), 1.

The great commission that Jesus gave the Church was to go and make disciples (Matthew 28:19). He said, "Be My witnesses in all the earth" (Acts 1:8). But what does it mean to witness for the Lord? This is what it means: "I pray that they may be one, Father, as We are one, that the world may believe." As much as Christians have spoken about Jesus, all the world has never believed, and will never believe until the Church enters into being a witness unto all the earth. It is time for the great witness of the Lord Jesus Christ to come forth in the earth, and according to John 17:21, that witness is the oneness of the Body of Christ.

This is the front line of the Kingdom of God. You may ask what God is doing in the earth today and where our focus should be. Our purpose is not just to bring the Word of God to the world. That Word of God must be manifested in a people. Distributing books and publishing the Word for the rest of our lives will not, in itself, cause people to believe. The true witness that causes the world to believe will be seeing our oneness in everything that we do.

When people visit our churches, I never hear them talk about how great our doctrines or our publications are. People have myriads of doctrinal writings and belief systems. Every belief system, without a living expression, is nothing but a platitude. What I do hear people talk about is what they see in us as a people. God has been working a maturity within us. The great focus of the Holy Spirit right now is to bring forth the Body of Christ into oneness. All of the walls, divisions, schisms, and denominations have to disappear until people are free to relate. Whether we are Baptists, Lutherans, or

---

Matthew 28:19 "Go therefore and make disciples of all the nations, baptizing them in the name of the Father and the Son and the Holy Spirit."

Acts 1:8 "But you shall receive power when the Holy Spirit has come upon you; and you shall be My witnesses both in Jerusalem, and in all Judea and Samaria, and even to the remotest part of the earth."

Catholics is not a limitation. God is bringing together His Body as it pleases Him (1 Corinthians 12:18).

According to Matthew 18:19, if just two are agreed on anything, it will be done for them. In other words, what is required is oneness and unity. Everything that happens in the spirit realm surrounds the ability of the believers to be one. The Body of Christ is oneness. This is the reason we focus on the diversities and the gifts, and encourage the different ministries to come forth. Our purpose is to help the Body of Christ recognize itself in its many members so that it is no longer disjointed because of its limited ability and maturity.

Throughout Christianity, we see a lack of maturity, a lack of ability to reach into this greater oneness. How do we get people to talk and relate together according to the scriptural pattern of speaking the truth in love? "But speaking the truth in love, we are to grow up in all aspects into Him, who is the head, even Christ" (Ephesians 4:15). That is the scriptural process of growth. It is a two-part process. You speak the truth in love, and growth is the result. However, if you cannot speak in love, then you hold your tongue until you can. Without love, you are going to voice something that will have one ultimate effect: it will break the unity. Whenever you speak with something wrong in your spirit, it separates you from one another. On the other hand, you can speak almost anything with a right spirit and draw people to yourself. People will feel an open door; they will feel that inclusion.

It is not a disaster that the Body of Christ has not attained this maturity; we are still growing. We cannot be too hard on ourselves, but neither do we want to wander around in confusion. In all

---

1 Corinthians 12:18 But now God has placed the members, each one of them, in the body, just as He desired.

Matthew 18:19 "Again I say to you, that if two of you agree on earth about anything that they may ask, it shall be done for them by My Father who is in heaven."

honesty before the Lord, we are not mature enough yet to function as the Body of Christ. If you look at the landscape of Christianity as it stands today, there are some positive aspects to it. We can see that various denominations exist, but it is as if everybody has gone to their own room so that they stop killing each other. Denominations emerged because infighting within groups caused separations. Rather than escalate the fighting into a holy war, many groups chose to go their separate ways. In a holy war, somebody is going to bleed; somebody is going to die. As you look at the sectarianism throughout most of Christianity, we have to acknowledge that at least all these people are still here. We have not killed each other yet!

The possibility for oneness in the Body still exists, and I believe it is going to happen. We do not have to go out into the world to bring down the walls of sectarianism. We bring down our own walls; we end divisions in our own fellowship. It is the principle of Noah building the ark in his own backyard; by doing so he affected the whole earth (Hebrews 11:7). Don't look at the division your church is going through as some little argument going on between a few people or factions. It is so much more.

Is it possible to bring down the principalities of division, and the demonic forces that have been set to stop the will of God for thousands of years? The whole fulfillment of Christ is His Body coming together in oneness. Without the Bride of Christ, there is no fulfillment (Revelation 19:7). This is not a minor issue; it has huge ramifications! We begin by realizing that our problems are not just little arguments. Creating oneness in the Body of Christ is probably the most difficult end-time event that will happen. After

---

Hebrews 11:7 By faith Noah, being warned by God about things not yet seen, in reverence prepared an ark for the salvation of his household, by which he condemned the world, and became an heir of the righteousness which is according to faith.

Revelation 19:7 "Let us rejoice and be glad and give the glory to Him, for the marriage of the Lamb has come and His bride has made herself ready."

the oneness of the Body is established, there is nothing left that we must accomplish; that oneness opens the door for every other fulfillment.

We are not a bunch of immature children, tossed to and fro by every wind of doctrine (Ephesians 4:14). Not only is this oneness possible, but we are mature enough to take the next step. First, realize that we have been lured into a trap of being divided one against another. The intent of this trap has been to perpetuate the lack of unity that keeps the Body of Christ ineffectual. Therefore, we repent and reach in for a greater level of maturity in our relationships until we have a real commitment to one another. And what is the commitment to one another that we need? Let's read some more from the book *Walking Together*:

> If you have any grievance or any occasion to grumble or complain against your brother that would loom up in your mind so great as to be a sin against the unity of the Body of Christ…you will stand guilty before God of the most heinous crime that can be committed against the Lord Jesus Christ Himself! Maintain unity with your brother. Help him.[7]

At this juncture, there is no greater violation than our breaking oneness with one another! If that is true, then there must be a way to move on into the will of God. Look again at this quote, but focus on the last two sentences: "Maintain unity with your brother. Help him."

To break oneness is the greatest sin. We can do this simply by grumbling against somebody, or gossiping. The very act of planting

---

Ephesians 4:14 As a result, we are no longer to be children, tossed here and there by waves, and carried about by every wind of doctrine, by the trickery of men, by craftiness in deceitful scheming.

[7] Stevens, "Operation Buddy," 1.

a negative thought into someone's thinking about another person **is** division. That is the most heinous crime that can be committed against the Lord Jesus Christ Himself. If people cannot stop speaking criticism, then the least you can do is stop listening to it. If someone talks to you about another person, stop and say, "Let's go talk to that person about this right now." That would stop the negative flow immediately.

Have enough integrity in your own being to encourage someone to go speak directly to the one who may have offended them. We cannot perpetuate what seems to be an unwritten law in many churches, which is to never sit down with someone you are having a problem with and talk to that person about it. Backbiting and avoiding one another are not acceptable. Don't skirt around each other. If a comment is worth saying to someone else, then it is worth saying directly to the person you are talking about. When we do not speak the truth in love, it creates an absolute misunderstanding of one another. Until you sit down and really spend some time talking to that person to hear what is in his or her heart, you cannot stop this cycle of misunderstanding and division.

Here is how that cycle works. If you have not developed honest relationships with others, then you are not free to honestly express your heart. Problems develop until you may completely avoid another person. Someone will make a careless remark, often with an underlying issue that they want to express, and you may be hurt or offended by it. But instead of speaking to the person you feel separated from, you talk to others about it. The problem is that those people are not in the position to do anything about the situation. And it only gets worse as you build up a mountain of ideas in your mind based upon something that may be nonexistent. The original problem may not be that bad, but you have blown it up into a larger issue.

We should stop backbiting, gossiping, and talking about people when they are not present. It is that simple. If you go talk with that person, it will open up a greater awareness of the problem within you. You will hit your own reluctance and face your own unwillingness. Choosing to put aside your own reluctance and have a conversation with that person is choosing oneness over your own wounds and hurt feelings. You may discover that the offense you perceived was not even intended. By the Holy Spirit, you might discover that there was no wrong motivation toward you, only a misunderstanding. Yet wounds and division had been allowed to grow. Words spoken and actions committed can literally sever our oneness and hurt the whole Body of Christ.

Putting up walls, walking away from a hurtful situation, or being unwilling to talk to that person in love: all of these reactions block our ability to worship the Lord. It is a scriptural principle. When you come to worship the Lord, and you remember that you have something against your brother, what do you do? You leave your offering and go talk to your brother (Matthew 5:23-24). What would happen if we actually put this principle into practice with each other? With a broken heart you should go talk to that person with whom you feel an offense. It is not what that person did to you, but how you reacted to them when it happened. Speaking the truth in love to one another allows our wounds to be healed.

Marriage relationships are an illustration of this principle. Hundreds of things happen during the course of a day between two people, any one of which can just set one partner off. It can hurt and become a wall. One partner can walk away maintaining that wall day after day, even if the other is doing nothing offensive or from a wrong

---

Matthew 5:23-24 "If therefore you are presenting your offering at the altar, and there remember that your brother has something against you, [24] leave your offering there before the altar, and go your way; first be reconciled to your brother, and then come and present your offering."

motivation. It is in the way you react to what you think is offensive. Before you begin to accuse people of offenses, you need to consider: was there really an offense at all, or did you merely take offense? The more you talk to others, the more you perceive yourself to be in the right, and the offense becomes even more horrible. These principles cannot be mere doctrines; they are the very life of our relationships! Do not be someone who simply identifies a word or action as division, but does nothing about it. Division will only exist if you let it!

> All of us have offended and been offended at some time or another. Yet the offenses should not rise up so great in our mind that we be unforgiving. We should not allow anything to detract from the unity of the Body of Christ and the flow of the Spirit of the Lord in this great army, which shall not break ranks nor thrust one another through (Joel 2:8). This unity does not just happen. There must be men and women who are dedicated to the prophecies, and dedicated to make the unity of the Spirit a way of life in the oneness with which we walk together.[8]

We must be dedicated to the relationships in the Body of Christ, just like being in a marriage. When a couple comes to the altar and stands next to each other, and makes a commitment of heart, they have just determined that there will be a solution to every problem that ever arises between them. That means a commitment to open up and do whatever is necessary to arrive at a solution to their problem. Two people have to want to do this. Many couples do not get married with this level of commitment anymore, but it can still become their reality. Even if they began with uncertainty, they can

---

Joel 2:8 They do not crowd each other; they march everyone in his path. When they burst through the defenses, they do not break ranks.

[8.] Stevens, "Operation Buddy," 2.

still pull together and face their problems with a gut-level refusal to give up.

Our young people need to know the level of dedication that it takes for successful relationships. We should not continue to promote a fantasy about relationships. If you love a person, then commit to that person and decide to find a solution together. Relationships are not just happy and wonderful, without any problems. Even when there is no conflict between two people in a marriage, something outside of them often arises that is set to rip them apart. Marriages endure because you refuse to give up on one another, and you determine that the relationship will last.

The Body of Christ is always envisioned as a marriage—the marriage of the Lamb (Ephesians 5:24-25). And the Body is going to function according to that same marriage principle. There must be a determination and a dedication of our hearts. We do not get there by vetting each relationship until we all get along with each other. That will never happen; we will never all be completely in agreement. Agreement is different than oneness. We have to come to the place where all the church authorities—apostles, prophets, evangelists, pastors and teachers, elders, deacons, as well as the other local church ministries—come together because they are determined to be one. We need to take our walls down and talk to one another until we really hear. We must be willing to hear each other's hearts, including the anger, the misunderstandings, and the hurts. No matter how frustrated we are, we must come together to function in a commitment to oneness, a dedication to the unity of the Body.

These conversations must be in an appropriate atmosphere, not in a public forum or a large meeting where people cannot be truly

---

Ephesians 5:24-25 But as the church is subject to Christ, so also the wives ought to be to their husbands in everything. [25] Husbands, love your wives, just as Christ also loved the church and gave Himself up for her.

open or honest with one another. Remember the admonition of the Scriptures that you first go to your brother (Matthew 18:15). We want to get to the bottom of the problems until we really hear each other and are willing to move toward the same goals. The Scripture says, "How can two walk together if they be not agreed?" (Amos 3:3, KJV). Walking together requires that we seek oneness among the leaders first; that will create a deep agreement about where we are going together as a people. One of the greatest objectives we have right now is to be one in the Body of Christ. Leaders really need to listen to one another, to talk things through. Then they need to refuse to keep hashing out their disagreements. We cannot stay out in the wilderness because we do not know which way to go. Once we reach a confirmed Word from God, we move from that place toward our goal.

We have a scriptural illustration of how to do this in Acts chapter 15, when the apostles and elders came together over the issue of the Gentiles. A question had arisen in the churches about how to deal with the Gentiles. Remember, the early Church had been entirely Jewish for fifteen years before the Gentiles began to be joined to the believers. Circumcision became a major issue of scriptural interpretation causing division among the churches. The apostles knew they needed to come together to get an answer from the Lord (Acts 15:2, 4-6).

Matthew 18:15 "And if your brother sins, go and reprove him in private; if he listens to you, you have won your brother."

Amos 3:3, KJV Can two walk together, except they be agreed?

Acts 15:2 And when Paul and Barnabas had great dissension and debate with them, the brethren determined that Paul and Barnabas and certain others of them should go up to Jerusalem to the apostles and elders concerning this issue.

Acts 15:4-6 And when they arrived at Jerusalem, they were received by the church and the apostles and the elders, and they reported all that God had done with them. [5] But certain ones of the sect of the Pharisees who had believed, stood up, saying, "It is necessary to circumcise them, and to direct them to observe the Law of Moses." [6] And the apostles and the elders came together to look into this matter.

This must be our precedent. If we have something that we are really disagreeing about, let's get the apostles and the elders together—not just from our own church, but from all over the region. A ministry from another locality can be very objective. So these early apostles called together the council and they began to speak their feelings and share scriptural illustrations. When James got up and spoke, there was one response: "That is a Word from the Lord." It bore witness to all of them. Even those who had come with a different point of view dropped it. Now when they walked out of that room and into their churches, it was as one man with one Word and one direction. No one said, "This is what was spoken, but I do not really agree with it." That would have destroyed the oneness.

To hold on to your own interpretation rather than choosing to be one is immaturity. It takes maturity to be able to drop your disagreement and honestly put all of your heart behind something that now is a confirmed Word from God. The early Church struggled with this. An earlier example was when the disciples ended up drawing lots to choose a new apostle (Acts 1:23-26). Why did it get to the point where they had to draw lots? Because they could not agree. That was probably a difficult process; some wanted this brother; some wanted that brother. Some may have felt that neither one of them was really qualified. These disciples who had been personally picked by the Lord and walked with Him for three-and-a-half years must have had a difficult time considering including someone else. But they had to work this out because the Day of Pentecost was approaching.

Acts 1:23-26 And they put forward two men, Joseph called Barsabbas (who was also called Justus), and Matthias. [24] And they prayed, and said, "Thou, Lord, who knowest the hearts of all men, show which one of these two Thou hast chosen [25] to occupy this ministry and apostleship from which Judas turned aside to go to his own place." [26] And they drew lots for them, and the lot fell to Matthias; and he was numbered with the eleven apostles.

When the Day of Pentecost arrived, Peter and the eleven stood up as one man (Acts 2:14). That oneness brought the power of the Holy Spirit to the Body of Christ in the first century. Do not lose sight of the fact that they had to pray and then draw lots to get to that point. It was a challenge to those men to walk away from drawing lots and agree on a new apostle. But they all backed it; they were determined to be one. A lot of room for division exists; it is easy to oppose the flow of oneness. Whatever your reasons are, it is not worth jeopardizing the flow of oneness in the Body of Christ. Mature sons who are reaching to have a Word from the Lord can resolve their problems and find the way to walk together with all their hearts.

In the days ahead, the Body of Christ will have to find answers to very difficult problems. We have just begun to be challenged with the problems that will face us as a people. When faced with finding answers, it is clear that the disciples considered it important that they be one. They may have been thinking, "I don't care who the lot falls on. As long as we're one, it will work. If this man is rough around the edges, he will still move as an apostle because we are backing him in that apostolic commission." They understood that once the oneness is broken, the power is gone. Now you can see why the power of the Church has been gone for so long: there is not the maturity in the Body of Christ to be able to lay down all of our individual thoughts and our own ways (Judges 21:25).

We see it in something as simple as leading a worship service. The Spirit may be really moving, but everyone has a different idea about what the next song should be, or they are critical of the one

---

Acts 2:14 But Peter, taking his stand with the eleven, raised his voice and declared to them: "Men of Judea, and all you who live in Jerusalem, let this be known to you, and give heed to my words."

Judges 21:25 In those days there was no king in Israel; everyone did what was right in his own eyes.

leading worship. Something is going to be lost in the worship if the authorities are not agreed. If we are one in our hearts and spirits, we can sing any song and have a breakthrough in worship. We will continue to seek for an exact Word from God, but we are going to miss it sometimes, or the leading of the Spirit may be clouded. We are not always going to have an absolute leading of the Holy Spirit as one man. That is our goal, but we are not there yet.

Sometimes the Lord will not give us a sure Word from God just to see if we will seek oneness. If we are sincerely reaching for unity, even if we take a wrong turn, God will make it right. That principle will work for us, but it is only going to work because there is a commitment in our hearts to pray together and find our answers as one. If, for some reason, we are not finding a confirmed Word from God, we should keep believing until God speaks to us. Then, without breaking ranks, and without pushing another from their place, we will all walk together in what God speaks (Joel 2:8). All through the Bible, people in some manner laid out a fleece before God when they could not find the leading of the Lord (Judges 6:36-40). That is a step of faith. Together, we put out a fleece before God. Then we trust the Lord in it, because we have done everything we could to get a Word from Him. Do not bog down in endless discussions or opinions. Once you have aired a subject, ask, "Do we have a Word? What is the witness here?" See if there is a confirmed Word. If not, then go to the next step, even if it means getting the lots out. Even that can work, if we determine to be one in the process.

Judges 6:36-40 Then Gideon said to God, "If Thou wilt deliver Israel through me, as Thou hast spoken, [37] behold, I will put a fleece of wool on the threshing floor. If there is dew on the fleece only, and it is dry on all the ground, then I will know that Thou wilt deliver Israel through me, as Thou hast spoken." [38] And it was so. When he arose early the next morning and squeezed the fleece, he drained the dew from the fleece, a bowl full of water. [39] Then Gideon said to God, "Do not let Thine anger burn against me that I may speak once more; please let me make a test once more with the fleece, let it now be dry only on the fleece, and let there be dew on all the ground." [40] And God did so that night; for it was dry only on the fleece, and dew was on all the ground.

This is the wall that we are up against right now in the Kingdom of God. We must have an intense drive of spirit—a demand before God that there will be a people who can be one with one another, who can literally commit to one another to the depth that they will not break oneness. The unity of the Spirit will become a way of life when we are determined to walk together.

Chapter 7

Tabernacles – The Great Ingathering

September 27, 1999
Church of the Living Word, North Hills, California

This message was spoken during the Feast of Tabernacles celebration as part of the series of messages on John 17:21: "That They May All Be One."

The Feast of Tabernacles, or Feast of Ingathering, was celebrated at the end of the late harvest in the land of Israel, when all of the crops were gathered in from the fields (Exodus 23:14-16). Historically, after the harvest, the Israelites would take their offerings and head to Jerusalem to celebrate the Feast of Tabernacles. You can imagine the wonderful sense of rejoicing that they had as they went up to the Feast together. All of the biblical feasts are filled with expectation, but the eighth and final day of the Feast of Tabernacles is called the Day of Rejoicing. This day celebrated the tremendous fulfillment

---

Exodus 23:14-16   "Three times a year you shall celebrate a feast to Me. [15] You shall observe the Feast of Unleavened Bread; for seven days you are to eat unleavened bread, as I commanded you, at the appointed time in the month Abib, for in it you came out of Egypt. And none shall appear before Me empty-handed. [16] Also you shall observe the Feast of the Harvest of the first fruits of your labors from what you sow in the field; also the Feast of the Ingathering at the end of the year when you gather in the fruit of your labors from the field."

of the ingathering of all the crops. If you have ever been around a farming community, you know that once the crop has been brought in, it must be safely stored away in the barns and granaries. As the Israelites went to Jerusalem, all of the work of harvest and storage was complete. Rather than approaching with an expectation for their crops, or praying for rain, or believing the Lord for a good harvest, they came with rejoicing because they literally had the fruit of the year gathered away into their barns. And so this Feast was a time of great focus upon the Lord. The Israelites were not worried about what was going on at home. They came to the Feast to worship the Lord for what He had done for them.

Today, God is about to bring an amazing fulfillment of the Feast of Tabernacles in a spiritual harvest beyond anything we have ever seen (Revelation 14:14-16). To understand this harvest, look at the New Testament parallel related to the ingathering of the fruit of Christ's ministry. When Christ came, His ultimate work was to die on the cross and be resurrected from the dead. When the experience of the cross was complete, His work was finished (John 19:30). Before He died, Christ directed the disciples to go and gather in the fruit that His work on the cross would bring forth (Matthew 9:37-38; John 12:24). Any time there is a great physical harvest, there has to

---

Revelation 14:14-16 And I looked, and behold, a white cloud, and sitting on the cloud was one like a son of man, having a golden crown on His head, and a sharp sickle in His hand. [15] And another angel came out of the temple, crying out with a loud voice to Him who sat on the cloud, "Put in your sickle and reap, because the hour to reap has come, because the harvest of the earth is ripe." [16] And He who sat on the cloud swung His sickle over the earth; and the earth was reaped.

John 19:30 When Jesus therefore had received the sour wine, He said, "It is finished!" And He bowed His head, and gave up His spirit.

Matthew 9:37-38 Then He said to His disciples, "The harvest is plentiful, but the workers are few. [38] Therefore beseech the Lord of the harvest to send out workers into His harvest."

John 12:24 "Truly, truly, I say to you, unless a grain of wheat falls into the earth and dies, it remains by itself alone; but if it dies, it bears much fruit."

be enough laborers to bring in the crops. Christ told the disciples to pray to the Father, the Lord of the harvest, that there would be enough laborers to gather in the great harvest of people from all over the earth. We have yet to experience this final ingathering of all that Christ was looking to bring forth. We are living in the time now of the spiritual fulfillment of the Feast of Tabernacles.

Following Christ's resurrection and just prior to His ascension, He told His disciples, "Go into all the world and preach the gospel to all creation. He who has believed and has been baptized shall be saved; but he who has disbelieved shall be condemned" (Mark 16:15-16). Christ was giving them what we call the great commission. Ever since that time, Christians have had this great commission resting upon them. It is a commissioning of ingathering. It is the same message: a command to go out into the fields and gather in the fruit for which Christ labored and died.

Luke the 24th chapter gives us another example:

> Then He opened their minds to understand the Scriptures, and He said to them, "Thus it is written, that the Christ should suffer and rise again from the dead the third day; and that repentance for forgiveness of sins should be proclaimed in His name to all the nations, beginning from Jerusalem. You are witnesses of these things. And behold, I am sending forth the promise of My Father upon you; but you are to stay in the city until you are clothed with power from on high." (Luke 24:45-49)

Christ was speaking of the Day of Pentecost. In the agricultural year, the time of Pentecost precedes the season of Tabernacles. In fulfillment of this scriptural pattern, on the Day of Pentecost, the believers were empowered to go out into the field and bring in the fruit, a harvest of souls (Acts 2:41). To accomplish this ingathering, the anointing of the Holy Spirit was given as the enabling. For thousands of years since, the witnesses of Christ have gone out into the world to gather this fruit, by the power of the Holy Spirit.

We read in Acts 1:8, "But you shall receive power when the Holy Spirit has come upon you; and you shall be My witnesses both in Jerusalem, and in all Judea and Samaria, and even to the remotest part of the earth." Here again, just before His ascension, we see this proclamation made by Christ that directed the purpose of the disciples: go out, and gather in the fruit. Reap for the Lamb the reward of His suffering. That is this concept of ingathering, the very heart of the Feast of Tabernacles.

The following was the Lord's prayer to the Father:

> "As Thou didst send Me into the world, I also have sent them into the world. And for their sakes I sanctify Myself, that they themselves also may be sanctified in truth. I do not ask in behalf of these alone, but for those also who believe in Me through their word; that they may all be one; even as Thou, Father, art in Me, and I in Thee, that they also may be in Us; that the world may believe that Thou didst send Me." (John 17:18-21)

The verb "believe" is in the Greek present subjunctive mood and means more than just "that they may believe in Me," but "that they should continually believe in Me." It is a progressive, eternal, unending process. Then Jesus says, "That they may all be one." Because of this oneness, "the world may believe that Thou didst send Me." By virtue of these people who are the witnesses, there is to be a continual bringing in of the harvest of believers. "And the

---

Acts 2:41 So then, those who had received his word were baptized; and there were added that day about three thousand souls.

glory which Thou hast given Me I have given to them; that they may be one, just as We are one" (John 17:22).

The Day of Pentecost was the fulfillment of Christ's prayer to the Father that the glory, the anointing, the Spirit which rested upon Him would also rest upon His witnesses in order that they might be one. We cannot become one on our own by working really hard at getting along. By virtue of the anointing of the Holy Spirit, we should be endued with power that brings about oneness within us as a people. We are in the midst of this Scripture being fulfilled: "And the glory which Thou hast given Me I have given to them; that they may be one, just as We are one." So it is possible for us, as the Body of Christ, to be one: "I in them, and Thou in Me, that they may be perfected into one" (John 17:23).

What is perfection? It is being brought together into one. In unity our perfection is completed. This does not mean that we will be free of personal problems. In God's eyes, perfection is not getting rid of all my needs or flaws. I may still need deliverances. Perfection, as the Lord is defining it here, is that we come into oneness: "I in them, and Thou in Me, that they may be perfected into one." What is the purpose of coming into oneness? "That the world may know that Thou didst send Me, and didst love them, even as Thou didst love Me" (John 17:23). The purpose of our perfection is to manifest the greatest glorification of the Lord Jesus Christ that the world will ever know. When we are perfected into one, then the world will believe that Christ came to the earth, died for their sins, and provided forgiveness and salvation.

As we read in Mark 16, Jesus said to them, "Go into all the world and preach the gospel to all creation. He who has believed and has been baptized shall be saved" (Mark 16:15-16). They will believe because those who preach the Gospel have an amazing, undeniable oneness. "I in them, and Thou in Me, that they may be perfected into one, that the world may know that Thou didst send Me" (John 17:23).

When people see the oneness among us, they will come to know the truth about Jesus Christ.

They are going to believe on the Lord Jesus Christ, not by virtue of the preaching, the witness, the words, or the doctrines, not even because of the signs and wonders.

> "And these signs will accompany those who have believed: in My name they will cast out demons, they will speak with new tongues; they will pick up serpents, and if they drink any deadly poison, it shall not hurt them; they will lay hands on the sick, and they will recover." (Mark 16:17-18)

The signs are the Holy Spirit confirming the words of the believers who are witnessing, to help them minister God's love and grace. However, people are not going to believe merely because of signs, wonders, and miracles.

Throughout history, this earth has had tremendous miracles and outpourings, and incredible signs on the natural level. Yet those outpourings, signs, and wonders have never brought down the walls in the Body of Christ, or created a great worldwide ingathering. We are still awaiting the great Feast of Tabernacles, the tremendous ingathering which is the fulfillment of what Christ spoke. Only one thing can create that ingathering: God's people becoming one, having been perfected in oneness. Then the world will be able to believe. What a beautiful picture!

The deepest frontline revelation of what God is doing in the earth today is this: our relationships in the Lord can bring us into oneness. It is beyond our human ability to comprehend. And that is why we must labor over the Word of oneness until we get it. Oneness is the centerpiece of completing the will of God in the earth. Nothing significant happens in the end time without this oneness of God's people. It is by the power of the Holy Spirit that we are enabled to be one. We should not be bluffed out of the reality that we can enter into this oneness which Jesus declared: "I in them, and Thou in Me, that they may be perfected into one, that the world may know." Here the word "know" is again the Greek present subjunctive mood: so that the world may continually know. This is not some little, insignificant revelation; this is the knowledge that transforms the world!

When this ingathering and oneness of the Body of Christ happens, a perpetual awareness of the presence of God will be turned loose in the earth. People will know, and keep on knowing, that Christ came to the earth, died for their sins, and opened a door for them to be reconciled to God (2 Corinthians 5:19). Through that awareness, they can be filled with the Holy Spirit, and come into the knowledge of the Father, through His Son. Can you imagine walking around the earth surrounded by a constant awareness that the Lord is alive? What an amazing atmosphere that would be to live in—continually aware of God's presence, aware of what He has given us, and all that He has done!

Instead, we often wake up wondering where God is. Even after receiving tremendous personal meetings with the Lord, those experiences can fade into a mist. Sometimes you even question whether they really happened. We live in a tremendous, incessant spiritual battle that tries to rob us of this knowledge, this awareness of God's love. How can we be judgmental of non-believers when they have a hard time getting a revelation of the Lord? We know that it takes a revelation from the Lord to walk with Him. But it is not easy, in this present world, to get a revelation of the Lord.

---

2 Corinthians 5:19 Namely, that God was in Christ reconciling the world to Himself, not counting their trespasses against them, and He has committed to us the word of reconciliation.

The knowledge of the Lord is constantly under attack, within us and outside of us (2 Corinthians 4:3-4).

However, we have the prophecy that the knowledge of the Lord will fill the earth, as the waters cover the sea (Isaiah 11:9). The impact of that prophecy is not alive until we realize how much we have faced a constant battle against our daily knowledge of the Lord. The Scriptures speak of the concept of the Parousia, the presence or coming of the Lord (Matthew 24:27; 1 Thessalonians 3:13). The Parousia, the dawning of the Lord's presence, does not happen out there somewhere; it happens within us as a growing experience of His presence with us (Luke 17:20-21).

What would change the atmosphere of this world more than anything else? It would be turning loose the knowledge of the Lord—for ourselves and for the entire world. How could we ever do that? Should we get together and have all nights of prayer? Should we fast over all these promises? No, we have the answer right here: "I in them, and Thou in Me, that they may be perfected into one, that the world may know that Thou didst send Me, and didst love them, even as Thou didst love Me" (John 17:23). Wouldn't you like to know

---

2 Corinthians 4:3-4 And even if our gospel is veiled, it is veiled to those who are perishing, [4] in whose case the god of this world has blinded the minds of the unbelieving, that they might not see the light of the gospel of the glory of Christ, who is the image of God.

Isaiah 11:9 They will not hurt or destroy in all My holy mountain, for the earth will be full of the knowledge of the Lord as the waters cover the sea.

Matthew 24:27 "For just as the lightning comes from the east, and flashes even to the west, so shall the coming of the Son of Man be."

1 Thessalonians 3:13 So that He may establish your hearts unblamable in holiness before our God and Father at the coming of our Lord Jesus with all His saints.

Luke 17:20-21 Now having been questioned by the Pharisees as to when the kingdom of God was coming, He answered them and said, "The kingdom of God is not coming with signs to be observed; [21] nor will they say, 'Look, here it is!' or, 'There it is!' For behold, the kingdom of God is in your midst."

that the Father loves you, just as He loved Christ? Wouldn't that awareness change your life? This atmosphere of love and oneness is the fulfillment of the Feast of Tabernacles, and it is the means by which the world will come to know the Lord.

Chapter 8

Our Prime Directive

September 29, 2000
Church of the Living Word, North Hills, California

During the annual gathering of churches for the Feast of Trumpets celebration, the series of messages surrounding John 17:21 continued. This word was a trumpet call for oneness.

Jesus prayed, "And for their sakes I sanctify Myself, that they themselves also may be sanctified in truth. I do not ask in behalf of these alone, but for those also who believe in Me through their word" (John 17:19-20). You are included in this prayer. Christ was talking to the Father about the people who were standing around Him, but He also said very specifically, "Father, I am not just talking to You about those around Me, but I am also talking about those who are going to believe." He was talking to the Father about you. What is the will of God for you? Christ did not leave the world without telling you exactly what He wanted you to do and to become. It is not a mystery; it is not some vague concept. He left very clear instructions for your Christian life.

> "I do not ask in behalf of these alone, but for those also who believe in Me through their word; that they may all be one; even as Thou, Father, art in Me, and I in Thee, that they also may be in Us; that the world may believe that Thou didst send Me." (John 17:20-21)

What is the will of God for us? That we all may be one. You should never again wonder what God's will is for you; your purpose is clear. Whatever specific direction you may have from the Lord for your personal life, do that in oneness with one another. Nothing that the Lord ever speaks, or has ever spoken, supersedes that prime directive.

This is one unchangeable directive. The principal purpose for everything else you are led to do in the Lord should be clear because of this one thing that Christ prayed for. It was neither vague nor conditional: "That they may all be one." Every one of us who believe are to be one with one another, as one as Christ and the Father are one. There is no vagary here. "That they may all be one; even as Thou, Father, art in Me, and I in Thee, that they also may be in Us; that the world may believe that Thou didst send Me."

This may shock the Christian world, but our current methods of evangelism are quite ineffective when compared to what Jesus directed the believers to do. They were first to remain in Jerusalem until they became one, and second, in their oneness they were to be endued with the power of the Holy Spirit. Being witnesses was the third step in Jesus' directions. The proof of Christ is only found in the oneness of His Body. When we attempt to be witnesses or evangelists without first being dedicated to experience the oneness of Christ and the Father, and without being filled with the Holy Spirit, our works are soulish attempts which fall short of the commission Christ gave us.

We may be a people with many spiritual directives and projects. Many churches have important outreach programs like schools or hospitals. Everything that the Lord leads us to do is simply for one ultimate purpose: that we use that activity to become one. We are mistaken if we think we have fulfilled a word or a directive when we have not become one as we complete that project. The Lord will just give us another project, with the same relentless intent that we become one.

Do you want to keep working on projects that really do not accomplish this purpose? "That the world may believe that Thou didst send Me." The Greek word for "believe" is in the present subjunctive mood: "That the world may **continually** believe that Thou didst send Me." Down through history, from the time of Christ's ascension into heaven until the time that He returns, the world should have been, and should still be, in a continual state of believing in Jesus Christ. If the Body of Christ had become and remained one, then the people of the world would have believed. What an interesting history this world would have had, if oneness had been firmly planted and grown in God's people. This may seem impossible for us to accomplish, but let's look again at the Scripture.

"And the glory which Thou hast given Me I have given to them; that they may be one, just as We are one" (John 17:22). Christ gave the provision for us to be one. He declared on the cross, "It is finished!" (John 19:30). What was finished? The provision of everything that we need to become one and to know Him, was finished. Christ gave us everything necessary for us to walk in oneness. "I in them, and Thou in Me, that they may be perfected into one" (John 17:23). Do you believe that we are supposed to be perfect? What does it mean to be perfect? How long have people been running around trying to perfect themselves? According to this verse, the very definition of perfection is oneness. God is perfecting us by making us one.

Jesus prayed for us that we be "perfected into one, that the world may know that Thou didst send Me, and didst love them, even as Thou didst love Me" (John 17:23). This is a beautiful Scripture; it tells us exactly what the will of God has been from before the

---

John 19:30 When Jesus therefore had received the sour wine, He said, "It is finished!" And He bowed His head, and gave up His spirit.

cross, down through this present age. It proves that we can do this; God has made the provision for us to do it. How do we work the works of God? Believe (John 6:28-29). By faith we reach into this Scripture and lay hold of a dedication and commitment to be one. Whether or not we have heard this before, we have not taken the full provision to become one. We are not there yet, but we cannot be so overwhelmed by unbelief that we do not even try to become one.

One of the most sobering, shattering revelations that we will ever receive is that there is no excuse for our disunity. We have developed a very systematic theology of excuses. In our minds, we have developed a very complex conscious, and subconscious, way of relating to the Lord. We are convinced that oneness among Christians is not possible. However, the responsibility for appropriating God's perfect provision is ours. On the day that we all stand before His throne, He will accept no excuses for the schisms, divisions and lack of oneness within the Church (Matthew 7:22-23). In truth, our oneness together is the building block of true theology. We should not be so quick to let go of our hope of oneness, or the promise God has given of our oneness.

The Kingdom of God is relationships—not in theory, not in doctrine, but in the practical, daily application of how we walk, relate, and function together. Our relationships should lead us into oneness in His love. Instead of absolving ourselves from the responsibility to be one, we should reach into God's perfect provision for it. His glory is the anointing that creates oneness. No matter what your

---

John 6:28-29 They said therefore to Him, "What shall we do, that we may work the works of God?" ²⁹ Jesus answered and said to them, "This is the work of God, that you believe in Him whom He has sent."

Matthew 7:22-23 "Many will say to Me on that day, 'Lord, Lord, did we not prophesy in Your name, and in Your name cast out demons, and in Your name perform many miracles?' ²³ And then I will declare to them, 'I never knew you; DEPART FROM ME, YOU WHO PRACTICE LAWLESSNESS.'"

personal problems are, there is a way for you to be one with those whom Christ has related you to. This may not work with thousands of people at one time, but try it at home first and see how that works. Realize that your family, even your fellowship or local church, is like a microcosm of the world. Oneness is a principle in the spirit, and if we can attain it on a small scale, then it can be applied to thousands that you personally may never know. Ultimately, this promise of oneness is for the whole Body of Christ. Rather than thinking it is not important, or absolving yourself of reaching into it in your own church, you have to believe that oneness can grow from where you are, and fill the earth (Matthew 13:33).

Lord, confront us with this. Each of us is responsible to find a way in our dedication, in our commitment, to be one. We cannot trade being one for other accomplishments. We cannot come to the end of all that the Lord has given us to do, and then try to prove to Him all we have accomplished. That would be substituting what He has assigned us to do in our projects for the real purpose of the project. Every project that the Lord gives us, even as small as cleaning the church, has behind it the purpose of bringing us together for oneness. We may even find ourselves in a project where working together brings out the worst in us. That is one of God's favorite kinds of projects, because it becomes an opportunity for us to reach in for more love and a genuine unity. Every time we begin a project that we are directed to do by the Lord, we become more aware of our lack of oneness and our need for one another.

The greatest power in the earth is born out of oneness; everything else is just a facsimile. Unless we are exercising our oneness together, we are not moving in authority in the Spirit; we are moving in a psychic substitute of power. We move by human power as a substitute for the fact that we do not have the oneness that allows us to move in

---

Matthew 13:33 He spoke another parable to them, "The kingdom of heaven is like leaven, which a woman took, and hid in three pecks of meal, until it was all leavened."

the real authority of the Holy Spirit. We have moved in our own abilities for too long; the Body of Christ must move in the authority of God.

Our prime objective is to be one. Of all the instruction that we have received, the only direction that Christ gave us before He left this world was for us to be one; that includes each one of us. I must be committed to oneness, and I must get rid of every excuse for not being one. We can either remain nominal churches, or we can move into the fullness of what God has for us. Those who are dedicated to this oneness are going to move into something different from anything that they have ever known. But first they must leave this spiritual plateau, this place of excuses and halfhearted dedication. There will be a people who walk in oneness. All of our projects will fade away unless they become vehicles for becoming one. We must let the Lord burn this reality into our spirits until we understand that if we know these things, happy are we if we do them (John 13:17, KJV).

This oneness existed in the early days of the first-century Church: "And the congregation of those who believed were of one heart and soul" (Acts 4:32). Imagine being so one with each other that your souls are one. Most of us are not even one with our own soul. We do not have our spirit, soul and body united in one purpose within our being. Not only is that possible, but oneness with each other is the promise for all of those who believe. Imagine this congregation of believers described in the Book of Acts and the thousands who had come into Christ at that time:

> And the congregation of those who believed were of one heart and soul; and not one of them claimed that anything belonging to him was his own; but all things were common property to them. And with great power the apostles were

---

John 13:17, KJV If ye know these things, happy are ye if ye do them.

giving witness to the resurrection of the Lord Jesus, and abundant grace was upon them all. (Acts 4:32-33)

It was in this atmosphere that Ananias and Sapphira were slain because of their attempt to break the oneness. This was the Church in power at its beginning. The 120 disciples in the upper room on the Day of Pentecost were one, and they continued to be one as thousands were brought in and miraculous manifestations of that oneness took place. They believed in the Lord, not because of the signs and wonders performed by the apostles, but because they witnessed the miracle and authority of the oneness in that congregation of believers. This is available to us today.

This word should be like a two-edged sword that reaches down and pierces our innermost being (Hebrews 4:12). We cannot hold the world back anymore just because we do not want to go to the trouble of becoming one. We cannot pretend that there is another way to evangelize the world into a faith in God. If our outreach does not come from a people who are one, it will be the same insipid evangelism that the world has seen too often from the Church for over 2,000 years. The world cannot wait for us to get over our petty little refusals to become one. Oh, that the world could "taste and see that the LORD is good" (Psalm 34:8).

In every place that we see division, let there be an intense, persistent drive in our hearts to tear down the barriers to oneness, rather than tearing down ourselves or our brothers. Even if it's just

---

Hebrews 4:12 For the word of God is living and active and sharper than any two-edged sword, and piercing as far as the division of soul and spirit, of both joints and marrow, and able to judge the thoughts and intentions of the heart.

Psalm 34:8 O taste and see that the LORD is good; how blessed is the man who takes refuge in Him!

Gideon's 300 (Judges 7:7), a people will walk in this Word from the Lord Jesus Christ to become one, even as Christ and the Father are one. I prophesy, in the name of the Lord, the provision of the glory of Christ to come upon us as the enabling of this oneness. I loose us to move in oneness, to live it and breathe it as a people, in order that God may be glorified and that the world may finally believe.

Be one. With all of your heart, make a covenant with the Lord to see this oneness work. Let the world have a witness that Jesus Christ has come into the earth as the reflection of the Father. Let the world understand that Christ died for their sins, a perfect provision, and that they can enter into that provision. Lord, let the world believe, so they can be drawn to You like a magnet, so that they can run to You (Song of Solomon 1:4), so that they can cleave to You and have the privilege of being overwhelmed by the knowledge of the Lord (Isaiah 11:9). The Lord has called us to oneness; let us answer the call.

Judges 7:7 And the Lord said to Gideon, "I will deliver you with the 300 men who lapped and will give the Midianites into your hands; so let all the other people go, each man to his home."

Song of Solomon 1:4 "Draw me after you and let us run together! The king has brought me into his chambers."

Isaiah 11:9 They will not hurt or destroy in all My holy mountain, for the earth will be full of the knowledge of the Lord as the waters cover the sea.

Chapter 9

Are We the Church That Christ Spoke Of?

June 5, 2005
Grace Chapel of Honolulu, Honolulu, Oahu, Hawaii

This message, spoken on a Sunday morning to the local church congregation, was part of a foundational teaching on the first-century New Testament Church that opened up a revelation about oneness.

John chapter 17 records the prayer of Jesus to the Father before His crucifixion, as He ministered to the disciples. In this prayer we have a glimpse of what would happen in the Church in the days following His ascension:

> "But now I come to Thee; and these things I speak in the world, that they may have My joy made full in themselves. I have given them Thy word; and the world has hated them, because they are not of the world, even as I am not of the world. I do not ask Thee to take them out of the world, but to keep them from the evil one. They are not of the world, even as I am not of the world. Sanctify them in the truth; Thy word is truth. As Thou didst send Me into the world, I also have sent them into the world. And for their sakes I sanctify Myself, that they themselves also may be sanctified in truth. I do not ask in behalf of these alone,

> but for those also who believe in Me through their word; that they may all be one; even as Thou, Father, art in Me, and I in Thee, that they also may be in Us; that the world may believe that Thou didst send Me." (John 17:13-21)

It is evident that Christ commissioned the disciples into the earth. Yet, He also spoke beyond the twelve apostles, beyond the disciples of that generation, and commissioned all who would believe through their Word. It is an eternal, ongoing commission to the Church. Christ intended for the Church to continue from generation to generation through impartation and through the ministry of the Spirit. How does that impartation happen? It is a miracle of oneness, an impartation that we receive from the Father through the Son, and then through one another.

Oneness is like the Trinity. In our humanity, we have difficulty understanding something that seems to make no sense. Is there one God, or three? How are Christ and the Father one? How does the Holy Spirit fit in? Although our human minds cannot grasp these truths, they were a reality, by revelation, to the early apostolic fathers. They accepted that the believer is also included in this process of oneness with the Father, Son, and Holy Spirit, becoming so much like the Lord that they are inseparable. This is the foundation of the Church: "that they may all be one; even as Thou, Father, art in Me, and I in Thee, that they also may be in Us; that the world may believe that Thou didst send Me."

Here is my one prayer for the universal Church: Lord, that we may all be one. Bring this oneness that You prayed to the Father for. Beyond the power to do miracles, beyond the anointing to heal or to perform any other sign or wonder, the most important work of the Holy Spirit is to make us one. Healings are child's play, in a spiritual sense, compared to us becoming one. Real, true oneness, in the context of the universal Church, is our goal—so that the world may believe. True evangelism is going to flood this earth when there is a restoration of the oneness (Isaiah 11:9).

They had such a oneness in the first-century New Testament Church. This fact is recorded in the Book of Acts. Those believers all stood in one accord, with one voice; and when they prayed, the place was shaken and then signs and wonders took place, not only through the apostles, but through the Body itself (Acts 4:23-24, 29-31). This happened out of their oneness. This oneness was at the very inception of the Church. "And when the day of Pentecost was fully come, they were all with one accord in one place" (Acts 2:1, KJV). Those who were arguing and cowardly before the crucifixion were now clothed with power from on high because they had become one (Luke 24:49).

Somehow they came together on that day, at that moment, and the Church of Jesus Christ was born through that miracle of oneness. It was an answer to Christ's prayer, "And the glory which Thou hast given Me I have given to them; that they may be one, just as We are one" (John 17:22). What is the purpose of the glory of God being given to the Church? It is not simply for miracles, signs, and wonders; the glory of God is given to the Church to create the miracle of

---

Isaiah 11:9 They will not hurt or destroy in all My holy mountain, for the earth will be full of the knowledge of the LORD as the waters cover the sea.

Acts 4:23-24 And when they had been released, they went to their own companions, and reported all that the chief priests and the elders had said to them. [24] And when they heard this, they lifted their voices to God with one accord and said, "O Lord, it is Thou who DIDST MAKE THE HEAVEN AND THE EARTH AND THE SEA, AND ALL THAT IS IN THEM."

Acts 4:29-31 "And now, Lord, take note of their threats, and grant that Thy bond-servants may speak Thy word with all confidence, [30] while Thou dost extend Thy hand to heal, and signs and wonders take place through the name of Thy holy servant Jesus." [31] And when they had prayed, the place where they had gathered together was shaken, and they were all filled with the Holy Spirit, and began to speak the word of God with boldness.

Luke 24:49 "And behold, I am sending forth the promise of My Father upon you; but you are to stay in the city until you are clothed with power from on high."

oneness. You may not see it or feel it tangibly, but the glory of God is at work when you see people's hearts being welded together in oneness. Oneness is the fruit of that glory; through it the Church is perfected into one. "I in them, and Thou in Me, that they may be perfected into one, that the world may know that Thou didst send Me, and didst love them, even as Thou didst love Me" (John 17:23).

Let's look for the oneness in everything that we pursue. If there is a purpose for the Church, it is for the world to know that Jesus Christ came to this earth as an expression of the love of God to save all mankind. If we can move into oneness, and by that oneness the world begins to believe on Jesus Christ and His saving work, then the Church will truly be what Christ prayed for it to be. Whatever names we want to use for our churches, whatever programs we want to have, our constant question must be, are we becoming one? Is the world coming to believe on Him? If it is, then we will be able to say, "We are the Church of which Christ spoke!"

Chapter 10

That They May All Be One

February 27, 2006
Caio Martins Stadium, Niteroi, Brazil

During the annual School of Prophets conference near Rio de Janeiro, this message was spoken at the Caio Martins stadium to thousands of believers of differing Christian backgrounds. This was a benchmark event, knitting together hearts within the Christian community in Rio de Janeiro state and other areas of Brazil.

God is getting ready to end the greed and division that we have seen so often in churches in the United States and all over the world. The last one hundred years have witnessed several occasions of the tremendous moving of God by the Spirit, phenomenal releases of spiritual gifts and authority, restoration of ministries, and restoration of the Church. However, it has been too long since we have seen such a moving, and we should grieve in our spirits over this. When you have not witnessed something in your own generation, it is difficult to believe that it can happen again. No matter how impossible it may seem, a great moving of God can happen again throughout the whole earth.

Do you remember the sign that was given to Elijah when he prayed for rain? He saw the little cloud the size of a man's hand, and said, "Everybody run! It's going to rain like you've never seen before!" (1 Kings 18:44). God is going to move again, and He is looking for a generation in which to move. Any time God has ever moved in the earth, it is because He has heard the cries of His people (Exodus 2:23-25). The prayer, the intercession, and the faith of a people have triggered an outpouring of His Spirit. When we come together, it is not just to have a nice worship; it is not just to have a few churches get together for fellowship. We have a greater purpose, a greater faith. We come together to take a step into a real release of God's presence and glory.

God is preparing the vessels for His next great moving in the earth. The services that bring together many pastors from different churches would never take place without a lot of intercession, without a lot of spiritual warfare. Many things have been set to stop such meetings, but the churches involved are more mature now than when they started planning such gatherings. God is teaching His sons how to make things happen together by virtue of faith and prayer. And I honor the pastors, true men and women of God, who are willing to drop the walls built around their own churches and ministries to allow oneness to come forth within the Body of Christ. That is the step of faith that will trigger something from God.

Christianity, in all of its division, has missed this opportunity. There is a difference between there being many churches, and the fact that those churches are divided. While there will always be thousands of churches in different locations, there should not be a spirit of division in the Body of Christ. Division has rendered the Body of

---

1 Kings 18:44   And it came about at the seventh time, that he said, "Behold, a cloud as small as a man's hand is coming up from the sea." And he said, "Go up, say to Ahab, 'Prepare your chariot and go down, so that the heavy shower does not stop you.'"

Exodus 2:23-25   Now it came about in the course of those many days that the king of Egypt died. And the sons of Israel sighed because of the bondage, and they cried out; and their cry for help because of their bondage rose up to God. [24] So God heard their groaning; and God remembered His covenant with Abraham, Isaac, and Jacob. [25] And God saw the sons of Israel, and God took notice of them.

Christ ineffectual in its attempts to evangelize the world. Most of Christianity agrees on the need for evangelism, for the saving of souls and the sending of the Word of God to the ends of the earth. Many programs try to bring people to a faith in Jesus Christ as their personal Savior, but we have yet to see the effectiveness of true evangelism. As people look at the Body of Christ, as it is today, they are left with more reasons not to believe, than to believe.

The scriptural pattern for evangelism will be fulfilled when the world sees the Body of Christ in oneness. If you search the Scriptures, you cannot find another plan for evangelism that works. The following Scripture makes this plain:

> "I do not ask in behalf of these alone, but for those also who believe in Me through their word; that they may all be one; even as Thou, Father, art in Me, and I in Thee, that they also may be in Us; that the world may believe that Thou didst send Me. And the glory which Thou hast given Me I have given to them; that they may be one, just as We are one; I in them and Thou in Me, that they may be perfected into one, that the world may know that Thou didst send Me, and didst love them, even as Thou didst love Me." (John 17:20-23)

How does the oneness happen? By His glory. Believers should be seeking the glory of God to manifest itself once again in their churches. We are never going to become one just because we work at it. No, Christ gave His glory to His believers in order to create them into one. It is time to declare, "Lord, restore Your glory to the Church!" We have a world that needs to believe that God sent Jesus Christ into the earth, and they will only truly believe that when they see oneness of spirit and true unity in God's people.

Release Your glory, Lord. Release the cry of intercession. Remember the parable in the Scriptures of the widow who came before the unjust judge and would not be denied (Luke 18:2-5). Let that determination be in our hearts. Creating opportunities for groups and churches to come together takes that kind of determination and persistence. God is teaching us that we cannot give up. You knock, and you keep knocking; you ask, and you keep asking, because you are determined that what the Lord has shown you, you are going to have (Matthew 7:7). We are not asking for something that God has not provided. Christ prayed, "Father, I am giving them My glory." We should cry, "Where did that glory go?"

We should begin to cry out, "Lord, restore Your presence in the Church, in the Body of Christ." By that glory we will become one, and when we are one the whole earth will believe that God sent Jesus Christ. We can no longer afford to see the Church exist without the power and authority of God, without the maturity of the believers that are able to move in the anointing of the Lord. Too long has the Church been satisfied with preaching a salvation message over and over again. When do we mature those who already believe? That process of maturity will begin in those churches that are willing to come together to be one.

When you give yourself to oneness, the maturity follows. How does God perfect His Church? He perfects it into one. The perfect Body of Christ is one Body, "perfected into one, that the world may know that Thou didst send Me" (John 17:23). When the hearts of leaders become involved together with the hearts of men and women who declare that the Body of Christ must come together as one, then

---

Luke 18:2-5 Saying, "There was in a certain city a judge who did not fear God, and did not respect man. ³ And there was a widow in that city, and she kept coming to him, saying, 'Give me legal protection from my opponent.' ⁴ And for a while he was unwilling; but afterward he said to himself, 'Even though I do not fear God nor respect man, ⁵ yet because this widow bothers me, I will give her legal protection, lest by continually coming she wear me out.'"

Matthew 7:7 "Ask, and it shall be given to you; seek, and you shall find; knock, and it shall be opened to you."

the knowledge of the Lord will cover the earth (Isaiah 11:9). It has been over 2,000 years; how long do we want to wait? Let there be a cry in us like there was in Moses: "Lord, show me Your glory!" (Exodus 33:18). Lord, release Your glory in the Church, until we are perfected into one.

We see a beautiful picture of this reality in Ephesians the 4th chapter:

> There is one body and one Spirit, just as also you were called in one hope of your calling; one Lord, one faith, one baptism, one God and Father of all who is over all and through all and in all. But to each one of us grace was given according to the measure of Christ's gift. (Ephesians 4:4-7)

When churches come together, each one of us has a measure of the grace of God in our gift. Christ has given each one of us something that others do not have, so that without one another, we are incomplete. In this age, the Body of Christ is incomplete, totally incapable of functioning, and will remain so until we become one. It is like the dry bones in the prophecy of Ezekiel. As Ezekiel prophesied, those bones began to rattle and come together (Ezekiel 37:7). That must have been an amazing sight to watch—all of those bones rattling and coming to life as they were drawn into one. The bones became bodies, they became whole. It is time for the Body of Christ to come together and be whole. If you listen, you can hear the bones rattling. But we are not going to stop at rattling bones. Like Ezekiel, we are going to prophesy until all of the bones come together in wholeness,

---

Isaiah 11:9 They will not hurt or destroy in all My holy mountain, for the earth will be full of the knowledge of the Lord as the waters cover the sea.

Exodus 33:18 Then Moses said, "I pray Thee, show me Thy glory!"

Ezekiel 37:7 So I prophesied as I was commanded; and as I prophesied, there was a noise, and behold, a rattling; and the bones came together, bone to its bone.

and stand as a great army on the face of the earth in the name of the Lord (Ezekiel 37:8-10).

The Body of Christ will be the greatest army that the earth has ever seen—one that moves not by might, but by the Spirit of the living God (Zechariah 4:6). This is the Body of Christ that brings in the Kingdom and crowns Him King. Jesus is waiting at the right hand of the Father until every enemy is made the footstool for His feet (Hebrews 10:12-13). And it is the army of God, the Body of Christ, that will accomplish this. The weapons of their warfare are not carnal, but mighty to the pulling down of strongholds (2 Corinthians 10:4, KJV). It will be amazing to see how the spiritual forces of wickedness, division, and hate in high places are brought down by a people who are one by the Holy Spirit (Ephesians 6:12). This is how we make way for the King (Isaiah 40:3-5). It is going to take all of our spiritual

---

Ezekiel 37:8-10 And I looked, and behold, sinews were on them, and flesh grew, and skin covered them; but there was no breath in them. [9] Then He said to me, "Prophesy to the breath, prophesy, son of man, and say to the breath, 'Thus says the Lord God, "Come from the four winds, O breath, and breathe on these slain, that they come to life."'" [10] So I prophesied as He commanded me, and the breath came into them, and they came to life, and stood on their feet, an exceedingly great army.

Zechariah 4:6 Then he answered and said to me, "This is the word of the Lord to Zerubbabel saying, 'Not by might nor by power, but by My Spirit,' says the Lord of hosts."

Hebrews 10:12-13 But He, having offered one sacrifice for sins for all time, SAT DOWN AT THE RIGHT HAND OF GOD, [13] waiting from that time onward UNTIL HIS ENEMIES BE MADE A FOOTSTOOL FOR HIS FEET.

2 Corinthians 10:4, KJV For the weapons of our warfare are not carnal, but mighty through God to the pulling down of strong holds.

Ephesians 6:12 For our struggle is not against flesh and blood, but against the rulers, against the powers, against the world forces of this darkness, against the spiritual forces of wickedness in the heavenly places.

Isaiah 40:3-5 A voice is calling, "Clear the way for the Lord in the wilderness; make smooth in the desert a highway for our God. [4] Let every valley be lifted up, and every mountain and hill be made low; and let the rough ground become a plain, and the rugged terrain a broad valley; [5] then the glory of the Lord will be revealed, and all flesh will see it together; for the mouth of the Lord has spoken."

gifts and every church coming together to make this happen. We mix our hearts together into the oneness of Christ's Body and speak with faith, like Ezekiel, "Bones, come together!"

> And He gave some as apostles, and some as prophets, and some as evangelists, and some as pastors and teachers, for the equipping of the saints for the work of service, to the building up of the body of Christ; until we all attain to the unity of the faith, and of the knowledge of the Son of God, to a mature man, to the measure of the stature which belongs to the fulness of Christ. As a result, we are no longer to be children, tossed here and there by waves, and carried about by every wind of doctrine, by the trickery of men, by craftiness in deceitful scheming; but speaking the truth in love, we are to grow up in all aspects into Him, who is the head, even Christ, from whom the whole body, being fitted and held together by that which every joint supplies, according to the proper working of each individual part, causes the growth of the body for the building up of itself in love. (Ephesians 4:11-16)

He gave the apostles, prophets, evangelists, and pastors and teachers for one purpose: for the equipping of the saints for the work of service. It is not the foundational ministries that build the Body. They equip each one, they perfect our spirits, but it is the Body that builds itself up in love. This is the maturity that comes when we move as one. Our spiritual service is the building up of the Body of Christ until we all attain to the unity of the faith, and of the knowledge of the Son of God, to a mature man. We are to be no more children; oneness brings forth sons who are matured to the measure of the stature which belongs to the fullness of Christ. This is possible, but we can only attain it together as one.

It is time for a moving of God. It is time for an outpouring of His Spirit, a manifestation of His glory that will bring us into the oneness that is truly the Body of Christ. This may be a day of small beginnings, but you cannot imagine what God can do with a small beginning (Zechariah 4:10)! He can take a few fish and a little bit of bread, and by the time He blesses it, it will feed the world (Mark 6:41-44). The Kingdom of God is like a little leaven (Matthew 13:33). This is the leaven of oneness that is being implanted and it is going to grow until many churches in every nation come together in their hearts to become one, and the knowledge of God's Word goes to the ends of the earth.

Zechariah 4:10 "For who has despised the day of small things? But these seven will be glad when they see the plumb line in the hand of Zerubbabel—these are the eyes of the LORD which range to and fro throughout the earth."

Mark 6:41-44 And He took the five loaves and the two fish, and looking up toward heaven, He blessed the food and broke the loaves and He kept giving them to the disciples to set before them; and He divided up the two fish among them all. [42] And they all ate and were satisfied. [43] And they picked up twelve full baskets of the broken pieces, and also of the fish. [44] And there were five thousand men who ate the loaves.

Matthew 13:33 He spoke another parable to them, "The kingdom of heaven is like leaven, which a woman took, and hid in three pecks of meal, until it was all leavened."

Chapter 11

Finding the Way Back Into Oneness

January 18, 2008
Igreja A Palavra Viva, Mount Zion, Niteroi, Brazil

This message was spoken at a gathering of local pastors in the Christian community, many of whom were meeting each other for the first time, all of them seeking the Lord for oneness in the Body of Christ.

After 2,000 years of Christianity, it is almost impossible to discern the true Church except by revelation and by letting the Lord extract it for us, with many confirmations from the Scriptures. The true Church is lost in the fog of history. And if the Church as we know it today continues in its current pattern, we will miss the anointing and the power that God intends for us to have. The opportunity is before us to change what has been the history of the Church, but it will only come by restoring Christ's Lordship to His Church. If we humble ourselves, submit our hearts one to another, and seek the Lord, we can seize this opportunity.

The Lordship of Christ over His Body cannot be established apart from the leadership in the Church. We must grasp on a deeper level what His Lordship means for us as ministries, and apply it to ourselves. It is time for us as leaders to take our own medicine. All of the problems within the Church have come from those at its head, the leadership past and present. That is what has brought the Church to where we are today. Only God, by His grace, can give us the leadership that is able to direct us out of the problems that have been created. And in order to lead effectively, we need to understand the diversity of the Body. Look at this explanation in 1 Corinthians chapter 12:

> Now there are varieties of gifts, but the same Spirit. And there are varieties of ministries, and the same Lord. And there are varieties of effects, but the same God who works all things in all persons. But to each one is given the manifestation of the Spirit for the common good. (1 Corinthians 12:4-7)

This vision of the "common good" has been lost to the Church. As we have been separated either by community or anointing or direction of the Holy Spirit, our various gifts have been misinterpreted as divisions among us. These distinctions were never meant to cause division. Diverse gifts and ministries are meant to feed back into the welfare of the Body of Christ for the common good. Our common purpose must become more important than our individual ministries. By the Spirit, we honor these gifts and ministries so that they can become conduits for God's love as we function together. God gave those gifts and ministries for the common good.

> But now God has placed the members, each one of them, in the body, just as He desired. And if they were all one member, where would the body be? But now there are many members, but one body. And the eye cannot say to the hand, "I have no need of you"; or again the head to the feet, "I have no need of you." On the contrary, it is much truer that the members of the body which seem to be weaker are necessary; and those members of the body, which we deem less honorable, on these we bestow more abundant honor, and our unseemly members come

> to have more abundant seemliness, whereas our seemly members have no need of it. But God has so composed the body, giving more abundant honor to that member which lacked, that there should be no division in the body, but that the members should have the same care for one another. (1 Corinthians 12:18-25)

We have to apply this to our different ministries and churches. God brings diversity with the intent that there be no division in the Body. When the human mind sees diversity, it finds ways to separate, to compare, to compete, and to create division. That must end in all of us as leaders, and throughout the Body of Christ.

Some may have a ministry to the poor, or a burden for evangelism. Some may have a ministry to pastors. Others may have a burden for intercession, for spiritual warfare, or for teaching. Entire churches may be built around specific ministries or distinct gifts. It is easy to look at your own gift and think, "What I'm doing is more important." When you realize that there is a common good, then you realize that without other churches and ministries, your church is lacking something. In yourself, or even in your local fellowship, you are not doing many things that the Holy Spirit wants done; you are incomplete. Whatever you have is only a piece of Christ's personality or burden. You must find the way to minister to the common good. God wants to restore His Church so that every area of ministry has His presence and power. It is up to us to look for the ways to bring the Body together so that there is no longer division. That is the first step.

Before His crucifixion, Christ envisioned the spreading of the Word to the Gentile world and the multitudes who would believe on His name. For thousands of people at the beginning of the Church, salvation was a response to the explosion of God's presence. The power to receive salvation was in the Church because of their oneness. Today we work so hard to minister salvation, but much of our effort is lost in the lack of oneness in the Body of Christ. Yet there is a way to return to the oneness that God created. We should come together as leaders and ministries and cry, "Lord, make us one, as You and the Father are one!" Our diversity, as it manifests in differences of gifts or even in doctrines, is not the point. God gave us these differences to make us one, so start believing that our differences are no longer going to divide us. By the anointing of the Holy Spirit, our differences will make us one. As the Church becomes one, God's presence will be restored. His coming to His Church in power is dependent on our oneness.

One of the greatest illustrations in the Bible of finding oneness together is in Acts chapter 15. It describes the early Church coming together to solve a great dilemma, which was how to deal with Gentiles being added to the fellowship of believers. How should the Jews relate to the new Gentile believers? They had nothing to guide them since the Church had only Jewish believers for the first fifteen years of its history. The issue was, should the new Gentile believers be circumcised, as was the requirement for the Jews under the Law? After Paul and Barnabas had great dissension and debate with those of the circumcision, they realized that the potential for confusion and division existed among the brethren (Acts 15:2). The leaders, the elders and the apostles, refused to use their individual churches as a platform for debate, and they came to Jerusalem to seek the Lord together. In the face of this challenge, they stopped what they were doing to find an answer that would preserve the oneness.

We have to remember how separate these people were. These ministries were widely separated geographically; some were ministering to the Jews and some were ministering to the Gentiles. There was an amazing diversity spread across natural divisions of

---

Acts 15:2 And when Paul and Barnabas had great dissension and debate with them, the brethren determined that Paul and Barnabas and certain others of them should go up to Jerusalem to the apostles and elders concerning this issue.

geography and culture. Yet somehow they stopped everything they were doing to come together and find the mind of the Lord. They came together in Jerusalem, they prayed, they sought the Lord, and they debated. They gave each other a place to speak, and everyone listened. But when James spoke, their hearts bore witness to the wisdom of the Lord (Acts 15:13-14, 19, 22).

We also must come together with enough humility, brokenness, and commitment to the common good that, regardless of who speaks the word of wisdom, we will have a willingness in our hearts to bear witness. Beyond our walls, our concepts, and our doctrines, we determine to hear the voice of the Lord out of the mouths of our brothers and sisters. The biggest hurdle is to see one another as Christ coming forth in the flesh of humans. Like Paul said, "We have this treasure in earthen vessels" (2 Corinthians 4:7). That does not make me anything in myself, but there is a treasure in me. How do we not only respect one another, but submit to one another? In small steps, God will begin to teach us how to submit in our spirits to one another.

It is easy to fake commitment and submission one to another and not really be knit together in our hearts. For years, pastors have been fellowshipping together in communities, yet changing very little. Rather than facing their difficult differences, they have found

---

Acts 15:13-14 And after they had stopped speaking, James answered, saying, "Brethren, listen to me. [14] Simeon has related how God first concerned Himself about taking from among the Gentiles a people for His name."

Acts 15:19 "Therefore it is my judgment that we do not trouble those who are turning to God from among the Gentiles."

Acts 15:22 Then it seemed good to the apostles and the elders, with the whole church, to choose men from among them to send to Antioch with Paul and Barnabas—Judas called Barsabbas, and Silas, leading men among the brethren.

2 Corinthians 4:7 But we have this treasure in earthen vessels, that the surpassing greatness of the power may be of God and not from ourselves.

leaders with whom they feel an affinity, and have settled for just fellowship. That may be good, but we are not looking to attain "good." We are seeking the oneness that is forged by the Spirit of God, despite all of our differences.

We can only change the way we function as the Body of Christ by our submission one to another. This is not easy. Within every church or group, the leaders must first work on this together. The sheep will follow the example of good shepherds and flourish. Each shepherd needs to ask the question, "When I think I have a Word from God or a revelation, who can tell me 'No'?" When they have the willingness, trust, and submission to be open to correction, God can move through a group of leaders as one.

That openness and trust was infused in the hearts of those early disciples, as you see in Paul's submission to the apostles:

> Then after an interval of fourteen years I went up again to Jerusalem with Barnabas, taking Titus along also. And it was because of a revelation that I went up; and I submitted to them the gospel which I preach among the Gentiles, but I did so in private to those who were of reputation, for fear that I might be running, or had run, in vain. (Galatians 2:1-2)

Despite Paul's own revelation, the Lord spoke to him, in effect, "It is not enough that you have heard from Me, that you have seen Me, that you have been caught up to the third heaven; you must go submit your heart to your brothers." Paul went and submitted to the other apostles his gospel, the very revelation of the ministry to the Gentiles that he cherished. He laid it all back on the table to make sure that what he had was a Word from God. Notice that Paul submitted his revelation to those who were of reputation. He had a witness in his own spirit, but he submitted to those whom he knew to be proven and commissioned as apostles of God. He avoided the false brethren, yet opened his heart to those in true authority (Galatians 2:4-6).

God is helping us find by revelation those to whom we can submit, not only our hearts, but even our very ministry and gospel. This group cannot be just a pastoral fellowship in which we rehearse our accomplishments and pat each other on the back. Somehow I have to find those to whom I can submit my heart. Then I must commit beforehand that when I have a word of direction, they can say, "Stop. This is not right. This is not the Lord." When we submit ourselves to the Lordship of Jesus Christ, as it is manifesting in His authorities, something is going to change. Our oneness will emerge; power and authority will be restored.

Another example of submission came shortly after this, when Paul rebuked Peter for moving in hypocrisy regarding the Gentiles.

> But when Cephas came to Antioch, I opposed him to his face, because he stood condemned. For prior to the coming of certain men from James, he used to eat with the Gentiles; but when they came, he began to withdraw and hold himself aloof, fearing the party of the circumcision. (Galatians 2:11-12)

Peter was eating with the Gentiles, probably sitting there at lunch having a nice pork chop. Then here come some of the brothers from Jerusalem, and Peter sneaks out the back door. When the Jews to whom he had been ministering saw this, they began to follow his example of hypocrisy. Paul was troubled about this and went to speak with Peter.

Galatians 2:4-6 But it was because of the false brethren who had sneaked in to spy out our liberty which we have in Christ Jesus, in order to bring us into bondage. [5] But we did not yield in subjection to them for even an hour, so that the truth of the gospel might remain with you. [6] But from those who were of high reputation (what they were makes no difference to me; God shows no partiality)—well, those who were of reputation contributed nothing to me.

The apostles gave each other the access to correct one another's spirit. It is too easy for us as leaders of our churches to not receive correction if we are only surrounded by those who are listening to our instruction and serving us, allowing us to determine on our own what God is speaking. I am sure Peter had a wonderful explanation for his actions, and no one within his own circle corrected him. Paul could see more clearly what Peter was doing; often distance gives us a fresh perspective. Paul spoke the truth to Peter, and Peter was willing in his openness to hear what Paul had to say. He submitted to it as a Word from God.

The gifts that Christ is looking to empower His ministries with in this hour might be too powerful for us yet. The early apostles spoke a Word of life and death. I doubt that God is willing to release that kind of power to us if we are loose cannons. Such anointing is being held back from the Church because there is no guard over our souls. We do not yet function in oneness with a sense of common purpose. We have to move beyond fellowship into real submission to one another. It has to be Christ's Lordship manifested in each one. As scary as that seems, by faith we will learn it through experience.

Consider again the example of the apostles and elders in Acts chapter 15. When they determined to come together in Jerusalem, not only did they find the Word of the Lord together; they also submitted their hearts to one another to follow it through in their local churches. They did not walk away from the table and say, "That was a good meeting, but now I'm going to go tell my church what I want. It was a great time in Jerusalem, but I've got to go home now, and there may be pressure there to circumcise the Gentiles." No, they were faithful to carry out that directive to all of their churches. There was an integrity to seek the Lord together, to honor the Word that they had received, and to walk it out in oneness. It was a monumental change, but that created the power that was in the early Church. Today we have an opportunity to see that power restored and to restore Christ's Lordship to the Church, as we find our way back into oneness.

Chapter 12

We Are Responsible for Oneness

January 26, 2008
Igreja A Palavra Viva, Mount Zion, Niteroi, Brazil

This message was spoken at a breakfast meeting with nearly a hundred leaders of the local Christian community who had gathered to seek oneness in the Body of Christ.

The history of the Church is not a history of oneness. It is a history of division, separation, infighting, and destroying one another. That cycle must end! In speaking about Israel and the Palestinians, one brother expressed something very beautiful. He said, "When the people involved want peace, there will be peace." It is the determination for peace that is the key. It is not a matter of who gives up what land, or any of the natural problems that exist with borderlines. When there is a desire, a drive, and a determination for peace, all of those issues will be worked out. As long as we have no desire for peace, we will live with an excuse for why we fight with one another. Christianity should be on the front lines of peace. We, as the Body of Christ, must find a way to achieve oneness. Our existence and our message depends on that.

As we read in John chapter 17, Jesus prayed to the Father for the disciples. In this prayer His will and direction for us becomes clear:

> "I do not ask Thee to take them out of the world, but to keep them from the evil one. They are not of the world,

even as I am not of the world. Sanctify them in the truth; Thy word is truth. As Thou didst send Me into the world, I also have sent them into the world. And for their sakes I sanctify Myself, that they themselves also may be sanctified in truth. I do not ask in behalf of these alone, but for those also who believe in Me through their word; that they may all be one; even as Thou, Father, art in Me, and I in Thee, that they also may be in Us; that the world may believe that Thou didst send Me." (John 17:15-21)

Just prior to Christ's death for the removal of our sin, His heart was expressed in this prayer to the Father. This prayer is for all who hear and believe, from generation to generation. We who believe in this day are the disciples of the great commission, and we must realize that Christ has sent us into the world with the same commission as those early disciples (Matthew 28:19-20). When I went to seminary, we were taught that the anointing stopped with the first apostles. So I went to the professor with this prayer, and I said, "It is clear that Christ was praying for the apostles and the other disciples that were standing around, but what about this idea that He was praying for all those who believe through their words?" If we are believers, then Christ's prayer is also for us, and it must have its fulfillment, and that might as well be in this generation.

In Christ's prayer, what is He sending us to accomplish? "That they may all be one; even as Thou, Father, art in Me, and I in Thee, that they also may be in Us; that the world may believe." We read in the great commission that Christ sent the disciples into the world to preach the Gospel. We all agree on that. But this prayer in John 17 tells us how the world will come to believe the Gospel. The impact of the Church on the world is not what it should be. A great revival is yet to happen—one in which the world believes, when hearts open

---

Matthew 28:19-20 "Go therefore and make disciples of all the nations, baptizing them in the name of the Father and the Son and the Holy Spirit, [20] teaching them to observe all that I commanded you; and lo, I am with you always, even to the end of the age."

and people receive the message of the Gospel. That is dependent on our oneness. It is one thing to be obedient to the great commission by preaching the Gospel to the ends of the earth, but I want the world to believe. And they will only believe when we, the believers, are one. This is why there has been such a battle against oneness. Satan's plan to stop the Gospel has been focused on keeping Christianity divided, because a kingdom divided against itself cannot stand (Mark 3:24).

The desire for division is not necessarily within the members of the congregation. We have many wonderful sheep who follow their shepherds. It is the shepherds who have the ability to stop the sectarianism and the criticisms that lead to division. We have many different ideas and beliefs. Yet if we were to write down the things that we all believe and agree upon, we would find there are many more things that make us one than issues that divide us. We believe in Christ. We believe in His blood that washes us of our sins and includes the Gentiles into the family of God. And we believe that Christ is coming again. The truths that are truly important are the same ones that we all agree upon.

We may have many different ideas about how Christ is coming again. Is there a "rapture"[9] or not? Will there be a thousand years of Christ's reign on earth? Maybe we would not agree on those details, but how important are they, compared to our oneness? Christ is

---

Mark 3:24 "And if a kingdom is divided against itself, that kingdom cannot stand."

[9.] Rapture is a term in Christian eschatology which was originally used as a synonym for the first resurrection as referred to in 1 Corinthians 15:51-52. In the Scriptures, the first resurrection occurs after the tribulation period. Therefore, the original use of this term was without the belief that a group of people is caught up to heaven before the tribulation. This definition is the view that has been held historically for the longest period of time. The current, most popular use of the term "rapture," especially among fundamentalist Christians in the United States, refers to a group of people "being caught up to meet the Lord in the air" as described in 1 Thessalonians 4:16-17, and being taken to heaven. This concept was introduced by John Nelson Darby in the 1830s. It moves the first resurrection forward chronologically, referring to it as a pre-tribulation event where one group of people is caught up to heaven while another is left behind on the earth to face the tribulation.

coming again; and when He does, we will all understand how He came. When He is here, we will all be able to agree how He got here. In the meantime, we should not let our concepts about His coming cause divisions in our midst. The job we have to do before He comes is much more important.

I believe there is a move of the Spirit happening, an anointing to begin to bring this level of oneness. It is wonderful to come together, shake hands, have coffee, share some food, and take Communion with one another. That is a good start, but what we look for is this oneness. Do not just look to have fellowship with one another; seek to become one. When our hearts are one, I believe the power of Christ in His Church will be released. It is not an easy thing. From the beginning of the Church, it was not easy to maintain oneness, but I want us to recognize that it can be done, if we determine it.

In Galatians chapter 2, Paul wrote about the council at Jerusalem. This was the coming together of the leaders of the Church about a great problem. The apostles called the council at Jerusalem because they did not know what to do with these Gentiles. The apostles and elders were spread all over the place preaching the Gospel when this Gentile issue emerged. What were they to do? Remember, for its first fifteen or twenty years, the early Church was made up of only Jews. God had to speak to Peter three times in a dream to convince him that the Gentiles were to be a part of God's family (Acts 10:9-16, 28),

---

Acts 10:9-16 And on the next day, as they were on their way, and approaching the city, Peter went up on the housetop about the sixth hour to pray. [10] And he became hungry, and was desiring to eat; but while they were making preparations, he fell into a trance; [11] and he beheld the sky opened up, and a certain object like a great sheet coming down, lowered by four corners to the ground, [12] and there were in it all kinds of four-footed animals and crawling creatures of the earth and birds of the air. [13] And a voice came to him, "Arise, Peter, kill and eat!" [14] But Peter said, "By no means, Lord, for I have never eaten anything unholy and unclean." [15] And again a voice came to him a second time, "What God has cleansed, no longer consider unholy." [16] And this happened three times; and immediately the object was taken up into the sky.

Acts 10:28 And he said to them, "You yourselves know how unlawful it is for a man who is a Jew to associate with a foreigner or to visit him; and yet God has shown me that I should not call any man unholy or unclean."

and years later the apostles and elders still had to come together to solve this issue (Acts 15:1-2). I think it is interesting that today the Church is trying to come back together and figure out how to relate to the Jews. Hopefully, our hearts will be as open, and we will have as much revelation as they had in Acts 15.

Think about their decision at that point. The apostles could have laid anything they wanted to on the Gentile believers (Acts 15:19-20). The males, in particular, really had something to lose if they would have submitted to circumcision. Paul wrote of this time,

> Then after an interval of fourteen years I went up again to Jerusalem with Barnabas, taking Titus along also. And it was because of a revelation that I went up; and I submitted to them the gospel which I preach among the Gentiles, but I did so in private to those who were of reputation, for fear that I might be running, or had run, in vain. (Galatians 2:1-2)

Prior to going up to Jerusalem, Paul had been ministering the Gospel to the Gentiles while the other apostles were spread across the nations. Still, they came together with the elders in Jerusalem. Paul wrote that he went up because of a revelation, for fear that he had run in vain. Paul was not afraid because of the Gospel he was ministering; it had come directly from the Lord. Jesus Christ had appeared to Paul on several occasions and given him his apostolic

---

Acts 15:1-2 And some men came down from Judea and began teaching the brethren, "Unless you are circumcised according to the custom of Moses, you cannot be saved." [2] And when Paul and Barnabas had great dissension and debate with them, the brethren determined that Paul and Barnabas and certain others of them should go up to Jerusalem to the apostles and elders concerning this issue.

Acts 15:19-20 "Therefore it is my judgment that we do not trouble those who are turning to God from among the Gentiles, [20] but that we write to them that they abstain from things contaminated by idols and from fornication and from what is strangled and from blood."

ministry (Acts 9:15; 1 Corinthians 15:8). He did not go to Jerusalem because he was afraid that he was preaching incorrectly. Paul's fear was that division was taking hold in the Church. He understood the principle of oneness, and he knew it was important to have confirmation from the other apostolic leaders and to establish a oneness with them. Otherwise, people would not believe their testimony. When you preach in oneness, then the world believes. So Paul went back to Jerusalem to confirm and strengthen the oneness.

The prayer of Christ was that we be one, and based upon that oneness, the world will believe. The reverse would also be true, that the impact of the Gospel is lost through our division. When Paul went up to Jerusalem, the apostles not only came into a oneness, but they also carried that agreement with them to their local churches. How do we heal the divisions along denominational lines, and problems of our faith and doctrines? It seems impossible. But nothing could have been more impossible or divisive than the issue of the Gentile believers. It did not even make sense that the Gentiles would be included in the early Church. Our doctrinal issues may not make sense either, but our determination to become one must take precedence. We are to be one Body, one family, one heart. Christ is to return to the oneness that He prayed for.

Imagine that when Christ returns, we all stand before Him and say, "I'm sorry about Your prayer in John 17; we didn't do that." I want Him to come back to one people, one Church, one Body. We are one Body, with many diversities. God gave us those diversities. It is up to the leadership to determine whether or not Christ's prayer in John 17 will have fulfillment. There is power in the prayer of Jesus Christ, and we believe for that power to be executed among us in creating oneness in the leadership of His Church.

Acts 9:15 But the Lord said to him, "Go, for he is a chosen instrument of Mine, to bear My name before the Gentiles and kings and the sons of Israel."

1 Corinthians 15:8 And last of all, as it were to one untimely born, He appeared to me also.

What result do we want to see from our coming together as leaders? Not just fellowship—oneness. God has a purpose in this hour: to see Christ's prayer fulfilled by a moving of His Spirit until the oneness of His Body becomes a reality. We take the responsibility to see oneness begin to spread like a fire that will consume the whole Church!

Chapter 13

We Are One Man

April 11, 2008
Church of His Kingdom, San Diego, California

This message was spoken in a service where pastors and believers of various cultural backgrounds from the surrounding communities gathered together to worship the Lord as one.

What is God's purpose for us in this generation? I believe one of the greatest purposes is our impact on the Church itself. One of the greatest problems we face is that we have lost the power of the early Church. How was that power lost? It disappeared in the conflicts arising from racism and the rejection of other cultures. Look at the earliest accounts of those who believed on the Lord. If you begin in Acts the 6th chapter, you will see the Church in its infancy. "Now at this time while the disciples were increasing in number, a complaint arose on the part of the Hellenistic Jews against the native Hebrews, because their widows were being overlooked in the daily serving of food" (Acts 6:1).

This is the first conflict that the Scripture itself points out in the Church, and it was completely focused on the cultural differences between the Hellenistic Jews and the native Hebrews. Isn't that strange? At that time, there were deeply rooted divisions which came to the surface as the believers began to live, eat, and worship together. We see the same pattern repeated today in our churches. It is so easy to find reasons why we allow our own walls of separation to stand.

From the moment of Christ's ascension until now, we see that satan has been set to destroy the Body of Christ through racism and cultural differences. For centuries, this plan has eventually thwarted or diminished many moves of God. Something has to break this destructive pattern. I believe it is possible. When a handful of people from a few different churches in one area get together, it is no small thing. There is the potential to change the landscape of Christianity as we have known it. I believe this is essential for the coming Kingdom of the Lord.

At this time, many believers are excited about Christ's return to the earth. However, we should probably be saying, "Lord, don't come yet. Hold on a minute. We have some work to do." Do we want Christ to return to a racially and culturally divided body of people and then say to Him, "This is the reward of Your suffering"? He died on the cross for us—for all of us. The Scripture teaches what we are to do with the talents that He gave us (Matthew 25:22-28). Each of us will have to face the Lord and answer the question, "What did you do with what I gave you?" Before that happens, we have some work to do. We are the only ones who can bring down the walls of division and end the hatred.

Matthew 25:22-28 "The one also who had received the two talents came up and said, 'Master, you entrusted to me two talents; see, I have gained two more talents.' [23] His master said to him, 'Well done, good and faithful slave; you were faithful with a few things, I will put you in charge of many things; enter into the joy of your master.' [24] And the one also who had received the one talent came up and said, 'Master, I knew you to be a hard man, reaping where you did not sow, and gathering where you scattered no seed. [25] And I was afraid, and went away and hid your talent in the ground; see, you have what is yours.' [26] But his master answered and said to him, 'You wicked, lazy slave, you knew that I reap where I did not sow, and gather where I scattered no seed. [27] Then you ought to have put my money in the bank, and on my arrival I would have received my money back with interest. [28] Therefore take away the talent from him, and give it to the one who has the ten talents.'"

To see how insidious this pattern has been in the Church, let's look at Acts chapter 15. After amazing manifestations of oneness, the second big challenge that faced the Church was a racial issue. What were the Jewish believers supposed to do with the other nations and races that were coming to believe on Christ? What about those Gentiles? The apostles and elders came together to find a confirmed Word from the Lord regarding this:

> And some men came down from Judea and began teaching the brethren, "Unless you are circumcised according to the custom of Moses, you cannot be saved." And when Paul and Barnabas had great dissension and debate with them, the brethren determined that Paul and Barnabas and certain others of them should go up to Jerusalem to the apostles and elders concerning this issue. (Acts 15:1-2)

> And the apostles and the elders came together to look into this matter. And after there had been much debate, Peter stood up and said to them, "Brethren, you know that in the early days God made a choice among you, that by my mouth the Gentiles should hear the word of the gospel and believe. And God, who knows the heart, bore witness to them, giving them the Holy Spirit, just as He also did to us; and He made no distinction between us and them, cleansing their hearts by faith. Now therefore why do you put God to the test by placing upon the neck of the disciples a yoke which neither our fathers nor we have been able to bear? But we believe that we are saved through the grace of the Lord Jesus, in the same way as they also are." (Acts 15:6-11)

Earlier, the Lord had given Peter a vision three times before he was able to open up to something new; he was so conditioned by his own viewpoints (Acts 10:9-16). Finally, Peter told the Gentiles at the house of Cornelius what God had shown him: "And he said to them, 'You yourselves know how unlawful it is for a man who is a Jew to associate with a foreigner or to visit him; and yet God has shown me that I should not call any man unholy or unclean'" (Acts 10:28).

The Gentiles were not to be considered unholy or unclean. Yet today we are still very conditioned by our racial and cultural viewpoints. We need to repent and change. If we believe the Bible literally, we know that God created Adam and Eve. The Scriptures show us that there is only one race on the earth; we are all descendants of one man, Adam (Genesis 5:1-2). Genetic advances have prompted scientists to examine whether or not the Genesis account is feasible: that one man and woman brought forth all the races now on the earth. Geneticists have actually been able to trace and confirm this genetic lineage. The conclusion of this research is that there was a genetic Adam and Eve. The DNA of the entire human race originated from a single woman and a single man.[10] Even according to science, we all share a common genetic makeup and lineage.

Lord, help us to see the Scriptures without our cultural and racial conditionings! We should all come before the Lord with this cry:

Acts 10:9-16 And on the next day, as they were on their way, and approaching the city, Peter went up on the housetop about the sixth hour to pray. [10] And he became hungry, and was desiring to eat; but while they were making preparations, he fell into a trance; [11] and he beheld the sky opened up, and a certain object like a great sheet coming down, lowered by four corners to the ground, [12] and there were in it all kinds of four-footed animals and crawling creatures of the earth and birds of the air. [13] And a voice came to him, "Arise, Peter, kill and eat!" [14] But Peter said, "By no means, Lord, for I have never eaten anything unholy and unclean." [15] And again a voice came to him a second time, "What God has cleansed, no longer consider unholy." [16] And this happened three times; and immediately the object was taken up into the sky.

Genesis 5:1-2 This is the book of the generations of Adam. In the day when God created man, He made him in the likeness of God. [2] He created them male and female, and He blessed them and named them Man in the day when they were created.

[10.] "The Search for Adam," *National Geographic Documentary*. 2005. DVD.

"Eradicate from us satan's lies, and our walls and divisions." The truth is, Christ is not divided. There is no division. Christ is not racially separated. We believe that He is returning and will establish His Kingdom on the earth, but His Kingdom is not going to be a world of separated racial communities. A kingdom divided against itself cannot stand (Mark 3:24). We will not drive through the landscape of the Kingdom with it segregated by cultures and races.

Only we can end division and hatred. One of the greatest purposes that we have as a people in this generation is to end the satanic lie that has entrenched itself in the Church from its beginning to bring division and schism. Paul faced that in Corinth:

> Now I exhort you, brethren, by the name of our Lord Jesus Christ, that you all agree, and there be no divisions among you, but you be made complete in the same mind and in the same judgment. For I have been informed concerning you, my brethren, by Chloe's people, that there are quarrels among you. Now I mean this, that each one of you is saying, "I am of Paul," and "I of Apollos," and "I of Cephas," and "I of Christ." Has Christ been divided? Paul was not crucified for you, was he? Or were you baptized in the name of Paul? (1 Corinthians 1:10-13)

Did Paul mean there were no divisions except race, culture, or denominations? No, he meant no divisions. Has Christ been divided? No, He is not divided. But in reality, we have chopped Christ up into such cultural, racial, and denominational divisions that it is almost impossible to see Him in the Body of Christ! Yet His promise is that if we abide in oneness, we will have whatever we ask for:

> "If you abide in Me, and My words abide in you, ask whatever you wish, and it shall be done for you. By this

---

Mark 3:24 "And if a kingdom is divided against itself, that kingdom cannot stand."

> is My Father glorified, that you bear much fruit, and so prove to be My disciples. Just as the Father has loved Me, I have also loved you; abide in My love." (John 15:7-9)

In oneness we see results to our prayers for the world, and we bear much fruit. The proof of our discipleship is in our oneness. This is why we come together in faith, to put Christ's Body back together again, and restore the power of the Church.

In John chapter 17, we see Jesus praying to the Father. Now, that is a prayer that has to be important to us. It was certainly crucial to the Lord. Jesus was asking the Father for something. What was the one thing He asked for just before His crucifixion?

> "I do not ask in behalf of these alone, but for those also who believe in Me through their word; that they may all be one; even as Thou, Father, art in Me, and I in Thee, that they also may be in Us; that the world may believe that Thou didst send Me." (John 17:20-21)

We are wasting our time on evangelism if we continue to be divided in our churches. It is only when we truly become one that the world will believe. That was what Jesus prayed for: "Father, make them one so that the world may believe." True oneness will be the conduit for God's power to return to His Church. True oneness will change our testimony; it will change our witness to the world.

We cannot profess to be Christians or have spiritual gifts, and yet be enemies of one another. You may not call your brother an enemy, but if you are divided from him it is the same thing.

> "But I say to you, love your enemies, and pray for those who persecute you in order that you may be sons of your Father who is in heaven; for He causes His sun to rise on the evil and the good, and sends rain on the righteous and the unrighteous. For if you love those who love you, what

reward have you? Do not even the tax-gatherers do the same? And if you greet your brothers only, what do you do more than others? Do not even the Gentiles do the same? Therefore you are to be perfect, as your heavenly Father is perfect." (Matthew 5:44-48)

All the Law and the Prophets depended on this principle: "You shall love your neighbor as yourself" (Matthew 22:39). We are taking a step into this love when pastors get together from different denominations to worship and seek the Lord. Even a small attempt at this can become a testimony to the world. As we genuinely seek to become one, it will be the evidence of Christ's love. Do we really want the world to believe that Jesus Christ is their Savior? If we do, then we must become willing to move into this oneness together.

We must be driven enough for God's Kingdom to repent to one another for our denominational walls, our racism, and our cultural divides. We must be so driven for the world to believe in Jesus Christ that we find the way to forgive one another. We must put our biases, our hatreds, and our offenses in the sea of God's forgetfulness (Micah 7:19; Jeremiah 31:34). This will not only heal the divisions in the Body of Christ; it will bring a oneness that will change the world!

Micah 7:19 He will again have compassion on us; He will tread our iniquities under foot. Yes, Thou wilt cast all their sins into the depths of the sea.

Jeremiah 31:34 "And they shall not teach again, each man his neighbor and each man his brother, saying, 'Know the Lord,' for they shall all know Me, from the least of them to the greatest of them," declares the Lord, "for I will forgive their iniquity, and their sin I will remember no more."

Chapter 14

A Case for Unity Between Christianity and Judaism

May 20, 2008
Igreja A Palavra Viva, Mount Zion, Niteroi, Brazil

God's heart for oneness between Christianity and Judaism was uncovered in this meeting with Christian pastors and leaders of the local community in Niteroi.

The main focus of this book is about oneness between believers in Christ. However, if our objective is to truly bring a death blow against satan's use of division, we must also recognize the absolute necessity of finding a place of reconciliation between Christians and Jews. Observant Jews are our "older brothers" in the family of God, and the principles of faith and our inclusion in the Scriptures have been handed down to Christianity through generations of faithful Jews.

If we are going to have a oneness of spirit with the Jewish community, we need to understand that it is both possible and pleasing to the Father to relate to them in love. Over the centuries, the Church has persecuted the Jews, destroyed their fathers, and participated in the Holocaust. Many of the Jews in Brazil are there because of the persecution of the Spanish during the Inquisition. Jews living in Spain were required to sign documents that they were Christian or else be killed; many saw their families killed. Of course they are not open to the Church today. Of course they do not like Christians. This historical picture of the Church is something we have to remove as an issue. If we have a testimony of Christ to the Jewish community, it should be in the way we live, not in what we say, because we have a lot of ground to recover from our own bad example. Peter's instruction to women who had unbelieving husbands was not for them to talk about Christ, but for their lives to be a testimony (1 Peter 3:1-2). This is a Word to the Church on relating to the Jews: let them see your example.

If we live Christ, that will be the Word of God that is recognizable to the Jewish people, because they love the Word. What is the Word of God? Christ is the Word made flesh (John 1:14). You cannot love the Word of God without loving Christ. But what Christians must understand is that God's chosen people already have the love of Messiah in their hearts. When the Messiah appears to them, they will receive Him without question. Our preaching often does nothing but drive the Jews away from Christ. We have to remember that the Church originally was Jewish. For the first fifteen years, there were no Gentile believers and the expression of the Church was as a synagogue. We know that Paul went to the Temple to pray and worship (Acts 21:26). Peter was going to the Temple at the time of prayer when he healed the lame man (Acts 3:1). So the expression

---

1 Peter 3:1-2 In the same way, you wives, be submissive to your own husbands so that even if any of them are disobedient to the word, they may be won without a word by the behavior of their wives, [2] as they observe your chaste and respectful behavior.

John 1:14 And the Word became flesh, and dwelt among us, and we beheld His glory, glory as of the only begotten from the Father, full of grace and truth.

Acts 21:26 Then Paul took the men, and the next day, purifying himself along with them, went into the temple, giving notice of the completion of the days of purification, until the sacrifice was offered for each one of them.

Acts 3:1 Now Peter and John were going up to the temple at the ninth hour, the hour of prayer.

of the services, the way that they lived their faith in Christ, was recognizable by the Jewish people as being Judaism.

Historically, the early Church was a branch of Judaism; Christianity was accepted by the Jews as a sect. Many Jewish sects, like the Pharisees, the Sadducees, and the Essenes, existed at the time of Christ. It was not an unusual concept within the faith of Judaism to embrace early Christian ways of thinking and believing, since the early Church way of worship and their way of relating within the community was basically the same as other Jewish sects. However, in a Jewish context, the way that the modern Christian Church has developed is something that they cannot even recognize as being from God. It has no connection to the Scriptures. To them, it has no connection to being the same faith as theirs. To bring Jews into what we call the Church today literally requires that they deny their existence, racially and spiritually, in order to become a part. That was not true of the original Church.

Jews in the original Church shared the same faith as Gentile Christians; but for Jews to be in the Church today they must eviscerate their faith. If a Jew becomes a Christian today, according to the Church he cannot celebrate the Sabbath. But remember his problem: the Bible tells him to celebrate the Sabbath. Sadly, there are many legalistic churches that believe strongly in replacement theology, which is the teaching that the Christian Church has replaced Israel in the fulfillment of God's promises. Believing this simply perpetuates the racist stance of the Church.

So what has the Church done? It has divided the Old Testament from the New Testament, when they are one continuous Word from God. Slowly, the Church began to separate itself from its Jewish roots, so that now Christians either do not celebrate the Sabbath, or it has degenerated into a form. Christians do not celebrate the feasts of Tabernacles, Passover, Pentecost, or Purim. The Church began to celebrate Christmas and Easter; yet where are Christmas and Easter in the Word of God? The modern Church is so far away from what the early Church used to be. The problem with the Jews is the Church's problem, not the Jews' problem. It is because we have strayed so far from where we began. We must live as an example of Christ. Christ is the Word and a believing Jew loves the Word! But at this point, the Church is not qualified to testify to the Jews, because our lives are not a clear testimony of Christ. We have a long way to go to get rid of the cultural influences that have been substituted for the moving and leading of the Holy Spirit. We need to hasten the process of the Restoration to bring us back to what the Lord is looking for (Acts 3:20-21). When we get there, the Jews will see a different picture; they will recognize the Word as it appears in us.

Christianity has a concept that Judaism is legalistic and restrained, but Christianity has been far more legalistic and restrictive than Judaism. We have gathered to ourselves doctrines and regulations that are far more cultural than spiritual. Look at the Crusades; look at the Inquisition. Christianity has burned people at the stake for not following the most trivial regulations. Over the years, unrighteous rulers and leaders made decisions that were not in the leading of the Lord, and which have put a heavy burden on people. The Church, as a whole, is far more legalistic in its rules and requirements than Judaism. In contrast, the Pharisees, known for their legalism, were just one sect at the time of Christ, and did not represent the whole belief system of the Jews. All of the disciples were Jews, and the women who followed Christ were Jews. Christians think of Jews as those who killed Jesus, yet the ones with Him at the foot of the cross

---

Acts 3:20-21 "And that He may send Jesus, the Christ appointed for you, [21] whom heaven must receive until the period of restoration of all things about which God spoke by the mouth of His holy prophets from ancient time."

were Jews (John 19:25-27). The one who gave Him a burial place was a Jew (Luke 23:50-53). When we look at those who were against Christ and we create that into a paradigm of all Jews, we are being racist. We have to be careful to recognize that the thousands of early believers in Christ were all Jews.

Progressing in the Restoration means that we begin to recognize that in Christ, we are all God's children, and I cannot cast you out or wall you off based upon our differences. Doing just that, unfortunately, has been our Christian tradition. However, in Judaism today, we are seeing an openness and acceptance of one another, the dropping of the sectarian rejection of different ways of worship and forms of government, so that they can come together and pray. Even in Christ's time, Judaism was very resilient to allow differences of interpretation and belief to exist within its confines. They were very advanced, because during the feasts all of the Jews of the Diaspora, which included different sects and cultures, came in oneness to the Temple to worship God together. Despite all of their differences, they came together and sought the Lord. Yet after hundreds of years, in Christianity we are just now coming to the place where we can all come to one place at one time and worship Christ together. Lord, deliver us from our sectarian heart, from our Christian legalism! We need to stop trying to evangelize our Jewish brothers; rather, we need to love and create a relationship with them. We need to

---

John 19:25-27 Therefore the soldiers did these things. But there were standing by the cross of Jesus His mother, and His mother's sister, Mary the wife of Clopas, and Mary Magdalene. [26] When Jesus therefore saw His mother, and the disciple whom He loved standing nearby, He said to His mother, "Woman, behold, your son!" [27] Then He said to the disciple, "Behold, your mother!" And from that hour the disciple took her into his own household.

Luke 23:50-53 And behold, a man named Joseph, who was a member of the Council, a good and righteous man [51] (he had not consented to their plan and action), a man from Arimathea, a city of the Jews, who was waiting for the kingdom of God; [52] this man went to Pilate and asked for the body of Jesus. [53] And he took it down and wrapped it in a linen cloth, and laid Him in a tomb cut into the rock, where no one had ever lain.

live the example that was given to us by our Jewish Messiah. Then, let's come back to the Church and clean up our own mess, and with humility love one another.

The deaths of Peter and Paul were very destructive to the early Church. They were the apostles to the Jews and the Gentiles; had they lived longer, they would have left us more of an example of the lifestyle and relationship of Jewish Christians and Gentile Christians living and relating in the Jewish community. In New Testament times, three groups began to emerge: Jews who were observant to Judaism, Jews who were believers in Jesus as the Messiah but were still functioning in the Temple, and Gentile believers in Jesus. Obviously Paul, as a Jewish believer, freely went to the Temple. A lot of people don't want to talk about it, but after the cross Paul still made sacrifices in the Temple. So he was not breaking, in our thinking, from the Jewish ways.

Ephesians 4 describes the reality of where the Lord is leading us:

> I, therefore, the prisoner of the Lord, entreat you to walk in a manner worthy of the calling with which you have been called, with all humility and gentleness, with patience, showing forbearance to one another in love, being diligent to preserve the unity of the Spirit in the bond of peace. (Ephesians 4:1-3)

This passage is describing the relationship of unity with humility and gentleness, which would allow Christians to walk together in oneness. It also describes the qualities necessary in our heart to preserve the unity of the Spirit in the bond of peace with our Jewish family. Remember, in Christ we were grafted in to the family of Abraham. Preserving the unity of the Spirit requires a lot of patience for one another and much love. The foundation will be love, but we must be diligent to preserve the unity. We have to recreate what has been lost, which is the unity of the Spirit among the leadership, among the men and women of God. It is possible to come to a place where we maintain our spirits in the unity of the Holy Spirit, being absolutely one. That is where we begin. It takes revelation; it takes faith, and seeking the Lord with fasting and prayer. Those of us who are leaders and authorities of the Church must believe for the Lord to continue what He has been doing for several hundred years in the Restoration of the Church, bringing it out of the Dark Ages and restoring it to a purity of worship. Let us come together in oneness of spirit and seek the Lord, outside of our walls of doctrines, and find the unity of the Spirit. Once we are able to walk in that, something else will begin to happen.

"Until we all attain to the unity of the faith, and of the knowledge of the Son of God, to a mature man, to the measure of the stature which belongs to the fulness of Christ" (Ephesians 4:13). If we can walk in the unity of the Spirit, then we will come to the unity of the faith. It will not happen by hammering out a belief system that we can all agree upon. No matter how sincere our efforts are to do that, we will end up disagreeing and arguing. One thing we know: we have too many different doctrines. But if we can come into a oneness of spirit, the Lord will bring us to a oneness of faith. The Holy Spirit will teach us all things (John 16:13-15). We do not have Paul and Peter; all we have is each other, but the Holy Spirit will lead us into oneness.

There is an amazing account in Acts 21 of Paul's meeting in Jerusalem with the apostle James. James told Paul,

> "And they have been told about you, that you are teaching all the Jews who are among the Gentiles to forsake Moses,

---

John 16:13-15 "But when He, the Spirit of truth, comes, He will guide you into all the truth; for He will not speak on His own initiative, but whatever He hears, He will speak; and He will disclose to you what is to come. [14] He shall glorify Me; for He shall take of Mine, and shall disclose it to you. [15] All things that the Father has are Mine; therefore I said, that He takes of Mine, and will disclose it to you."

em not to circumcise their children nor to walk
to the customs. What, then, is to be done? They
will certainly hear that you have come. Therefore do this
that we tell you." (Acts 21:21-23)

Paul listened to James and purified himself along with four Jewish men who were under a vow. Paul went with these men to the Temple, and made the sacrifice according to the Law (Acts 21:23-26). This is a key Scripture. Together, they corrected any question among the Jews that Paul had been teaching people to stop Jewish practices. Paul went to great lengths to show that believing in the Messiah did not mean to separate from their Jewish roots, or to stop their Temple worship.

Later in the Book of Acts, we read about Paul speaking to the Jews about Jesus:

> And when they had set a day for him, they came to him at his lodging in large numbers; and he was explaining to them by solemnly testifying about the kingdom of God, and trying to persuade them concerning Jesus, from both the Law of Moses and from the Prophets, from morning until evening. And some were being persuaded by the things spoken, but others would not believe. (Acts 28:23-24)

In this passage, Paul was not just declaring Jesus as the salvation of their sins; the issue was broader than that. He was speaking about

---

Acts 21:23-26 "Therefore do this that we tell you. We have four men who are under a vow; [24] take them and purify yourself along with them, and pay their expenses in order that they may shave their heads; and all will know that there is nothing to the things which they have been told about you, but that you yourself also walk orderly, keeping the Law. [25] But concerning the Gentiles who have believed, we wrote, having decided that they should abstain from meat sacrificed to idols and from blood and from what is strangled and from fornication." [26] Then Paul took the men, and the next day, purifying himself along with them, went into the temple, giving notice of the completion of the days of purification, until the sacrifice was offered for each one of them.

the Kingdom of God. Was Jesus the Messiah? We tend to think of that in church terms. Our priority has been thinking of Jesus as the Savior: when you accept Him, He saves you from your sins. That really is not the entire context of the New Testament. Christ preached the Kingdom of God (Mark 1:14-15). John the Baptist, in preparing the way for Christ, preached the Kingdom (Matthew 3:1-2). The apostles preached the Kingdom, not church or salvation as we think of them today. So Paul was speaking to these Jews about the Kingdom of God, and of Christ's Lordship.

The Jewish understanding of Messiah follows the pattern and prophecies about David. Thus, the Messiah comes to establish a government on this earth. According to the Jewish mind, Jesus had violated the core concept of being the Messiah when He left the earth. Even the disciples said after His resurrection, "Lord, is it at this time You are restoring the kingdom to Israel?" (Acts 1:6). The Kingdom of God includes the Messiah who has an earthly reign as the King. Paul was not constantly dealing with the Jews about whether Christ brought forgiveness and died on the cross for them. The Jews' question was, where did He go? If He is the Messiah, then He must be here in this earth, reigning over us just as David had done as king.

Christ is returning to establish His Kingdom on the earth in this day. When He returns, Christians are going to have a whole new perspective where the Jews are concerned. The Jews will be able to recognize the Messiah who comes to reign. I have talked with many rabbis and we have reached a oneness. At the heart of the matter is a shared belief: we both believe in the Messiah. Christians believe

---

Mark 1:14-15 And after John had been taken into custody, Jesus came into Galilee, preaching the gospel of God, [15] and saying, "The time is fulfilled, and the kingdom of God is at hand; repent and believe in the gospel."

Matthew 3:1-2 Now in those days John the Baptist came, preaching in the wilderness of Judea, saying, [2] "Repent, for the kingdom of heaven is at hand."

He has come; the Jews believe He is yet to come. We all agree there is one Messiah, and both Christians and Jews are presently waiting for His appearing. There is a great deal of oneness there, and at the Messiah's appearing, Jews and Christians will all be one under the reign of His Lordship.

Where some Christians have a problem is with their end-time teaching. Many believe that a "rapture" will occur and that Christians will be pulled out of this earth to be with Jesus in heaven, waiting for the great redemption of the Jews. This teaching leaves out the Kingdom of God with the Messiah on the earth reigning over His people. Racism is inherent in this belief that all the Christians go to heaven while two-thirds of the Jews are destroyed on the earth during the tribulation. The arrogance of Christianity looks at the Jewish people as those who need to suffer for crucifying Christ, and for not opening their hearts initially to Jesus as the Messiah. This is not the picture we see in the Scriptures of the loving Father's heart for the Jews, His chosen people.

Paul speaks of a hardness that rests upon the chosen people. This is only a partial hardening, because many Jews have believed and do believe that Jesus is the Messiah (Romans 11:25). At some point, this hardening will come to an end, and I believe that the return of Christ to rule on the earth will obliterate it. We, as Gentile believers, cannot be arrogant about our standing, or allow it to separate us from our Jewish brethren. Christians and Jews will both be here on the earth as believers while the Messiah rules in a physical Kingdom.

As Christians, we should see Christ's coming as creating oneness between Jews and Christians. Some of the greatest barriers to creating oneness between Jews and Christians are the eschatological

---

Romans 11:25 For I do not want you, brethren, to be uninformed of this mystery, lest you be wise in your own estimation, that a partial hardening has happened to Israel until the fulness of the Gentiles has come in.

beliefs widely-held by Christians today. These doctrines require division between Christians and Jews in order to be fulfilled. Such teaching perpetuates our separation rather than creating oneness as we come to know the Messiah. I believe a true messianic revelation brings oneness between Jews and Christians. The Christ is more than our Savior; He is the King who is coming to rule and reign, gathering all of His people, both Jews and Gentiles, into His Kingdom (Ephesians 2:14-16).

Christian doctrine, as it has developed throughout history, has a purposeful drive to separate Christianity from Judaism. This began very early and was based upon the persecution of the Jews which preceded the destruction of the Temple in 70 AD. The Gentiles did not want to be part of that persecution, so many said, "No. We are not like the Jews." The separation grew from that point on. We must recognize that as Christians, we are the ones that have created the separation and division. Our church fathers after the apostles did this through calculated actions and doctrines. Many Scriptures have been interpreted in ways that tend to divide us from the Jews. We must seek, in the Holy Spirit, to find the truth in the Bible, and not use Scriptures simply to create or support doctrines.

From the Jewish perspective, based upon many prophecies in the Old Testament, Christ's ascension did not fit the Jews' expectations of the Messiah. But as believers, we know that Christ is coming back. When He comes back, the question over why He went away will be resolved, even for the Jewish people. Remember, in this age we are experiencing the coming and establishment of His Kingdom on earth. People will be believing and accepting Christ as King even

---

Ephesians 2:14-16 For He Himself is our peace, who made both groups into one, and broke down the barrier of the dividing wall, [15] by abolishing in His flesh the enmity, which is the Law of commandments contained in ordinances, that in Himself He might make the two into one new man, thus establishing peace, [16] and might reconcile them both in one body to God through the cross, by it having put to death the enmity.

after He returns. Many will see and receive Him; others will reject Him. But His coming remains an open door until the time of the judgment.

Lord, give us grace, patience, and the love that we need to be one in spirit with one another. And do not let us be influenced by the things that divided our church fathers from the Jewish people. We are beginning a new day, like the day of oneness that existed at the very beginning when Peter stood up with the eleven (Acts 2:14). Lord, let there be one heart, one voice, one purpose, and one faith!

Acts 2:14 But Peter, taking his stand with the eleven, raised his voice and declared to them: "Men of Judea, and all you who live in Jerusalem, let this be known to you, and give heed to my words."

Chapter 15

Our Unity Brings His Anointing

February 19, 2009
Igreja A Palavra Viva, Mount Zion, Niteroi, Brazil

During an annual gathering with the pastors and leaders of the local Christian community, another step was taken toward oneness in the Body of Christ.

We read about the process of coming into oneness in Ephesians chapter 4:

> I, therefore, the prisoner of the Lord, entreat you to walk in a manner worthy of the calling with which you have been called, with all humility and gentleness, with patience, showing forbearance to one another in love, being diligent to preserve the unity of the Spirit in the bond of peace. (Ephesians 4:1-3)

This Scripture describes the attitude we must have as the Lord begins to bring various groups of believers together. The Lord is connecting us together, bone to bone, joint to joint, ligament to ligament, as He sets us together in His Body (Ezekiel 37:7-8; 1 Corinthians 12:18).

Ezekiel 37:7-8   So I prophesied as I was commanded; and as I prophesied, there was a noise, and behold, a rattling; and the bones came together, bone to its bone. [8] And I looked, and behold, sinews were on them, and flesh grew, and skin covered them; but there was no breath in them.

1 Corinthians 12:18   But now God has placed the members, each one of them, in the body, just as He desired.

As we go through that process, the attitude we must have as leaders, as those in authority, is an attitude of humility, so that we can truly hear one another.

There is a tremendous humility and gentleness that each one of us must have in our relating together. It takes a great deal of humility to position ourselves before one another and seek to understand, listen with our hearts, and reach beyond the walls and divisions that have existed for so long between denominational leaders in the Church. We cannot be abrupt or dismissive. Rather, we must move in a gentleness that is inclusive. For example, when children speak out, it is easy to chide them or demean them. But that does not work. With gentleness, you should let them know that you understand what they are saying, and let them into your heart. There has to be patience, forbearance, and most of all, love.

God is raising up a fathering anointing in these ministries to be diligent to preserve the unity of the Spirit. We may not agree on doctrines, we may not agree on projects, we may not like each other's personalities, and certainly we do not all speak the same language, but there is a carefulness to guard the basic unity of the Holy Spirit. There is one Body, one Lord, and one Holy Spirit who dwells in all of us (Ephesians 4:4-6). According to 1 Corinthians 12, it is very clear that the Spirit distributes gifts and ministries in many different kinds of expressions, yet we all can be one.

> Now there are varieties of gifts, but the same Spirit. And there are varieties of ministries, and the same Lord. And there are varieties of effects, but the same God who works all things in all persons. But to each one is given the manifestation of the Spirit for the common good. For

---

Ephesians 4:4-6 There is one body and one Spirit, just as also you were called in one hope of your calling; [5] one Lord, one faith, one baptism, [6] one God and Father of all who is over all and through all and in all.

to one is given the word of wisdom through the Spirit, and to another the word of knowledge according to the same Spirit; to another faith by the same Spirit, and to another gifts of healing by the one Spirit, and to another the effecting of miracles, and to another prophecy, and to another the distinguishing of spirits, to another various kinds of tongues, and to another the interpretation of tongues. But one and the same Spirit works all these things, distributing to each one individually just as He wills. For even as the body is one and yet has many members, and all the members of the body, though they are many, are one body, so also is Christ. For by one Spirit we were all baptized into one body, whether Jews or Greeks, whether slaves or free, and we were all made to drink of one Spirit. (1 Corinthians 12:4-13)

In human thinking, in order for a group to be unified, all of the members would have to be the same so that there is no argument. But when God wanted to make His Body one, He gave us the Holy Spirit through His Son, and the Spirit brings about diversity. On a human level, diversity always brings division. Look at all the wars generated in the world because of differences in countries. That is why Christian groups have kept separate all of these years, because the ability did not yet exist to preserve the unity of the Spirit in the bond of peace. Now, we have to trust that God knows what He is doing. If He says diversity brings oneness, then we trust the Holy Spirit to do His job.

That is one reason God is moving the way He is in Brazil. There is a gift of love in this country that is the first step to being able to preserve the unity in the bond of peace. Lord, endue us with an anointing and power to preserve the unity of the Holy Spirit in the bond of peace, and let there be such a great love. Give us the ability, as spiritual fathers, to find the way in the Holy Spirit to believe in what You are doing. We take the responsibility from this moment on, even if others will not, to preserve the unity of the Spirit in the bond of peace.

> And He gave some as apostles, and some as prophets, and some as evangelists, and some as pastors and teachers, for the equipping of the saints for the work of service, to the building up of the body of Christ; until we all attain to the unity of the faith, and of the knowledge of the Son of God, to a mature man, to the measure of the stature which belongs to the fulness of Christ. (Ephesians 4:11-13)

If we can hold on to the unity of the Spirit and promote it, then at some point, we will come into the unity of the faith. We will all see eye to eye when the Lord builds again Zion (Isaiah 52:8, KJV). Attempting to jump directly into the unity of the faith will not work. We must first preserve the unity of the Spirit; then, in an atmosphere of oneness, God can move in our hearts. If we try to start with the unity of the faith, we will become mired in our human thinking. We will talk about all those issues that we disagree on, and it will create more confusion and discord. The whole attempt will explode and we will be right back where the Church has been for a thousand years. But the Lord is leading us into a different day, into something new.

There is something the Lord has been speaking to us out of Psalm 133:

> Behold, how good and how pleasant it is
> For brothers to dwell together in unity!
> It is like the precious oil upon the head,
> Coming down upon the beard,

Isaiah 52:8, KJV Thy watchmen shall lift up the voice; with the voice together shall they sing: for they shall see eye to eye, when the Lord shall bring again Zion.

> Even Aaron's beard,
> Coming down upon the edge of his robes.
> It is like the dew of Hermon,
> Coming down upon the mountains of Zion;
> For there the Lord commanded the blessing—life forever.

There is an anointing when brethren come together. If we can come into this unity, we will have an anointing that will allow us to move through the problems, through the divisions, through the lack of understanding, and come to the place where the Lord will finally bring the unity of the faith. We read in Isaiah chapter 10, "And it shall come to pass in that day, that his burden shall be taken away from off thy shoulder, and his yoke from off thy neck, and the yoke shall be destroyed because of the anointing" (Isaiah 10:27, KJV). Some translations read that the yoke will be broken; but the word "destroyed" in the King James Bible is closer to the original Hebrew. The Hebrew word has a stronger meaning than "broken." It is more accurately stated, "The yoke of oppression is **shattered** because of the anointing."

This prophecy declares that God is releasing us from the oppressions that have been on us. And the greatest oppression on the Church has been this inability to come into oneness. We have to end the spiritual oppression that brings division in the Body of Christ, rendering us incapable of working together, of loving each other, and of being one in the Spirit. Yet it is a reality of spirit that we cannot do this in our human flesh. In Isaiah 10:27, the word "anointing" in Hebrew literally means "the face of His presence in the anointing." That is what is beginning to happen in our midst: the face of Christ and His anointing is resting upon us as we determine to come into unity. Here is the picture that came from the Lord: this little anointing that begins on the head just keeps increasing and increasing, until it covers every aspect of the Body. The anointing oil is flowing down and covering us completely. And it is that anointing that will break this yoke. The anointing from Christ's face, from His presence, brings the authority that breaks the yoke of oppression that has held His Body in division. Now it will bring the oneness.

Let it grow, let it increase, until every bit of us is covered with the anointing that enables us to move together in our gifts and ministries. Christ was the Anointed One from the Father. The Body of Christ, in order to minister this release to the earth, must be the anointed of God. Lord, release Your anointing to take dominion over every yoke, every bondage, and every separation that has kept Your leaders divided one from another. Release the anointing of oneness to work among us in this day!

Chapter 16

He Is Gathering the Nations

July 3, 2010
Shiloh Church, Kalona, Iowa

This message culminated a series of messages that were spoken during the Shiloh School of Prophets, an annual conference with international attendance.

As believers, we often look to have individual spiritual experiences in the Lord. Without taking away from these individual experiences, let's consider the unique experience of the believers on the Day of Pentecost. This was a corporate experience. God moved suddenly upon a whole group of believers. Now, once again, we are ready to see the Lord move upon us as a group. The truth is we lose a great deal when we try to function as individuals. Whenever any one of us is singled out, our problems and needs become very evident. However, when we move together as a body of people, our individual shortcomings are minimized by the principle of Body ministry. God is not emphasizing the individual in this day. Our own anointing, power, and enabling will come to each of us as we move together in oneness.

If you look at the Old Testament pattern, you begin to see how church mentality falls short of what God is really after. Under God's direction, the tribes and families of Israel became a nation with their own identity among all the nations of that day. He took

His people and made them able to stand up and face greater and mightier nations than themselves (Deuteronomy 9:1). God is still raising up a people today. His purpose is not just to have a group of disconnected individuals that are collectively called the Body of Christ. Rather, the purpose of His dealings upon us individually is to bring us into a oneness as a people, as a nation. Individually, we join the great nation that makes up the people of God.

This concept is important, because God wants to do something unique concerning our approach to praying for the world scene. Let's look at how God thinks about, and relates to, the nations of the world:

> "But when the Son of Man comes in His glory, and all the angels with Him, then He will sit on His glorious throne. And all the nations will be gathered before Him; and He will separate them from one another, as the shepherd separates the sheep from the goats; and He will put the sheep on His right, and the goats on the left. Then the King will say to those on His right, 'Come, you who are blessed of My Father, inherit the kingdom prepared for you from the foundation of the world.'" (Matthew 25:31-34)

This is a different vision of the return of the Lord than a lot of people talk about. Most of us have the picture of the "great white throne judgment," with every individual standing before the Lord to be judged (Revelation 20:11-12). But prior to that, He deals with the nations of the world, not with individuals. The truth is we are not

---

Deuteronomy 9:1 "Hear, O Israel! You are crossing over the Jordan today to go in to dispossess nations greater and mightier than you, great cities fortified to heaven."

Revelation 20:11-12 And I saw a great white throne and Him who sat upon it, from whose presence earth and heaven fled away, and no place was found for them. [12] And I saw the dead, the great and the small, standing before the throne, and books were opened; and another book was opened, which is the book of life; and the dead were judged from the things which were written in the books, according to their deeds.

waiting for this final judgment, because the return of the Lord is already in progress. The process has already begun. According to this Scripture in Matthew 25, Christ is coming and all the nations are gathered to Him, and then He begins to separate the nations. Prophetically, it is extremely necessary for us to grasp the fact that God is already in motion gathering the nations.

As Christians, we have been stuck in an "all about me" focus on our individual ministries and our individual meetings with the Lord. But God is gathering us together as a people. He not only brought Israel together as a people; He also established them as a nation. A nation is composed of many individuals, but they have one identity. We need to think of the Body of Christ like a national identity that is emerging in a global sense. It is not going to be acceptable or effective any longer to function as isolated groups of believers.

Today, Israel represents God's chosen people being drawn together as a nation in fulfillment of countless prophecies and promises in the Old Testament. What God has done with Israel is the prelude of what He is wanting to do with the entire Body of Christ. This illustration should speak to each of us, because we all understand what it is to be a citizen of a nation and part of a national identity. Even as we struggle to fulfill our individual destinies, God is drawing us together to accomplish a greater vision. Those individuals, groups, and nations who respond to being gathered together will feel the blessing of the Lord (Isaiah 2:2).

I prophesy that the Body of Christ will begin to come together as a national identity on a global scale. We are going to see nations drawn together because they are an atmosphere, or an incubator, in which the sons of God can come forth. And those nations will be

---

Isaiah 2:2 Now it will come about that in the last days, the mountain of the house of the LORD will be established as the chief of the mountains, and will be raised above the hills; and all the nations will stream to it.

blessed. That was the original promise to Abraham: "And in your seed all the nations of the earth shall be blessed" (Genesis 22:18). Not just individuals, but nations shall be blessed. God's thoughts are not our thoughts (Isaiah 55:8). We wrestle with coming into the Kingdom individually, but God is looking at a much bigger picture. He is focused on nations to raise up and to bless that will inherit the Kingdom prepared for them from before the foundation of the world. This is part of what Israel represents to us. It is a nation drawn together that started with one man, Abraham. It began with his children going into Egypt and growing into a people that were as great as the sands of the seashore (Genesis 22:17). Then God brought them into the land that He promised to them and created them into a nation. We are seeing this pattern repeated again.

There are nations that are being drawn together, amassing nuclear weapons, and being an arrogant affront to the rest of the international community. Even though it may appear that these nations are doing this by their own initiative, in the realm of spirit God is gathering them based on decisions each one has made, and is still making. That is part of the concern right now for the United States. We bless our rulers to get on the right side of God's purposes. We must rise up in our faith and start praying that the sheep nations of the earth be drawn together.

This picture of what God is doing with the nations is not just seen in a few verses of Matthew 25; let's look at the 2nd Psalm, which is also about the nations:

> Why are the nations in an uproar,
> And the peoples devising a vain thing?

Isaiah 55:8 "For My thoughts are not your thoughts, neither are your ways My ways," declares the LORD.

Genesis 22:17 "Indeed I will greatly bless you, and I will greatly multiply your seed as the stars of the heavens, and as the sand which is on the seashore; and your seed shall possess the gate of their enemies."

> The kings of the earth take their stand,
> And the rulers take counsel together
> Against the LORD and against His Anointed:
> "Let us tear their fetters apart,
> And cast away their cords from us!" (Psalm 2:1-3)
>
> Now therefore, O kings, show discernment;
> Take warning, O judges of the earth.
> Worship the LORD with reverence,
> And rejoice with trembling.
> Do homage to the Son, lest He become angry,
>   and you perish in the way,
> For His wrath may soon be kindled.
> How blessed are all who take refuge in Him! (Psalm 2:10-12)

This Psalm is a warning to the rulers of the earth in every nation to turn to the Lord, and become part of the inheritance of the Son. The nations that do so will be gathered together as His possession.

We also see this picture in Isaiah 2:4:

> And He will judge between the nations,
> And will render decisions for many peoples;
> And they will hammer their swords into plowshares,
>   and their spears into pruning hooks.
> Nation will not lift up sword against nation,
> And never again will they learn war.

With this picture in our hearts, we must acknowledge how important it is for us as individuals to impact the nations. You cannot stop at just being concerned about yourself, your family, your projects, or even your own country. As the Body of Christ, we have the ability to influence what is going to happen globally. As we take a stand in the spirit, the nations where we live will change. We cannot hide fearfully from these days. God has raised up each one of us as part of our individual nation, to determine how God is going to relate to that nation.

In Matthew 13 is the parable of the wheat and the tares. This is a parable about the Kingdom of God, and is dealing with the world on a global scale. The field in which the good seed was planted is the world, where also the enemy planted tares. Jesus said, "Allow both to grow together until the harvest; and in the time of the harvest I will say to the reapers, 'First gather up the tares and bind them in bundles to burn them up; but gather the wheat into my barn'" (Matthew 13:30). Now, at the end of the age, it is time for the wheat to be gathered out of every nation in the world. Every nation on earth is going to be engaged in this. "So you will again distinguish between the righteous and the wicked, between one who serves God and one who does not serve Him" (Malachi 3:18). That is something that will manifest on an international level.

Before we see whole nations come to serve God, we will first see governments and leaders open their hearts to allow a liberty in those nations for God to move among the people. The United States is not really a Christian nation, but it has been an atmosphere in which Christians can grow and thrive. There has been a level of safety and lack of outright persecution of believers in the United States. The nations that protect God's people will activate His blessing. We prophesy a joining together of nations by the hearts of the peoples of those nations. The world scene is going to change very quickly. We need to be watching the nations with an eye to see what God is doing. As His sons, we can be engaged without becoming activists carrying placards, because we are drawing from a higher source. We must begin to function like a company of prophets to prophesy with faith for the nations.

The sheep nations must find a way to league together in a symbiotic relationship one with another. There is a destiny that we must fulfill. Who will stand in faith to bind the elements of wickedness in every nation, and set them free to follow after the Lord? Why should God have to come and judge the nations of a continent because they are overwhelmed with wickedness? The truth is that there are many hungry hearts in the countries of the world. Realize that Christ is coming in this age to deal with the nations, to draw them unto Himself, and to separate out those who will not do His will. Just as we believe for individuals to be saved, we should look for whole nations to be saved. When we reach out to witness to someone about Christ, we believe that they are saved from the judgments to come. In the same way, nations need to be saved from the judgments to come.

John Stevens, a visionary of the Kingdom, spoke of this in a message titled "Lift Up Your Voice and Prophesy Against…":

> There will be some sheep nations as well as goat nations when the Lord comes to establish His Kingdom. According to Matthew 25, He will gather all the nations before Him, and some will be the sheep nations which will enter into the Kingdom; others will be banished and destroyed. We are in that period now. America can be a sheep nation; but that does not mean that God will not bring down every wrong thing in it. The only hope is the remnant that can lead America into the Kingdom of God. There are no military forces, no weapons, no finances, no statesmen at this present time that could actually lead the country into what God has for it in the future. Prophesy that things will change, and make the changes happen![11]

The answers will have to come from another level: an authority resting upon the Body of Christ by God's Spirit. As you look at the nations now, it is clear that they are facing problems that are

---

[11.] John Robert Stevens, "Lift Up Your Voice and Prophesy Against…," *This Week, July 4, 1976* (North Hollywood, CA: The Living Word, 1976), 20.

unsolvable. Terrorism is an example; it operates in such a way that no one has a solution for it. If anybody could have found a solution to quell terrorism, it would have been Israel.

So what can you do when you face problems that are unsolvable? Cry out to God. Look for answers that are different from anything you have known in the past. In many different locations, events are imminent that will draw government leaders to a place of humbling themselves. God wants to humble us, not to demean us, but so that we will cry out to Him. The Bible is filled with examples of God humbling nations to give them an opportunity to turn to Him (Deuteronomy 8:2-3). We will see national leaders brought to their knees to seek God because there will not be any other solutions.

There are answers in God for every single disaster and conflict that is facing the world today. But national leaders will have to drop their resistance to the Lord, get rid of their arrogance, and receive the answers that God will provide. Every nation will have its own opportunities. How should we respond? We should pray for our leaders, our country, and the citizens of other nations when disasters or challenges come: "Lord, open their hearts to the answers, because You are the answer." Solutions will not come from the wisdom of man or the abilities of the flesh.

Here is another excerpt from "Lift Up Your Voice and Prophesy Against…" by John Stevens:

> As Christians we are not required to believe a certain way politically. Our only effective approach will be that of

---

Deuteronomy 8:2-3 "And you shall remember all the way which the Lord your God has led you in the wilderness these forty years, that He might humble you, testing you, to know what was in your heart, whether you would keep His commandments or not. [3] And He humbled you and let you be hungry, and fed you with manna which you did not know, nor did your fathers know, that He might make you understand that man does not live by bread alone, but man lives by everything that proceeds out of the mouth of the Lord."

> faith before God. The systems and the trends have gone too far to be corrected through political channels, but we can do something; we can stand before God, and God can bring change. Remember that this is entirely a spiritual approach. Physical force will not bring these changes. We are not to be revolutionaries who go out and destroy. It would be anarchy, and God is not the source of anarchy.[12]

Christ is the source of raising up a global spiritual force. As the nations are blessed, it will create an atmosphere for that force to grow, so that the Body of Christ can come together. Elijah was a prophet who affected the political scene, but not because he ran for office. He had a higher source; he moved by the Spirit of God (1 Kings 17:1). Elijah dealt with kings, armies, and peoples, all by the power of the Spirit. In this day, there will be companies of prophets, moving in oneness, that will have the spiritual perception and authority to see the nations of this world change.

We must let go of the arrogance of our thinking and the smallness of our vision. Christ is not coming to be King over only the United States or some other individual nation. "The earth is the LORD's, and the fulness thereof" (Psalm 24:1, KJV). Christ is coming to rule all the nations of the earth; His Kingdom is a global kingdom (Revelation 11:15). "He is Lord of lords and King

---

1 Kings 17:1 Now Elijah the Tishbite, who was of the settlers of Gilead, said to Ahab, "As the LORD, the God of Israel lives, before whom I stand, surely there shall be neither dew nor rain these years, except by my word."

Revelation 11:15 And the seventh angel sounded; and there arose loud voices in heaven, saying, "The kingdom of the world has become the kingdom of our Lord, and of His Christ; and He will reign forever and ever."

[12.] Stevens, "Lift Up Your Voice," 21.

of kings" (Revelation 17:14). As the Body of Christ, we are being called together into a spiritual nation that will globally impact the establishment of God's Kingdom on this earth.

Revelation 17:14 "These will wage war against the Lamb, and the Lamb will overcome them, because He is Lord of lords and King of kings, and those who are with Him are the called and chosen and faithful."

Chapter 17

Oneness Triggers the Outpouring

October 3, 2012
Church of the Living Word, North Hills, California

This message came during an annual gathering of churches for the celebration of the Feast of Tabernacles.

From the four corners of the earth have come reports that the Body of Christ is engaging in intercession for the nations. Here in North America, many have been into fasting and prayer that God would heal our land, based upon the scriptural principle in 2 Chronicles chapter 7:

> Then the LORD appeared to Solomon at night and said to him, "I have heard your prayer, and have chosen this place for Myself as a house of sacrifice. If I shut up the heavens so that there is no rain, or if I command the locust to devour the land, or if I send pestilence among My people, and My people who are called by My name humble themselves and pray, and seek My face and turn from their wicked ways, then I will hear from heaven, will forgive their sin, and will heal their land." (2 Chronicles 7:12-14)

We believe that the Body of Christ is called by His name, just as all of Israel is called by His name, and that is the rallying point of our prayer. It is time for all who are called by His name to begin to humble themselves and find a deeper connection with the Lord. That humility, that seeking of His face, will evoke a response from God, and He will heal our land. As we begin to pray for our country, however, we sense the focus shifting onto something for the whole world; it becomes an expression of a worldwide burden. The truth is that it is not just our own country that is in need. All nations, all tongues on the planet are in need. The Kingdom of God is not a single culture, country, nation, or tongue. All of the earth is the Lord's (Psalm 24:1, KJV). He is giving us a global burden.

Look again at 2 Chronicles 7:13: "If I shut up the heavens so that there is no rain, or if I command the locust to devour the land, or if I send pestilence among My people." A lack of rain for the crops, locusts, pestilence—God can use whatever our circumstances are to get our attention. The Father has a wonderful ability to manipulate your individual circumstances to bring you to the place where you fall on your face before Him. In the same way, God is using circumstances in the nations to cause us to see what is wrong in our spirits and to humble ourselves before Him.

We know that God can heal our land. We know that He can move in power, by signs and wonders, by the outpouring of His Spirit, as He begins to deal with the whole earth. The more we reach in to walk with God, the more He will answer our cry, uncover the sources of our circumstances, and shine a spotlight on our needs. And one of the offenses that God is exposing is the spirit of division. The Holy Spirit is putting His finger on the spirit of division in the Body of Christ that continues to destroy God's ability to move among us.

The history of every Christian fellowship or denomination is riddled with division. In spite of all the teaching we have heard on divisiveness and being judgmental and unforgiving, we still try to

---

Psalm 24:1, KJV The earth is the Lord's, and the fulness thereof; the world, and they that dwell therein.

extract the little speck out of everyone else's eye while ignoring the beam in our own eye (Matthew 7:3-5). This is a pattern of divisive relating that we have allowed ourselves to indulge in. On the other hand, we could flip that coin over and say there is a lot of oneness within the Church, and that would also be true. But when God is perfecting something, He does not pat you on the back for what you have attained by grace. He emphasizes the need that remains. It is like somebody trying to lose 300 pounds. They think, "Great, I have lost 150 pounds!" But there are still 150 pounds to go. The Body of Christ has not finished purging itself of the spirit of division.

We need to understand how the spirit of division operates. The truth is that division is innate to satan's nature. It is in his DNA; he works through division. That is why God is putting His finger on that same spirit within us; He wants to root out whatever levels of division still exist. It is not enough to be forgiven; we must be cleansed. "If we confess our sins, He is faithful and righteous to forgive us our sins and to cleanse us from all unrighteousness" (1 John 1:9). Our hearts, our minds, and our spirits must be washed clean of division. As His Body, Christ is ready to do something through us on a higher plane, for a greater destiny. It is time to let go of the good for the better, and the better for the best. We can be free of division.

How do we get division out of our spirits, and out of our midst? One thing we are learning is that there really can be disagreement without division. One issue that has plagued churches is that when someone wants to leave a local fellowship, or disagrees with what the church believes, both parties often feel they have a point to prove. They feel the need to justify themselves, and therefore they

---

Matthew 7:3-5 "And why do you look at the speck that is in your brother's eye, but do not notice the log that is in your own eye? [4] Or how can you say to your brother, 'Let me take the speck out of your eye,' and behold, the log is in your own eye? [5] You hypocrite, first take the log out of your own eye, and then you will see clearly to take the speck out of your brother's eye."

criticize one another. Satan uses this situation to create division and continue to destroy the Body of Christ. If the one who wants to leave comes and talks with the leadership, the response should be, "We love you. If that is really what you want to do, we bless you. We will minister to you. We will help you find a church that is really a fit for you." The Kingdom is relationships, and sometimes there are very deep relationships in which people have walked together for years. However, once the Lord brings a change, or someone is going another direction, the correct response is to love one another and thank each other for the time they had, and their relationship together. Then keep on doing the will of the Lord and blessing each other.

Shepherds need to listen, to talk, and to work with people. Don't settle for people simply withdrawing from your church. Initiate a conversation with them to find out what the problem is, and honestly discern if anything needs to be corrected on your part. If apologies are called for, then make them and forgive each other. If the Lord is leading a person in another direction, even if you do not understand or agree, you still should love each other. Look that person in the eye and say, "Jesus Christ died on the cross for me and for you; the blood of the Lamb covers both of us. Let's take Communion together. I bless you to go do what you need to do."

God has given us missions and commissions, and we need to get on with them. We need to be transforming into prophetic communities, maturing the sons of God, and breaking through into authority in the Spirit. None of those things work in an atmosphere of division. We have a very biblical illustration in the story of Abraham and Lot, who were relatives. Abraham said, "It is not good that we are arguing among ourselves. Take your children and all of your herds and choose a land to dwell in, because we are not going to argue or fight. We must be one." So they parted company (Genesis 13:7-9).

We can be diverse, we can have disagreements over doctrine, we can even go separate ways, and still be one. Allowing the spirit of division to persist is just following in the footsteps of Christianity for the last 2,000 years. Realize that it is satan's plan for the Body of Christ to be eviscerated and nullified by virtue of division. Where are the outpourings of the Holy Spirit? Where is the ability to retain those outpourings when they come? Where is the authority in the Body of Christ that is able to bind, to loose, and to take dominion? God's people should be the ones moving the world, creating by prophetic proclamation, and framing the ages to come by speaking His Word (Hebrews 11:3). Where has the power gone? It has been consumed in the division that satan has fomented. If we are swimming around in a cesspool of division, we have no power.

When the children of Israel journeyed together through the wilderness, the anointing, the power, and the very presence of God dwelt in their midst. They had no diseases; there was no futility (Exodus 15:26). So if we have disease and a sense of futility, we must attribute it to this division that finds its way into our midst. No matter how long the history of division has been with us, we

---

Genesis 13:7-9 And there was strife between the herdsmen of Abram's livestock and the herdsmen of Lot's livestock. Now the Canaanite and the Perizzite were dwelling then in the land. ⁸ Then Abram said to Lot, "Please let there be no strife between you and me, nor between my herdsmen and your herdsmen, for we are brothers. ⁹ Is not the whole land before you? Please separate from me: if to the left, then I will go to the right; or if to the right, then I will go to the left."

Hebrews 11:3 By faith we understand that the worlds were prepared by the word of God, so that what is seen was not made out of things which are visible.

Exodus 15:26 And He said, "If you will give earnest heed to the voice of the Lord your God, and do what is right in His sight, and give ear to His commandments, and keep all His statutes, I will put none of the diseases on you which I have put on the Egyptians; for I, the Lord, am your healer."

can break it through repentance. To whatever degree you have been a part of this pattern, you can end it. Do it at the simplest levels: within your family, within your church, within your fellowship of churches. Wherever we see division, we should be going after it. We should be repenting of it, rejecting it, and refusing it. Once we end division, then we can see it replaced with the oneness of spirit.

Let's look at examples of division in relationships. We have been taught that divorce is sin. Divorce creates division between two people by breaking the oneness of the marriage covenant that was made. If you participate in a divorce, you should repent until you get the thing out of your spirit that created the division. Then there should be no condemnation once there has been adequate repentance. The repentance sets you free to relate in oneness with others. A spirit of division is based upon the same principle as divorce; it breaks relationships. In response, there should be repentance until whatever brought about that division is thoroughly removed out of your heart and from the realm of spirit. You cannot pull the water back once it has gone under the bridge. So start from where you are. Drive a stake into the ground to say, "This is the day that we replace division with oneness and reconciliation." Find a level of agreement in your spirits that can be a bridge for God's love to be expressed.

This does not mean that you should run out and talk with everyone that you have been divided from. In your prayer before the Father, go into the spirit realm and by faith cancel out every expression of anger and every word that may have caused harm. If God wants you to have a face-to-face repentance or conversation, then by the Holy Spirit, He will bring about that opportunity. When the blood of Christ cleanses you of your sin, you are clean. Do not go back and try to undo what you have done, as if it were a bundle of knots that you are mentally trying to unravel.

From the very outset of the early Church, with all of its power and apostolic anointing, there were widows who complained about not getting enough food (Acts 6:1). The seeds of satan were already planted to bring division to the Church. Another example was the story of Ananias and Sapphira; satan again attempted to divide the young Church (Acts 5:1-5). The enemy's devices are still at work among us to cause division. We should determine not to bite on those hooks anymore. The whole of the Body of Christ needs to be released from division, but that seems to be beyond our individual control. What can you do as an individual member? Declare, "As for me and my house, we will serve the Lord" (Joshua 24:15). If each one of us will do this, we can literally create a force that will begin to flow out to the rest of the Body of Christ in the realm of spirit.

Remember the story of Noah and the ark? He built a boat in his backyard and judged the world (Hebrews 11:7). That is a classic example of executing a spiritual principle. In your own group or church, begin to take a stand to end division. By this stance of

---

Acts 6:1   Now at this time while the disciples were increasing in number, a complaint arose on the part of the Hellenistic Jews against the native Hebrews, because their widows were being overlooked in the daily serving of food.

Acts 5:1-5   But a certain man named Ananias, with his wife Sapphira, sold a piece of property, [2] and kept back some of the price for himself, with his wife's full knowledge, and bringing a portion of it, he laid it at the apostles' feet. [3] But Peter said, "Ananias, why has Satan filled your heart to lie to the Holy Spirit, and to keep back some of the price of the land? [4] While it remained unsold, did it not remain your own? And after it was sold, was it not under your control? Why is it that you have conceived this deed in your heart? You have not lied to men, but to God." [5] And as he heard these words, Ananias fell down and breathed his last; and great fear came upon all who heard of it.

Joshua 24:15   "And if it is disagreeable in your sight to serve the Lord, choose for yourselves today whom you will serve: whether the gods which your fathers served which were beyond the River, or the gods of the Amorites in whose land you are living; but as for me and my house, we will serve the Lord."

Hebrews 11:7   By faith Noah, being warned by God about things not yet seen, in reverence prepared an ark for the salvation of his household, by which he condemned the world, and became an heir of the righteousness which is according to faith.

faith, you can impact the world. One act of obedience can change everything. That is what it means to be a prophetic community. Let's position ourselves in prayer, in humbling ourselves, in calling upon the name of the Lord, and in finding His presence in all that we are doing.

Something beyond our understanding happens when we break into oneness. There is a release of life, of power, and of anointing. In the Church today, and all over the globe, people are talking about a new outpouring of the Holy Spirit. How is it triggered? Psalm 133 portrays the unity as that which triggers the outpouring:

> Behold, how good and how pleasant it is
> For brothers to dwell together in unity!
> It is like the precious oil upon the head,
> Coming down upon the beard,
> Even Aaron's beard,
> Coming down upon the edge of his robes.
> It is like the dew of Hermon,
> Coming down upon the mountains of Zion;
> For there the Lord commanded the blessing—life forever.

This psalm illustrates the preparation of the high priest to minister in the tent of meeting in the wilderness, and in the Temple at Jerusalem (Leviticus 8:12). The anointing oil was poured over his head, dripping down over his whole body, all the way to the edges of his robe. This is a picture of the coming great outpouring of the Holy Spirit. Every part of the Body of Christ will be covered by the Holy Spirit. The great outpouring of the Spirit in this age is going to be triggered by a determination of oneness on the part of God's people. It will happen when those who are called by His name begin to seek Him and cry out, "God heal my land." When God hears that

---

Leviticus 8:12   Then he poured some of the anointing oil on Aaron's head and anointed him, to consecrate him.

cry, He begins to reveal that He cannot bring life to the land in the midst of division.

Does that mean we will all become one big, homogenized Church? No, I don't think that God will ever get rid of diversity. Human reasoning tells us that you have to put everything in a blender and have it come out looking the same. The Ecumenical Movement did not work because it was based upon finding an absolute agreement on the Bible and on doctrines. By the time you cut out of the Bible all the doctrines that you can't agree on, instead of a Holy Bible, you end up with a Bible full of holes. By the time you have finished removing every doctrine you're not sure about and what the other person isn't sure about, before you know it there will be nothing left. That is not what Psalm 133 is depicting: "Behold, how good and how pleasant it is for brothers to dwell together in unity!" (Psalm 133:1). This is a unity of heart and of spirit.

We will find unity before we find agreement. We will find oneness and understanding of who we really are as the Body of Christ; then, in that atmosphere, the Holy Spirit can lead us into all the truth (John 16:13). He will teach us all things (John 14:26). A Body of Christ that is filled with the Holy Spirit will be in the process of having all of its little wrinkles ironed out. Because of the flow of the Spirit, He will be able to teach us and lead us. Do we have doctrines that we believe that are not exactly correct? I am sure that we do. How do we find out what they are? The natural reaction is to say, "Let's get a group of pastors together in a room around the Bible and fast and pray for forty days." I don't think that would allow God to show us what is wrong with us; He has another way. We see it

---

John 16:13 "But when He, the Spirit of truth, comes, He will guide you into all the truth; for He will not speak on His own initiative, but whatever He hears, He will speak; and He will disclose to you what is to come."

John 14:26 "But the Helper, the Holy Spirit, whom the Father will send in My name, He will teach you all things, and bring to your remembrance all that I said to you."

illustrated in John 17, when Jesus prayed to the Father, "That they may be perfected into one" (John 17:23).

Only in true unity does the Body of Christ come together and function properly. God created the diversity of the Body so that, as it comes into oneness, it is able to accomplish many different projects and ministries at the same time. It does not look like chaos when the diversity is brought about by the Holy Spirit. The Scripture depicts the Body of Christ as being like a natural body (1 Corinthians 12:12). If the organs and parts of our physical body were not attached to each other, it would look crazy. It would look like puzzle pieces that bear little or no resemblance to one another. The pieces would not seem as though they could even attach to each other. How in the world could you take all these different, diverse, weird-shaped and single-purposed pieces and put them together into one functioning body? The Father who created the body knows how it all fits together.

As the different parts of the Body of Christ begin to connect, it may look even more diverse than it looks now; yet it will be one Body, one unit, without schism or division. The oneness will turn the Body loose to function; the Holy Spirit will be the circulatory system flowing around and through each member, bathing every cell in the nutrients of His life. At the same time, the Spirit will be carrying away the refuse while the whole Body functions as one performing many activities. Now, transfer that picture to the whole earth, and you will see how all of those diversities will be necessary to establish the Kingdom of God. Think of all the things that have

---

John 17:23 "I in them, and Thou in Me, that they may be perfected into one, that the world may know that Thou didst send Me, and didst love them, even as Thou didst love Me."

1 Corinthians 12:12 For even as the body is one and yet has many members, and all the members of the body, though they are many, are one body, so also is Christ.

to be done in people's lives around the world, and the diversity that it will require.

We are living in an urgent hour. Our intercession will create the atmosphere for the Body of Christ to hear this word of direction. God is bringing us into an understanding of how to spark the outpouring of the Holy Spirit. Historically, every great outpouring of the Holy Spirit was initiated by a people crying out in intercession, coming together determined to seek the Lord with repentance and faith, until God moved with power in their midst. First, we must get out of the death process by ending division. Then, in our own individual lives and churches, we must embrace this oneness. We must determine to see the Body of Christ come together, which will set free the cleansing, empowering flow of the Holy Spirit. Our oneness will trigger this outpouring. Then the anointing oil of the Holy Spirit will flow over every diverse part of the Body of Christ, bringing it into new life.

Chapter 18

There Is No Division in Christ's Body

January 13, 2013
Church of the Living Word, North Hills, California

This message, which was spoken in a Sunday morning service, sparked a series of messages focusing on the leaders of the Body of Christ.

The concept of the Body of Christ is an idea whose time has come. However, we need a breakthrough that releases it from being an idea into a functional reality. This reality can be seen in the prayer that Jesus prayed just before He went to the cross. This prayer needs to be declared and, by faith, brought into existence. When Jesus prayed this prayer, He was surrounded by His disciples, and yet He was including all of us:

> "Sanctify them in the truth; Thy word is truth. As Thou didst send Me into the world, I also have sent them into the world. And for their sakes I sanctify Myself, that they themselves also may be sanctified in truth. I do not ask in behalf of these alone, but for those also who believe in Me through their word; that they may all be one; even as Thou, Father, art in Me, and I in Thee, that they also may be in Us; that the world may believe that Thou didst send Me.

> And the glory which Thou hast given Me I have given to them; that they may be one, just as We are one; I in them, and Thou in Me, that they may be perfected into one, that the world may know that Thou didst send Me, and didst love them, even as Thou didst love Me." (John 17:17-23)

"As Thou didst send Me into the world, I also have sent them into the world." Our commission is to the world. Jesus is concerned that we be in the world, not that we be taken out of the world. Then He said, "I do not ask in behalf of these alone, but for those also who believe in Me through their word." Jesus makes it clear that this prayer did not just apply to those disciples around Him, but to all those down through the ages who would believe because of their word. Next, He reveals how the world will come to believe. The world will believe when we are one. Christianity that is so given to evangelism and saving souls will never see the true fulfillment until there is a oneness in the Body of Christ. Our burden for souls, for a great outpouring of the Spirit, for salvation to sweep the land, is all triggered by the fulfillment of Christ's prayer: that His glory will rest on us, so that we may be perfected into one.

What we see in this prayer that Jesus made to the Father is what was burning in Jesus' heart for us. We should be looking for its manifestation to be a part of God's Kingdom coming to the earth. The greatest expression of the Kingdom of God is in the oneness of His people. Maybe it is past time for that to happen, but all it takes is one group of believers to pick up the burden and release it into existence. The fulfillment of Christ's prayer will be our functioning together as one Body.

> But one and the same Spirit works all these things, distributing to each one individually just as He wills. For even as the body is one and yet has many members, and all the members of the body, though they are many, are one body, so also is Christ. For by one Spirit we were all

baptized into one body, whether Jews or Greeks, whether slaves or free, and we were all made to drink of one Spirit. For the body is not one member, but many. (1 Corinthians 12:11-14)

The Body of Christ is like a natural body; the members have different gifts and different functions. "The same Spirit works all these things, distributing to each one individually just as He wills," so each individual has something. "For even as the body is one and yet has many members, and all the members of the body, though they are many, are one body, so also is Christ." Christ **is** His Body, and He is made up of individual members, distinct anointings, which are one manifestation. This is always hard for humans to deal with; we do not do well with diversity. Diversity to us signals division. That is why it is so easy for satan to destroy the idea of the Body of Christ. When we look at the landscape of Christianity right now, with all of its different manifestations, we see schisms and divisions which have, over time, become acceptable to us. In our belief system, the Body of Christ is just divided. We look at all of its diversity and distinctions and assume it to be division. For example, as people walk together in a fellowship, various burdens emerge. The direction for the group fragments; therefore, the group splits apart. Perhaps there are misunderstandings and hurt feelings, so the differences are cemented into division.

Is it possible that God could take Christianity just as it is right now, with all of its denominations and expressions, without changing anything, and make it one by the Spirit? Is it possible that all of these differences that we count as division are actually diversities of the Holy Spirit? I believe it is possible. Much of what has happened that is considered division has actually grown out of man's inability to understand both diversity and oneness. Therefore, the distinctions have often unnecessarily become a cause for separating from one another. On a human level, our answer to bring the Body of

Christ into oneness today would be to take every manifestation of Christianity, get the biggest blender that we could find, stuff all of us into this blender, turn it on extra high, and blend everyone together until each one is indistinguishable from the other. We would all just become homogeneous. But God does not work that way. Look at the example of Abram and Lot. Abram told Lot to take his family and his herds and go elsewhere, so that there would be no division or conflict between them (Genesis 13:7-9). Distinction does not mean that there is division.

It is clear that each part of your physical body is very distinct. Your liver definitely does not look, act, or feel the same as your eyeball. And your brain is completely different in appearance and function. Your body is absolutely diverse, with thousands of parts and pieces. Honestly, if you were to take all the parts of the body and lay them on a table, and then bring somebody into the room who had never studied anatomy, that person would never believe that all of those weird and different parts came out of one physical entity. It doesn't seem to make any sense. But God, in His wisdom, uses our physical body as an illustration of the Body of Christ, which reveals that for the oneness to come in the Body, two different steps need to take place.

The first step is that you must accept who and what you are spiritually, the unique part of the Body that you are. The Holy Spirit imparts gifts and ministries, enabling each one individually as He wills, and no one else can provide the part that you specifically provide to the Body of Christ. Functioning as that part is a struggle all its own. As you learn to accept yourself and get a revelation of how to

---

Genesis 13:7-9 And there was strife between the herdsmen of Abram's livestock and the herdsmen of Lot's livestock. Now the Canaanite and the Perizzite were dwelling then in the land. [8] Then Abram said to Lot, "Please let there be no strife between you and me, nor between my herdsmen and your herdsmen, for we are brothers. [9] Is not the whole land before you? Please separate from me: if to the left, then I will go to the right; or if to the right, then I will go to the left."

move in your gifts, you sometimes feel that God could have done it differently, or that He has ruined you somehow. Nevertheless, you have to come to grips with who and what you are as a manifestation of the Holy Spirit. To do this, you must become one with the Father in how He made you.

Secondly, you have to ask yourself whether you will function with the other members where God has placed you in the Body of Christ. Do you accept them, and will you function with them? What would happen if your kidney said, "I'm not going to function any more. You can circulate all the blood through me that you want, but I'm not going to clean it"? Your body would become a polluted mess in a very short time. What happens when someone's liver or heart stops functioning? In the natural, this means certain disease or death. All the members functioning together correctly is crucial to the life of the physical body. But when it comes to the Body of Christ, sometimes we stop functioning together by choice. We either refuse to take our own part in the Body, or we do not see the importance of the other parts. Something has to happen for us. It is a good thing that Jesus prayed for our oneness, because we need that impetus. He is the one who proclaimed it; He set it up this way. Christ is His Body, with the many individual parts and pieces. The Body of Christ already exists, but we have to get rid of the division, so that it can function. That is really what the world is waiting for.

If the members of the Body of Christ would begin to really move as mature sons of God, they would become a mighty people. We have to pick up the burden for this, and prophesy with a revelation of how important the Body of Christ is in this hour. We can recognize and honor our distinctions and break the division that exists. There must be an understanding of who we are and a willingness to play our part in this great Body that He is bringing forth. We see this as we continue reading in 1 Corinthians chapter 12:

> If the foot should say, "Because I am not a hand, I am not a part of the body," it is not for this reason any the less a

> part of the body. And if the ear should say, "Because I am not an eye, I am not a part of the body," it is not for this reason any the less a part of the body. If the whole body were an eye, where would the hearing be? If the whole were hearing, where would the sense of smell be? But now God has placed the members, each one of them, in the body, just as He desired. (1 Corinthians 12:15-18)

This goes back to the first step of accepting yourself. Maybe you are complaining, "I don't want to be a foot. I just can't function as a foot." Well, if you are not a foot, then find out who you are and be that. God has made you a part of the Body, literally Christ in the earth. That should be enough. "If the whole body were an eye, where would the hearing be? If the whole were hearing, where would the sense of smell be?" How weird would that look if your entire body was an eye? And if your entire body was only an ear for hearing, you could not even tap your toe to the music—you wouldn't have a toe! Every part has to participate. We have to trust that God has placed the members in the Body, each one, just as He desired. Each of us only has a part; we do not have it all. And if we are disconnected in our spirits from the whole, then we become useless.

> And if they were all one member, where would the body be? But now there are many members, but one body. And the eye cannot say to the hand, "I have no need of you"; or again the head to the feet, "I have no need of you." On the contrary, it is much truer that the members of the body which seem to be weaker are necessary; and those members of the body, which we deem less honorable, on these we bestow more abundant honor, and our unseemly members come to have more abundant seemliness. (1 Corinthians 12:19-23)

When we think of the idea that members of the Body who seem to be weaker are more necessary, our concept is that those weaker people need to be given more abundant honor. Look more closely at the wording of this Scripture: "On the contrary, it is much truer that the members of the body which **seem** to be weaker." In the Greek that word is *dokeo*, and it does not mean "seem" in the sense of appearance. It means that we suppose they are weak, or we believe that they are weak. That is the picture of Christianity today. We look at these different, diverse aspects of the Body and we say, "There is something wrong over there. Those people are in trouble; they lack this or that. We are stronger." The member whom you **perceive** as weaker is a full member of the Body of Christ, with a function that is essential to you. That is the truth of it. Again we read, "And those members of the body, which we deem less honorable." The word "deem" here is the same Greek word *dokeo*. Whether it is "seem" or "deem," it means that is the way we think about someone, not necessarily the truth of that person's value.

We need to change this broken way that the Body thinks about itself. It is destroying our ability to reflect the Father to the earth. There is not necessarily a problem with others; the problem is in the way we view them, or relate to them. We wall people off because we "deem" there is a problem with them. Instead, we should bestow more abundant honor on them. The unseemly members should come to be more valuable to us. We should apply this to individuals, ministries, groups, and denominations throughout the Body of Christ. We should begin to see them as the parts that we need.

This concept of the Body of Christ is an idea whose time has come. It is time for there to be a people who stand up and say, "If Jesus prayed for this, then we will be those who become it. We are going to prophesy it into existence. We are going to give ourselves to it in every way that we can." That does not mean that you need to be a part of everyone else's ministry. Find where God has placed you, whether you are a liver or an eyeball, and function there. We are not looking to homogenize, but to recognize the distinctions. We are looking to break the lie of division that separates us, that makes us refuse to function with the rest of the Body, or that makes the rest of the Body refuse to function with us.

As we begin to understand that there is no division in the Body of Christ, we will seek to be one. In that process of oneness there will be a purification. Don't be fearful that you are going to enter into deception. Part of the great commission is that if you drink any deadly poison it will not hurt you (Mark 16:18). There may be a lot of deception within the Body of Christ, but God will straighten those issues out as we walk together. We will not attain perfection by trying to perfect our doctrine. Jesus prayed that we would be perfected into one. The only true way for us to be free from all of our issues is to be willing to move into a oneness in the Body of Christ. As our hearts believe this Word, it will be initiated. Our faith will bring it into existence. We will create it by speaking a Living Word from God. As we stand on the reality that there is no division in the Body of Christ, we will become one in the Lord.

Mark 16:18 "They will pick up serpents, and if they drink any deadly poison, it shall not hurt them; they will lay hands on the sick, and they will recover."

Chapter 19

Oneness – Our Authority to Bind Satan

February 2, 2013
Igreja A Palavra Viva, Mount Zion, Niteroi, Brazil

This message was spoken to an annual gathering of hundreds of Pentecostal, Evangelical, and Catholic Church pastors and leaders who had come to Mount Zion from all over Brazil.

How does the worldwide Body of Christ come into a true oneness? It may seem impossible. Yet God has a purpose far beyond what we have seen. When Christ ascended, He left apostles, prophets, evangelists, pastors and teachers on earth with His anointing. This is the mantle of Christ as Emmanuel—"God with us"—that was never to leave the earth. That truth must be real to church leaders who will then be able to lead the Church into true oneness. In Ephesians 4, Paul explains:

> I, therefore, the prisoner of the Lord, entreat you to walk in a manner worthy of the calling with which you have been called, with all humility and gentleness, with patience, showing forbearance to one another in love, being diligent to preserve the unity of the Spirit in the bond of peace. There is one body and one Spirit, just as also you were called in one hope of your calling; one Lord, one faith, one

baptism, one God and Father of all who is over all and through all and in all. But to each one of us grace was given according to the measure of Christ's gift. Therefore it says, "When He ascended on high, He led captive a host of captives, and He gave gifts to men." (Now this expression, "He ascended," what does it mean except that He also had descended into the lower parts of the earth? He who descended is Himself also He who ascended far above all the heavens, that He might fill all things.) And He gave some as apostles, and some as prophets, and some as evangelists, and some as pastors and teachers, for the equipping of the saints for the work of service, to the building up of the body of Christ; until we all attain to the unity of the faith, and of the knowledge of the Son of God, to a mature man, to the measure of the stature which belongs to the fulness of Christ. (Ephesians 4:1-13)

Christ ascended far above all the heavens that He might fill all things. Having ascended, He provided everything we would need to see the Body of Christ grow and mature. He gave us apostles, prophets, evangelists, and pastors and teachers. As leaders we too often get lost in our individual churches and forget that our ministries are what God gave to the entire Body of Christ. These ministries are for the building up, the training, and the creating of the Body of Christ. We should be more concerned with the overall purpose of the Body of Christ than we are with the goals and burdens of our individual congregations. We read at the beginning of Ephesians 4, "I, therefore, the prisoner of the Lord." I also believe that we are prisoners of the Lord in these anointings and these gift ministries which He has given us. We are prisoners of God to follow through with His purpose. The Holy Spirit is speaking this to us as our instructions for today.

"Walk in a manner worthy of the calling with which you have been called, with all humility and gentleness, with patience, showing forbearance" (Ephesians 4:1-2). In the Greek this Scripture more accurately means, "Put up with each other." Forbearance sounds so wonderful, but the Holy Spirit is saying, "Would you please try to put up with each other?" Parents say that to their children when they are arguing: "At least put up with each other." So it is not difficult to understand what it means to show forbearance to one another in love. It is something that should begin with church leaders. The Body of Christ will follow their leaders, and if there are problems in walking out this directive, it starts with the leaders. If anyone is a teacher, he will incur a stricter judgment (James 3:1). And so we must take responsibility. As leaders, God is holding us responsible for the condition of the global Body of Christ.

As we read in Ephesians 4, we need to be walking in a manner that is worthy of this calling, with all humility, gentleness, and patience, showing forbearance to one another in love. God give us a level of love that we have never known before. It is difficult for us because all our gifts are different, and our visions are different. But Paul gave us another example in the Scriptures to help us. He likens the Body of Christ to the physical body (1 Corinthians 12:12). The human body is a strange thing. The liver is very different from the kidney; the eyeballs are very different from the heart. But they have one thing in common: they have the blood that circulates through every part of the body. It feeds, cleanses and causes every cell to grow. The Holy Spirit is the blood of the Body of Christ; it flows through every one of us, despite all our differences and all our diversities.

James 3:1 Let not many of you become teachers, my brethren, knowing that as such we shall incur a stricter judgment.

1 Corinthians 12:12 For even as the body is one and yet has many members, and all the members of the body, though they are many, are one body, so also is Christ.

To the human mind, difference means division. Most of the wars that happen in the world today are not country against country; they are brother against brother within the same country or region. Even within tribes or families it can be difficult to come together. But the Holy Spirit is trying to knit us together on another level, so division is no longer an option for the Church. We must be "diligent to preserve the unity of the Spirit in the bond of peace" (Ephesians 4:3). We must get out of the questioning, the division, and the separation. We all have different churches, organizations, and burdens, but we must see our earthly function as more than just authority over these individual areas. We are authorities over the entire Body of Christ.

How did Jesus teach us to pray? "Thy kingdom come. Thy will be done, on earth" (Matthew 6:10). The ministry of the Body of Christ is to the earth. This means that we are like a company of John the Baptists who are preparing the way. We are concerned about the dips in the road; we must make straight the way of the Kingdom (Matthew 3:1-3). We are here to prepare the way for Jesus to dwell in the earth and establish His Kingdom. In order to do that job, there must be a spiritual oneness among God's people.

The unity of the Spirit that Paul spoke of is an actual step in this process. We must first come into the unity of the Holy Spirit, which is the circulatory system of the Body of Christ, and by virtue of that, we will be drawn together and become one. In the next step after the unity of the Spirit, "we all attain to the unity of the faith" (Ephesians 4:13). The more we grow into oneness, the more we are going to have a knowledge of what God is really doing. There will be a time when we come into the unity of the faith where we all believe

---

Matthew 3:1-3 Now in those days John the Baptist came, preaching in the wilderness of Judea, saying, ² "Repent, for the kingdom of heaven is at hand." ³ For this is the one referred to by Isaiah the prophet, saying, "THE VOICE OF ONE CRYING IN THE WILDERNESS, 'MAKE READY THE WAY OF THE LORD, MAKE HIS PATHS STRAIGHT!'"

the same things, we all understand the same things, and we all know the same things.

Currently, we all see different truths in the Scriptures. Since the Holy Spirit is teaching us those truths, they should not lead to division. Do not accept division; believe in the oneness of the Spirit. In our hearts we commit, by the faith we have been given, to a oneness of the Spirit, and then we grow into the unity of the faith. The unity of the faith leads to the knowledge of the Son of God. Do you believe that there is a perfect knowledge of the Son of God that we can come into? This is what the Lord is leading us all into. But it is not possible to attain if we are isolated in our own little churches trying to find the perfect knowledge of God. We will find that knowledge together, as a result of the unity and the oneness of the Body of Christ.

Paul says this leads to a mature man. When we are born into Christ, when we first become believers, it says we are children (Ephesians 4:14). But we are not supposed to stay children. We are to grow up into "the measure of the stature which belongs to the fulness of Christ" (Ephesians 4:13). Can we really mature into the fullness of Christ right here, right now, in this earth? Or is it something afar off, only in heaven? I believe it is available for us right now, and it is triggered by our determination to be one, to grow up and become all that God has for us. We must stop being the creators of division among the Body of Christ. Instead, we must teach our people to love one another; not just in our own churches, but love one another in each other's churches. We are one in our Lord Jesus Christ; we must prophesy and proclaim it until it manifests.

Ephesians 4:14 As a result, we are no longer to be children, tossed here and there by waves, and carried about by every wind of doctrine, by the trickery of men, by craftiness in deceitful scheming.

Let's look at John chapter 17 to see the source of this oneness. Here Jesus is not just speaking or teaching; He's praying to the Father. Nothing can stop the Father from answering this prayer of His Son:

> "I do not ask in behalf of these alone, but for those also who believe in Me through their word; that they may all be one; even as Thou, Father, art in Me, and I in Thee, that they also may be in Us; that the world may believe that Thou didst send Me. And the glory which Thou hast given Me I have given to them; that they may be one, just as We are one; I in them, and Thou in Me, that they may be perfected into one, that the world may know that Thou didst send Me, and didst love them, even as Thou didst love Me." (John 17:20-23)

If we take that last sentence and put it in the negative, is it possible to say that the world will **never** believe if we are not one? Sometimes our message to the world is not believed because people look at the Church and do not see the truth of what we preach. They think, "You can't even get along with each other. Why would I want to join the Church?" That is a good point.

"And the glory which Thou hast given Me I have given to them; that they may be one." We will not come into this oneness on our own. Christ gave us the Holy Spirit, He gave us the glory that the Father gave to Him that we may be one. "That the world may know that Thou didst send Me." I want the world to know that the Father sent Jesus Christ into the earth. The question is, do I want this badly enough that I will be willing to be one with you to make it happen? The power of the early Church to reveal the Father to the earth was in their oneness. That will be the source of our power also.

Let's look at what is called the great commission (Matthew 28:18-20). Sometimes we forget that the great commission was really step two. First of all, Christ did not call it the great commission; that name was assigned later by theologians. True, the Lord definitely commissioned the believers to make disciples of the nations, but it was not the first thing they were to do. Before His ascension, Jesus said, "Don't leave Jerusalem." He did not allow the disciples to begin to evangelize yet. He said, "Stay there until you are endued with power from on high" (Acts 1:4, 8). When we read about the outpouring of the Holy Spirit on the Day of Pentecost, there were 120 believers there in one place, in one accord (Acts 1:15; 2:1, KJV).

We know that the disciples were not in one place, in one accord, immediately after Jesus was crucified. They were all scattered (Matthew 26:56). Jesus Himself would not allow them to evangelize and tell the story of what had happened until they went into that upper room, prayed, and sought God. When they had come into a oneness, Jesus poured out upon them the promised Holy Spirit. The oneness had to come first; yet the Church today looks at the

---

Matthew 28:18-20 And Jesus came up and spoke to them, saying, "All authority has been given to Me in heaven and on earth. [19] Go therefore and make disciples of all the nations, baptizing them in the name of the Father and the Son and the Holy Spirit, [20] teaching them to observe all that I commanded you; and lo, I am with you always, even to the end of the age."

Acts 1:4 And gathering them together, He commanded them not to leave Jerusalem, but to wait for what the Father had promised, "Which," He said, "you heard of from Me."

Acts 1:8 "But you shall receive power when the Holy Spirit has come upon you; and you shall be My witnesses both in Jerusalem, and in all Judea and Samaria, and even to the remotest part of the earth."

Acts 1:15 And at this time Peter stood up in the midst of the brethren (a gathering of about one hundred and twenty persons was there together), and said.

Acts 2:1, KJV And when the day of Pentecost was fully come, they were all with one accord in one place.

Matthew 26:56 "But all this has taken place that the Scriptures of the prophets may be fulfilled." Then all the disciples left Him and fled.

great commission as overriding every other responsibility. No, first we must walk in a manner worthy of being the witnesses. We must walk in love and oneness.

In Acts 4, the disciples prayed together in one accord, all saying the same thing. When they finished, they all spoke the Word of God with boldness, and signs and wonders were taking place though the apostles (Acts 4:24, 29-31). The power was in their oneness. Why do we need power today? The Body of Christ is to bind satan and plunder his house (Matthew 12:29). When Jesus talked about casting out the devil, He said, "If I do this by the hand of God, then the Kingdom of God has come upon you" (Matthew 12:28). He was saying that the ability to bind satan and cast him out is a manifestation of the Kingdom of God. If we are going to manifest the Kingdom in this earth, then we are going to have to bind the strong man and plunder his house.

We are not here just to evangelize and save a few souls. I want us to stop thinking, "I have a church in a particular location." Instead, think, "My church is part of the Kingdom of God. I am here as an authority, as an apostle, prophet, evangelist, pastor, or teacher, and I have a congregation which is part of the global Body of Christ." We are not trying to save a few souls in a particular location. We

---

Acts 4:24 And when they heard this, they lifted their voices to God with one accord and said, "O Lord, it is Thou who DIDST MAKE THE HEAVEN AND THE EARTH AND THE SEA, AND ALL THAT IS IN THEM."

Acts 4:29-31 "And now, Lord, take note of their threats, and grant that Thy bond-servants may speak Thy word with all confidence, [30] while Thou dost extend Thy hand to heal, and signs and wonders take place through the name of Thy holy servant Jesus." [31] And when they had prayed, the place where they had gathered together was shaken, and they were all filled with the Holy Spirit, and began to speak the word of God with boldness.

Matthew 12:29 "Or how can anyone enter the strong man's house and carry off his property, unless he first binds the strong man? And then he will plunder his house."

Matthew 12:28 "But if I cast out demons by the Spirit of God, then the kingdom of God has come upon you."

are binding the strong man, binding satan, and casting him out. Do not settle for your church saving a few souls. Take the city! It is not satan's city anymore; it has been won by the blood of Christ (Colossians 1:13-14).

Who is going to bind the strong man and take over his house? We have not yet seen multitudes of people saved simultaneously all over the globe. Why not? Because they are bound up in the house of the strong man. Our responsibility as authorities is to bind the strong man and plunder his house. Part of that plunder is the souls that are under satan's control. Yet it is more than just souls; it is whole cities and countries. They belong to Jesus Christ. He is the King of kings and the Lord of lords (Revelation 17:14).

We are here to create a place for Christ to dwell, for Him to rule and reign. I do not think we are supposed to wait for His return to get rid of the devil and create the atmosphere of the Kingdom. The Lord expects that to be done by the time He gets here! I cannot just sit and pray, "Lord, I am waiting for You. I want Your return. Oh Lord, please return!" He will look down and say, "Don't worry about Me coming back; worry about your job. I need you to do your job." We may be waiting for Jesus' return, but according to the Scriptures, Jesus is the one waiting until His enemies are made a footstool for His feet (Hebrews 10:12-13).

Colossians 1:13-14 For He delivered us from the domain of darkness, and transferred us to the kingdom of His beloved Son, ¹⁴ in whom we have redemption, the forgiveness of sins.

Revelation 17:14 "These will wage war against the Lamb, and the Lamb will overcome them, because He is Lord of lords and King of kings, and those who are with Him are the called and chosen and faithful."

Hebrews 10:12-13 But He, having offered one sacrifice for sins for all time, SAT DOWN AT THE RIGHT HAND OF GOD, ¹³ waiting from that time onward UNTIL HIS ENEMIES BE MADE A FOOTSTOOL FOR HIS FEET.

According to Luke chapter 19, Jesus was walking along near Jerusalem with many people following Him. Some of those in the crowd were wondering, "When is the Kingdom coming?" Jesus got so frustrated that He gave them this parable:

> And while they were listening to these things, He went on to tell a parable, because He was near Jerusalem, and they supposed that the kingdom of God was going to appear immediately. He said therefore, "A certain nobleman went to a distant country to receive a kingdom for himself, and then return. And he called ten of his slaves, and gave them ten minas, and said to them, 'Do business with this until I come back.'" (Luke 19:11-13)

In the parable, the nobleman went away to receive a kingdom and he was planning to come back. When he did return, what was he interested in? "What did you do with what I gave you?" (Luke 19:15). That is how he judged them. And then those who resisted him, he killed (Luke 19:27). It is not worth being disobedient to Him! This parable is the Lord telling us, "Occupy till I come" (Luke 19:13, KJV). In other words, "Be focused here. Use your gifts to build My Kingdom here on the earth."

What are the "minas" that the Lord has given us? He has given us the gift ministries: apostles, prophets, evangelists, pastors and teachers. When He returns, He is going to ask us, "What did you do with all that the apostle Paul instructed you to do? Did you walk

---

Luke 19:15 "And it came about that when he returned, after receiving the kingdom, he ordered that these slaves, to whom he had given the money, be called to him in order that he might know what business they had done."

Luke 19:27 "But these enemies of mine, who did not want me to reign over them, bring them here and slay them in my presence."

Luke 19:13, KJV And he called his ten servants, and delivered them ten pounds, and said unto them, Occupy till I come.

in a manner worthy? Did you preserve the unity of the Spirit? Did you grow that unity of the Spirit into the unity of the faith? Did you come to the knowledge of the Son of God?" God has given us what we need; now He is waiting for us to grow up. He is waiting for us to bind satan and plunder his house.

How do we get the anointing and power to do this? When brothers are dwelling together in unity, the anointing comes (Psalm 133:1-2). We can sit in our individual churches and pray for the anointing, pray for power, but if we come into oneness, there will be an outpouring of God's Spirit. There will be a return of the power that the early apostles knew. Look at Acts chapters 2 through 5. There was tremendous oneness, power, anointing, miracles and boldness. The Word of God was flowing, not just from the apostles, but from all of the believers. The entire Body of Christ was moving in a way that we long for.

The global Body of Christ is in our hands. Our stance should be, "We are going to deal with the division. On our watch, division will not be allowed among the leaders, or in our fellowships. We are going to reach into a oneness that brings authority and anointing. We don't care which church the people that get saved go to. It's not just about the people finding salvation. The Kingdom of God is a greater vision than just our churches or a few souls."

"The earth is the LORD's, and the fulness thereof" (Psalm 24:1, KJV). We bind the strong man; satan's rule is over! He does not own our cities, our regions, or our nations. If Jesus prayed for us to be one, then by the name of the Father, we will be one. Jesus already created this by His prayer in John chapter 17, and He ever lives to make

---

Psalm 133:1-2 Behold, how good and how pleasant it is for brothers to dwell together in unity! ² It is like the precious oil upon the head, coming down upon the beard, even Aaron's beard, coming down upon the edge of his robes.

intercession for us (Hebrews 7:25). The Holy Spirit will create this oneness; all we have to do is not resist it or reject it. We must open our hearts to follow the Holy Spirit as He leads us into oneness. Oneness is our authority to bind satan and to prepare the way for God's Kingdom on earth.

Hebrews 7:25 Hence, also, He is able to save forever those who draw near to God through Him, since He always lives to make intercession for them.

Chapter 20

Oneness – The Enabling to Fulfill Our Purpose

February 3, 2013
Igreja A Palavra Viva, Mount Zion, Niteroi, Brazil

This message was spoken during the School of Prophets, an annual, international conference at Mount Zion.

The Words of Jesus in John chapter 17 are as important for us in our generation as they were for those disciples who first heard them. Rather than reading this Scripture as mere verses, take it as the Lord speaking directly to you in a very personal way. He is giving us direction and understanding of how to walk in the days ahead. Nothing that you will read here is new, but I want it to touch you in a new way, impacting another level of your spirit. This passage should become the expression of our lives together in the Body of Christ, an impartation by the Holy Spirit to our hearts.

> "And I am no more in the world; and yet they themselves are in the world, and I come to Thee. Holy Father, keep them in Thy name, the name which Thou hast given Me, that they may be one, even as We are. While I was with them, I was keeping them in Thy name which Thou hast given Me; and I guarded them, and not one of them perished but the son of perdition, that the Scripture might be fulfilled." (John 17:11-12)

"And I am no more in the world." Jesus is no longer in His singular body, in the flesh, here with us in this world. He ascended to the right hand of the Father. What He was saying to those disciples is our truth today: He is no longer here. "And yet they themselves are in the world." We are here. Our lives and what we relate to, are in this world. Jesus is in one place; we are in another place. That is one of the most difficult things to live with. We could protest that and say we want to be where He is. Or better yet, we want Him to be where we are, because we are not sure where He is! We may call it heaven, but we really don't understand heaven. We understand this world because we live in this world. This separation is our reality. But there is a purpose for this reality, and we must learn to live with it.

When we look at the reality of us being here and Christ being with the Father, our great hope must be to understand Christ's prayer; there is much more to be grasped. There are certain keys or principles to living in any age. How are we to live? What are we to believe and reach for in God? How are we to pray? These things should become very much our concern as believers today. While we live on the earth, on the natural level, we must deal with certain realities, such as the principle of gravity. Everything we do—the way we walk and act—is always with the awareness of gravity. Gravity may not exist tomorrow, but I must live in the world as it is right now. If I do not pay attention to gravity, I could destroy myself. Similarly, oneness is a principle that must be reckoned with because of our physical separation from Christ. Jesus explained that He is with the Father, and we are here, but He also said, "Holy Father, keep them in Thy name…that they may be one" (John 17:11). We must have oneness in order to exist in this earth spiritually and not be destroyed, just as on the natural level we must deal with gravity or be destroyed.

Will the world always be this way? No. Christ is not always going to be in heaven, separated from us who live here on the earth. The time is coming when He will set up His Kingdom here. When that happens, we really do not know what will change. There may be no need for gravity. It is possible that many principles that rule the earth in this age may change. Right now, satan is the prince of the power of the air (Ephesians 2:2). That will change. Our environment will not always be the same. The world we live in now is not the world that Adam and Eve lived in. At that time, they did not worry about death. There was no death in the Garden of Eden until there was transgression. When there was transgression, then death began to reign (Romans 5:17).

The very elemental principles that rule the atmosphere of the world in which we live are changeable. Jesus had the ability to function according to principles of the Kingdom while He was still on the earth. He walked on water (Matthew 14:25). We are subject to gravity, but He was freed from certain natural principles. Keep this concept in mind when you read that He asked the Father "that they may be one, even as We are" (John 17:11). If Jesus was asking the Father for that oneness as our answer to live in this world, then that oneness must include a provision much greater than we have ever imagined.

It cannot be too much for us to ask the Father for the same thing: "Let us be one." Let us be one with the Father, one with Christ, and one with one another. If we do not have this oneness, we are missing a necessary element to successfully live in this world. There is no condemnation; Jesus Himself said it would be this way. He said He would no longer be here, but we would be here. If we are to live in

---

Ephesians 2:2 In which you formerly walked according to the course of this world, according to the prince of the power of the air, of the spirit that is now working in the sons of disobedience.

Romans 5:17 For if by the transgression of the one, death reigned through the one, much more those who receive the abundance of grace and of the gift of righteousness will reign in life through the One, Jesus Christ.

Matthew 14:25 And in the fourth watch of the night He came to them, walking on the sea.

this world apart from Him, then the necessary ingredient is that we become one.

We may have a measure of unity, but that is not the oneness that Jesus was asking for. We must cry out for the exact oneness that Jesus prayed for. There is something in that oneness that allows us to function spiritually while being separated physically from our Lord. Do you think Jesus and the Father have left us in this situation for no reason? It does not matter that this has been the reality in the earth since Christ's ascension; God is looking for something new. The Father sent Jesus to earth to die on the cross as the sacrifice for our sin; and He remained in the earth, in His physical body, until He fulfilled His purpose as the Son of God, as our Savior. Once He died and was resurrected, everything changed for us on this earth. From that moment onward, we began this new phase, or epoch.

Jesus remained on the earth until His purpose was fulfilled. He ministered faithfully until He went to the cross, completing what God sent Him here to do. Then when Christ fulfilled the purpose of God in the earth, the age was able to change. Today, everyone is waiting for this current age to change; they are focused on Christ's return and the Kingdom of God being established on this earth. Christianity is waiting for this new epoch, so that we will no longer be separated from Christ as our King. That change of age will not happen until God's purpose for this time period is fulfilled. Then Christ's return and the establishment of His Kingdom will trigger the change of an age. If we want the page to turn on a new age, we must be willing, in the same way as Christ, to fulfill the purpose of God for our lives in this epoch. Today, that purpose does not rest on Jesus the individual; it rests on the whole Body of Christ. He is waiting until every enemy be made a footstool for His feet (Hebrews 10:12-13). How long can Jesus wait? How long can

---

Hebrews 10:12-13 But He, having offered one sacrifice for sins for all time, SAT DOWN AT THE RIGHT HAND OF GOD, ¹³ waiting from that time onward UNTIL HIS ENEMIES BE MADE A FOOTSTOOL FOR HIS FEET.

the Father wait? Another 2,000 years? How long will it be until the Kingdom comes? That is up to us. There is a purpose in the plan of God for this age, and it must be fulfilled through us.

> "But now I come to Thee; and these things I speak in the world, that they may have My joy made full in themselves. I have given them Thy word; and the world has hated them, because they are not of the world, even as I am not of the world. I do not ask Thee to take them out of the world, but to keep them from the evil one. They are not of the world, even as I am not of the world." (John 17:13-16)

Remember, this prayer is a conversation between Jesus and the Father, and those around Him were listening. Are we listening? He is talking to us today. This verse explains how we can be joyful while we are living in the world. We get so agitated living under these conditions, but there is a joy we can have as we embrace God's purpose for us. "I have given them Thy word; and the world has hated them, because they are not of the world, even as I am not of the world." Now, look carefully at the following words: "I do not ask Thee to take them out of the world." If you are praying for a "rapture," you are praying for something different than what Jesus prayed for. You can talk to Him about this, but I think He is going to win. We need to come to grips with the fact that we long to get out of this world situation. Even if you are not looking for a rapture, you may still be looking for the Kingdom to hurry up, without recognizing your part in making that happen. Jesus did not want us to be taken out of the world, but He prayed that we be kept from the evil one.

Let's look at how Jesus taught His disciples to pray: "Pray, then, in this way: 'Our Father who art in heaven, hallowed be Thy name. Thy kingdom come. Thy will be done, on earth as it is in heaven'" (Matthew 6:9-10). That sounds a lot like what Jesus was asking for in His prayer to the Father. He said, "I am not asking You to take them out of the world." That is why He taught the disciples to pray, "Thy

Kingdom come, on earth as it is in heaven." If we pray this prayer in our hearts daily, then we will not be looking for a way out. But we should pray, "Keep us from the evil one, because we are not of this world, just as Christ was not of this world."

We are ambassadors for Christ (2 Corinthians 5:20). God put us here because we are the ambassadors of a new age. That is why there is something in us that is yearning for the Kingdom, but we must understand that it is not out there somewhere apart from us. Christ sent us as His ambassadors to bring the Kingdom here. We are not of this world. Take that deep into your hearts. Don't get caught up in the things of the world. Satan tries to tempt us and to pull us into the things of the world, but we are here to bring the things of the world into subjection to the Lordship of Jesus Christ. We are His ambassadors who are removing all other authority, all other rule, so that the Kingdom of God is free to fill the earth.

> "Sanctify them in the truth; Thy word is truth. As Thou didst send Me into the world, I also have sent them into the world. And for their sakes I sanctify Myself, that they themselves also may be sanctified in truth. I do not ask in behalf of these alone, but for those also who believe in Me through their word; that they may all be one; even as Thou, Father, art in Me, and I in Thee, that they also may be in Us; that the world may believe that Thou didst send Me. And the glory which Thou hast given Me I have given to them; that they may be one, just as We are one; I in them, and Thou in Me, that they may be perfected into one, that the world may know that Thou didst send Me, and didst love them, even as Thou didst love Me." (John 17:17-23)

---

2 Corinthians 5:20 Therefore, we are ambassadors for Christ, as though God were entreating through us; we beg you on behalf of Christ, be reconciled to God.

"As Thou didst send Me into the world, I also have sent them into the world." Let that sink in. No one would argue with the truth that the Father sent Jesus into the world with a very distinct mission and purpose. But Jesus said, "As [just like] Thou didst send me into the world, I also have sent them into the world." Again, this time in which we live is not a mistake. It is an epoch with a purpose in God as real, as distinct, and as important as the age in which Jesus walked in the earth. Today, Jesus is not here, but His mantle of the Word made flesh is still here. We are sanctified in the truth, the Word made flesh in us, as it was made flesh in Jesus Christ (John 1:14).

As the Father sent Jesus into the world, He has sent us. He did not go away to leave us as orphans (John 14:18). You were born into this world as one who was sent. Just as Jesus began as a baby in the arms of His mother, so did you. You came with a distinct purpose that through you the Word of God would be manifested to the earth. Christ fulfilled His purpose and so will you.

> "For God so loved the world, that He gave His only begotten Son, that whoever believes in Him should not perish, but have eternal life. For God did not send the Son into the world to judge the world, but that the world should be saved through Him." (John 3:16-17)

The Father sent Christ to save the world. Now He has sent us to execute the salvation that He won on the cross. Are we willing to be sent into the world to fulfill our purpose? "For their sakes I sanctify Myself, that they themselves also may be sanctified in truth" (John 17:19). We have the ability to be sanctified in the truth, just as He was sanctified in the truth.

John 1:14 And the Word became flesh, and dwelt among us, and we beheld His glory, glory as of the only begotten from the Father, full of grace and truth.

John 14:18 "I will not leave you as orphans; I will come to you."

"I do not ask in behalf of these alone, but for those also who believe in Me through their word; that they may all be one; even as Thou, Father, art in Me, and I in Thee, that they also may be in Us; that the world may believe that Thou didst send Me." (John 17:20-21)

We also can be one as Christ and the Father are one. Then He said, "And the glory which Thou hast given Me I have given to them; that they may be one" (John 17:22). Why is there a need for glory? It creates a oneness between us that can never be produced by our human efforts.

Now we understand the purpose of this age that we live in, the purpose of our lives. And we understand the tribulation that we go through. Jesus said, "The world has hated them" (John 17:14). Satan hates you because you are the instrument of his destruction. You are the ones who take the victory of the cross and apply it in this generation. When the victory of the cross is applied in this age, then a new page will turn. We are able to enter into the age of the Kingdom because, by the victory of the cross, we bind the strong man and plunder his house (Matthew 12:29). Just as David desired to build a house for the Lord, and his son Solomon was driven to see it built (2 Samuel 7:1-3, 27; 1 Kings 5:5), Christ has opened the door

---

Matthew 12:29 "Or how can anyone enter the strong man's house and carry off his property, unless he first binds the strong man? And then he will plunder his house."

2 Samuel 7:1-3 Now it came about when the king lived in his house, and the Lord had given him rest on every side from all his enemies, ² that the king said to Nathan the prophet, "See now, I dwell in a house of cedar, but the ark of God dwells within tent curtains." ³ And Nathan said to the king, "Go, do all that is in your mind, for the Lord is with you."

2 Samuel 7:27 "For Thou, O Lord of hosts, the God of Israel, hast made a revelation to Thy servant, saying, 'I will build you a house'; therefore Thy servant has found courage to pray this prayer to Thee."

1 Kings 5:5 "And behold, I intend to build a house for the name of the Lord my God, as the Lord spoke to David my father, saying, 'Your son, whom I will set on your throne in your place, he will build the house for My name.'"

of salvation for all mankind and we are driven as His ambassadors to see humanity reconciled to the Father. We must look at this earth, and this age, with new eyes. It breaks our heart that Christ has to be in heaven when the earth should be His home (Acts 3:20-21). This is our declaration: we will create a dwelling place for Him on this earth.

Christianity has been very concerned about saving souls. We will retrieve those souls; they are locked up in satan's house. When we plunder his house, we will rescue those souls. Everyone that has been taken captive by satan blinding their eyes and hearts, we will retrieve. They are like the furnishings of the house. When Christ comes to dwell in the house, He will possess all those beautiful souls that have been created.

"The glory which Thou hast given Me I have given to them; that they may be one" (John 17:22). God's glory knits us into one, a oneness that opens our eyes to see our purpose in God. It is not a problem to us that Christ is out of our view, if we realize that we also are not of this world. We are His ambassadors that He has sent here with a purpose. We must execute the victory He won. It is up to us to make every enemy the footstool for His feet. Within the oneness that Jesus prayed for is our enabling to be effective. He prayed, "Father, I want them to be one, just as You and I are one." What made Jesus successful when He was here? It was His oneness with the Father. By that oneness with the Father, He had authority and power. He spoke Words that brought life. He was able to quiet the winds, deal with elemental spirits, and rebuke satan and tell him, "Begone!" Jesus knew that His oneness with the Father made Him effective, and He knew that only that same oneness would equip us.

Acts 3:20-21 "And that He may send Jesus, the Christ appointed for you, [21] whom heaven must receive until the period of restoration of all things about which God spoke by the mouth of His holy prophets from ancient time."

Jesus' prayer to the Father was also His commission to us; He has equipped us. We reach for the glory that imparts this oneness for us to fulfill our purpose. When Jesus was in His final hour, ready to go to the cross, His face was fixed on Jerusalem to complete His purpose (Luke 9:51). We, too, are coming to the moment of the fulfillment of the purpose for which we were sent. This age is ready to change. It is time for a new age to be ushered in, and that will only happen as we fulfill our destiny. Oh Lord, let everything You asked the Father for be manifested in us!

Luke 9:51 And it came about, when the days were approaching for His ascension, that He resolutely set His face to go to Jerusalem.

Chapter 21

Our Faith for the Catholic Church

February 17, 2013
Igreja A Palavra Viva, Mount Zion, Niteroi, Brazil

In a time of significant transition for the Catholic Church upon the announcement of Pope Benedict XVI's resignation, this message of faith was spoken to the local congregation at Mount Zion.

There is a tremendous move within Catholicism today to see the outpouring of the Holy Spirit, to see the fullness of the Spirit work throughout the Church and become the driving force behind the Church. I believe that Pope Benedict XVI is being led by the Holy Spirit concerning what needs to be done for the benefit of the Catholic Church. Our response is to bless the Pope and bless the people of the Catholic Church. There are those, of course, who criticize us for taking this position; they focus primarily on the history of the Catholic Church, or even recent events involving issues and violations with members of the Catholic clergy. There is no question that the Catholic Church has gone through many troubles in its nearly 2,000-year history. By standing with the Pope we are not denying or trying to absolve every problem and every troubling historic event that has taken place in the Catholic Church. Do their problems mean that the Catholics are not Christians? Do their problems mean that the Catholics, according to the Scriptures, are disqualified from the Body of Christ? No. They are a part of the

Body of Christ. Many Protestants have a real issue with Catholics over their doctrines and past actions. However, such problems are not limited to the Catholics. If you really want to be fair, you should study the church history of the Protestants also. It is just as bad. If we were to look closely at the history of any Protestant denomination—whether they are Spirit-filled, Pentecostal, Charismatic, or traditional denominations—I don't think any of us would want to be a part of them.

In the same way, there are many things in our history as a people that I am not proud of, that do not reflect Jesus Christ, in what He taught us to be, and in how we are to walk. But in taking on the leadership of our fellowship, I understood that I must own the bad with the good. I take responsibility for things I was not even responsible for, because they are part of our history. But I do that because I believe there is much more that is good than bad. Many of these situations that do not reflect Christ are part of the natural process of spiritual growth. People do things wrong. There have been people and leaders in our fellowship who never genuinely reflected our founder, John Stevens, in the way that he walked or in what he said. As a result, some people have focused on a negative picture of our fellowship, painted by the fleshly actions of these individuals, instead of seeing a true representation of what God has been doing with us. We just have to deal with that. As leaders, we have to be forceful in removing that which is not following the Word; but at the same time, we are to have faith for people. We must let them repent, let them grow, and let them become. We are all children in the Gospel, and we all need to grow out of our problems.

What parent does not have children who do things they are not proud of? But when those children grow up and become men and women of God, the parents can look back and say, "Those actions weren't really them. It was just something they went through. We're not proud of those actions, but we are proud of them. They grew up and became an expression of the will of God." The Body of Christ is much the same. If we are going to evaluate one another by virtue of church history, then no one is worthy; everyone has fallen short. But there is a heart that God is bringing forth in this day, a heart to walk with God, to know the Lord, to be filled with His Spirit, and to do His will (Jeremiah 31:33-34). As we believe that and embrace it, we can change everything. We can become something different.

In the fifth chapter of Galatians is a passage that explains how we are to walk and how we are to live as the Body of Christ: "For you were called to freedom, brethren; only do not turn your freedom into an opportunity for the flesh, but through love serve one another" (Galatians 5:13). Throughout the history of the Church, the flesh has always surfaced and created problems: sin, stumbling, and failing. As any of us begin to follow the Lord, the flesh can be overwhelming. The flesh is the greatest force that comes against us; it is something that we constantly wrestle with. We know that in Christ we are born into freedom. However, many times that freedom has become a problem for our flesh. We know that is not what God wants, or what Christ has called us to be. What He wants is that we, through love, serve one another.

We can all look at the nearly 2,000-year history of the Catholic Church and read about things like the Inquisition and the Crusades, but that still does not mean the sin committed is too great to forgive. Without question, there were horrible injustices done by the Catholic Church, but we have seen many horrible violations done by Protestant churches as well. Today, we have all the same sins and failings going on in the Protestant movement, with

---

Jeremiah 31:33-34 "But this is the covenant which I will make with the house of Israel after those days," declares the LORD, "I will put My law within them, and on their heart I will write it; and I will be their God, and they shall be My people. [34] And they shall not teach again, each man his neighbor and each man his brother, saying, 'Know the LORD,' for they shall all know Me, from the least of them to the greatest of them," declares the LORD, "for I will forgive their iniquity, and their sin I will remember no more."

some of the greatest iniquity including misappropriating people's money, mishandling designated funds, and committing sexual improprieties. Instead of focusing on people and their failings, we need to focus on the real enemy. We are pursuing this enemy, satan, seven ways into seven realms (Deuteronomy 28:7). And one of those seven realms is religion. Rather than pointing to the problems in the Catholic Church, or in any other religion, let's chase satan out of it completely. We need to get rid of the real source of the problem: satan reigns in the earth in religion, in all of its forms. Somebody has to end that reign, and we cannot do that by throwing rocks at one another. Jesus said, "He who is without sin should throw the first stone" (John 8:7). If we continue to throw stones of criticism, we will kill each other. If we make sin the basis, then we all deserve to die. The Scriptures give us a different way: "But through love serve one another. For the whole Law is fulfilled in one word, in the statement, 'YOU SHALL LOVE YOUR NEIGHBOR AS YOURSELF'" (Galatians 5:13-14).

Are the Catholics our neighbors? They are much more than that; they are our brothers and our sisters. They are part of the Body of Christ. But even if they were only neighbors, the whole Law is fulfilled in loving your neighbor as yourself. As much as I am believing for our own freedom and release in becoming men and women of God, I must also believe for my neighbor. As much as I am believing for us as a group to bring the Kingdom of God into this earth, I must believe for my neighbor to have the same fulfillment. I want nothing more for us than to become an expression of the Lordship of Jesus Christ in the earth. His Lordship must reign over my heart, and over your heart. If I believe that for me, and believe that for you, how can

---

Deuteronomy 28:7 "The LORD will cause your enemies who rise up against you to be defeated before you; they shall come out against you one way and shall flee before you seven ways."

John 8:7 But when they persisted in asking Him, He straightened up, and said to them, "He who is without sin among you, let him be the first to throw a stone at her."

I not believe the same for our Catholic brothers and sisters? I cannot honestly believe in Christ's Lordship becoming a reality for me if I do not believe, with the same intensity of spirit, for it to become a reality for my neighbor.

One of the greatest things I could ever picture is the Lordship of Jesus Christ ruling and reigning in the Catholic Church. What an amazing manifestation that would be. Yet an attitude has crept into Protestant circles to regard the Catholic Church as Babylon, or to see it as the antichrist. What about **my** sin? I want Jesus to forgive it. How does the Lord's Prayer go? "Forgive me my trespasses, as I forgive those who trespass against me" (Matthew 6:12). If we refuse to forgive the sins of the Catholics, then the Father will refuse to forgive our sin (Matthew 6:15). Jesus did not come to provide selective salvation. His blood is good for all, for every violation, for every sin—including that within the Church.

When satan was cast down, he began to invade the Church and has relentlessly continued this assault (Revelation 12:12-13). What can we say? "Begone, Satan!" (Matthew 4:10). Let's get rid of him, here, and in every place that the *ekklesia* of Christ exists. The Scripture is clear: "But if you bite and devour one another, take care lest you be consumed by one another" (Galatians 5:15). We cannot bite and devour one another. If we look at the Catholics and assume that because they have problems we are justified in biting and devouring

---

Matthew 6:12 "And forgive us our debts, as we also have forgiven our debtors."

Matthew 6:15 "But if you do not forgive men, then your Father will not forgive your transgressions."

Revelation 12:12-13 "For this reason, rejoice, O heavens and you who dwell in them. Woe to the earth and the sea, because the devil has come down to you, having great wrath, knowing that he has only a short time." [13] And when the dragon saw that he was thrown down to the earth, he persecuted the woman who gave birth to the male child.

Matthew 4:10 Then Jesus said to him, "Begone, Satan! For it is written, 'YOU SHALL WORSHIP THE LORD YOUR GOD, AND SERVE HIM ONLY.'"

them, then we are taking on the mantle of satan, the accuser of the brethren (Revelation 12:10). It is time for the Body of Christ to take off this mantle of accusation. It is time that we stop biting and devouring one another, both in our individual churches, and in the whole Body of Christ. In every area we must stop this, because the result is that we will be consumed by one another. I contend that the power of the Church has evaporated because we ourselves have devoured it. We have devoured it by devouring one another.

"But I say, walk by the Spirit, and you will not carry out the desire of the flesh" (Galatians 5:16). This is what the Pope is trying to do. In all that he is doing, he believes to be led by the Spirit and to walk by the Spirit. It is the only answer we have. This drive for love, for walking by the Spirit, has been the basis of our connection with our Catholic brothers and sisters. We are believing to see a new outpouring of the Holy Spirit in the Catholic Church, and we are not even the ones who started this burden of intercession. I wish we had been that aware. Instead, some Catholic brothers came to us and said, "Can you help us? We are believing to see new outpourings, new releases of the Spirit." This outpouring of the Spirit that the Pope is believing for is the ultimate answer for the Body of Christ. How do we stop our problems? How do we end the destructive history of the Church born out of problems of the flesh living and breeding in our organizations? By walking in the Spirit. When we walk in the Spirit, we will not fulfill, we will not promote or continue, the desires of the flesh.

Hopefully, by getting involved in this vision together with the Catholic Church, we will all be filled anew. God grant us a double portion of His Spirit. "For the flesh sets its desire against the

---

Revelation 12:10 And I heard a loud voice in heaven, saying, "Now the salvation, and the power, and the kingdom of our God and the authority of His Christ have come, for the accuser of our brethren has been thrown down, who accuses them before our God day and night."

Spirit, and the Spirit against the flesh; for these are in opposition to one another, so that you may not do the things that you please" (Galatians 5:17). That is a good description of the history of the Church. We have never been able to do what we really wanted to do because of this battle between flesh and spirit. The deeds of the flesh have been seen in every aspect of Church history up to this current day. The answer for that is an outpouring of the Holy Spirit.

> But if you are led by the Spirit, you are not under the Law. Now the deeds of the flesh are evident, which are: immorality, impurity, sensuality, idolatry, sorcery, enmities, strife, jealousy, outbursts of anger, disputes, dissensions, factions, envying, drunkenness, carousing, and things like these, of which I forewarn you just as I have forewarned you that those who practice such things shall not inherit the kingdom of God. (Galatians 5:18-21)

All of the deeds of the flesh have been evidenced in the Church. We cannot deny the source; we cannot hide from it. We realize that this has been our history. Envying, drunkenness, carousing—those who practice such things will not inherit the Kingdom of God. Now we know why we have had such difficulty doing what the Lord taught us—bringing the Kingdom of God into this earth (Matthew 6:9-10). Yet there is a way.

> But the fruit of the Spirit is love, joy, peace, patience, kindness, goodness, faithfulness, gentleness, self-control; against such things there is no law. Now those who belong to Christ Jesus have crucified the flesh with its passions and desires. If we live by the Spirit, let us also walk by the Spirit. (Galatians 5:22-25)

Matthew 6:9-10 "Pray, then, in this way: 'Our Father who art in heaven, hallowed be Thy name. [10] Thy kingdom come. Thy will be done, on earth as it is in heaven.'"

That is what we are doing in our connection with the Catholic Church; we are walking by the Spirit. But what about all that history? There is one answer: the blood of Jesus Christ. What about tomorrow? Walk by the Spirit. We are believing for the whole Body of Christ to walk by the Spirit. Rather than looking for problems to criticize, let's look at the heart. The Pope has a heart to walk with God and to bring to birth a walk in the Spirit for his church. I believe that what he is doing is in full faith that he is being led by the Spirit. Therefore, the result will be a greater level of infilling of the Holy Spirit into the Catholic Church. We bless that to happen.

I believe that in the days ahead, with all the strength that he has, this pope is going to move things in a direction so that the right people are in charge. The apostle Paul chose Timothy to follow after him. Since the Pope has a similar heart, he will be successful in appointing leaders that have this same determination that the Catholic Church will be led by the Spirit into a new day. It will be a new beginning in the history of the Catholic Church, in which a deep humility will emerge.

"Listen to me, you who pursue righteousness, who seek the Lord: look to the rock from which you were hewn, and to the quarry from which you were dug" (Isaiah 51:1). Our failures humble us and cause us to appropriate the Spirit. All of these terrible problems can have a very positive result in humbling the leadership of the Church. I pray that these problems humble all of us as part of the Body of Christ. We bless the Pope to accomplish the drive that the Lord put in him to see a fresh outpouring of the Holy Spirit in the Catholic Church.

Lord, let there be a new leadership of those who will walk by the Spirit, not by the flesh, who will lead the Catholic Church out of yesterday and into a new day. A new day does not mean modernization or liberalization, but rather a day of the Spirit. Let there be the leading and the power of the Holy Spirit, so that the multitudes who are part of the Catholic Church can have a true walk in the Spirit. We believe for it; we create it together with them. Once again we emphasize, "Begone, Satan!" (Matthew 4:10). You no longer have any place in the Catholic Church, in the Protestant denominations, or anywhere in religion. We cast you out, in the name of the Lord. Father, pour out Your Spirit upon the Catholic Church, and upon all the Protestant churches. Let there be a double portion of Your Spirit which rests upon us. Let this be a beginning of seeing the whole Body of Christ released to come forth in a new day, in the name of the Lord.

Chapter 22

We Celebrate Christ's Coming in His Many-Membered Body

March 23, 2013
Our Lady of Fatima Church, Meier, Rio de Janeiro, Brazil

This message was brought on Palm Sunday to leaders of the New Catholic Communities in the local area.

The greatest moment for all of us who love the Lord Jesus Christ is His resurrection. Most believers celebrate His resurrection on Easter Sunday while others celebrate it as part of the Passover observance. Part of this celebration for many churches is to observe Palm Sunday before Easter. The Holy Spirit made real to me that it is important for us to focus on this celebration of Jesus' triumphal entry into Jerusalem. There is something very deep in this that the Holy Spirit can impart to us to guide our lives. We will begin by reading out of two different accounts of this event in the Gospels. The first is in Mark 11:7-11:

> And they brought the colt to Jesus and put their garments on it; and He sat upon it. And many spread their garments in the road, and others spread leafy branches which they had cut from the fields. And those who went before, and those who followed after, were crying out, "Hosanna!

> Blessed is He who comes in the name of the Lord; blessed is the coming kingdom of our father David; Hosanna in the highest!" And He entered Jerusalem and came into the temple.

The next account of this event is in Luke 19:35-44:

> And they brought it to Jesus, and they threw their garments on the colt, and put Jesus on it. And as He was going, they were spreading their garments in the road. And as He was now approaching, near the descent of the Mount of Olives, the whole multitude of the disciples began to praise God joyfully with a loud voice for all the miracles which they had seen, saying: "Blessed is the King who comes in the name of the Lord; peace in heaven and glory in the highest!" And some of the Pharisees in the multitude said to Him, "Teacher, rebuke Your disciples." And He answered and said, "I tell you, if these become silent, the stones will cry out!" And when He approached, He saw the city and wept over it, saying, "If you had known in this day, even you, the things which make for peace! But now they have been hidden from your eyes. For the days shall come upon you when your enemies will throw up a bank before you, and surround you, and hem you in on every side, and will level you to the ground and your children within you, and they will not leave in you one stone upon another, because you did not recognize the time of your visitation."

This was a triumphant time. Those who had eyes to see were rejoicing and worshiping God because they saw the Christ. They recognized Jesus as the Messiah, the promised One who was to come; therefore, they were thankful. They cried, "Hosanna!" which in the Greek was derived from a Hebrew word meaning "save us," or "redeem us." They recognized the redemption that Jesus brought, and their worship reflected their anticipation of what was to take place in His sacrifice for our sins.

But Jesus also recognized that there were many who did not see Him as Lord during that triumphal entry. He heard those who were worshiping, yet His heart went out to those who were not seeing. He recognized that, because their eyes were closed and their hearts were not open, there would be terrible days ahead. And we know that terrible days did come upon Jerusalem.

We read in Matthew chapter 23 that Jesus was looking out over Jerusalem and His heart was breaking over it.

> "O Jerusalem, Jerusalem, who kills the prophets and stones those who are sent to her! How often I wanted to gather your children together, the way a hen gathers her chicks under her wings, and you were unwilling. Behold, your house is being left to you desolate! For I say to you, from now on you shall not see Me until you say, 'Blessed is He who comes in the name of the Lord!'" (Matthew 23:37-39)

This is what they were crying out at His entry into Jerusalem: "Blessed is He who comes in the name of the Lord." They recognized Jesus as being sent by the Father into the world. He was the Word of God made flesh in the earth (John 1:14), which they were acknowledging with their praises. However, Jesus was so concerned with those who did not recognize Him that He said, "You shall not see Me until you say, 'Blessed is He who comes in the name of the Lord!'"

When we look at the many aspects of this triumphal entry into Jerusalem, the origin of Palm Sunday, it is hard not to recognize that this was the presentation of Christ to the world. Yet many missed

---

John 1:14 And the Word became flesh, and dwelt among us, and we beheld His glory, glory as of the only begotten from the Father, full of grace and truth.

it; and Jesus said to them, "The things which make for peace… have been hidden from your eyes" (Luke 19:42). In the Greek, this doesn't just mean lack of physical sight; it means not perceiving or understanding. The same thing applies when it comes to our oneness. The truth is that we will not know the coming of Christ until we are able to look at other believers and say, "Blessed is He who comes in the name of the Lord." When I look in the eyes of believers, I see Jesus; so how can we deny that we are one? Why is it important for the different communities and expressions of the Church to come together? We are not trying to make ourselves one; Jesus Christ has already made us one. We do not come together as an ecumenical movement. It cannot be that we try to figure out doctrines or belief systems, or determine who thinks rightly and who is in error. History has tried to make enemies of Catholics and Protestants and of various sects of the Church, but that does not have to be. We are one.

There were those of the sect of the Pharisees, having a religious spirit, who wanted to deny Christ's entry into Jerusalem. They tried to deny it, but He was still the Messiah. Your denial does nothing except block your own entry into the things that God has for you. God has something for His Body in this day, but if you cannot see Jesus in the midst of His believers, then you will miss what God is doing in this hour. Jesus' triumphal entry was a tremendous day. It was a wonderful time of worship and rejoicing for those who recognized Jesus, for those who proclaimed Him as the Messiah. They entered into the blessing. But to those who missed it, as Jesus warned, there were days of judgment coming. It is time for the Body of Christ to wake up. It does no good to deny our oneness, because we are one. We are not here to create something. Oneness is.

> For even as the body is one and yet has many members, and all the members of the body, though they are many, are one body, so also is Christ. For by one Spirit we were

all baptized into one body, whether Jews or Greeks, whether slaves or free, and we were all made to drink of one Spirit. For the body is not one member, but many. (1 Corinthians 12:12-14)

Paul said it emphatically—the Body of Christ is one. On that day heralding Jesus' triumphal entrance into Jerusalem, there were those who rejoiced because they recognized Jesus. In this day, we must recognize Jesus in His many-membered Body. Paul said, "Even as the body has many members, so also is Christ." Christ **is** His many-membered Body, because He has identified Himself with that Body. "For by one Spirit we were all baptized into one body."

We are in a time when the Holy Spirit is being poured out afresh. We have seen many outpourings of the Holy Spirit throughout history that have included various manifestations. There have been tremendous miracles where people were sent out to preach the Gospel and they actually spoke in the tongues of nations that they did not know. In every instance, there was some outward display or evidence of the outpouring of the Holy Spirit. We must open our hearts to this reality, and see it released on a greater level in this day.

What then is the sign of the outpouring of the Holy Spirit in this generation? It is the oneness of the Body of Christ. It is a sign. On the Day of Pentecost, the Holy Spirit was poured out, but the disciples were already one. It says, "They were all with one accord in one place" (Acts 2:1, KJV). They had been seeking the Lord and becoming one, and that triggered the Holy Spirit being poured out upon them. We are in the beginnings of a fresh outpouring of the Holy Spirit upon the Church, and the necessary outcome must be our oneness. "For by one Spirit we were all baptized into one body, whether Jews or Greeks, whether slaves or free, and we were all made to drink of one Spirit." No matter how we try to divide ourselves up, God is not bringing a different Holy Spirit to each group of believers. There is one Spirit. And the truth is, there is one Body. We are all baptized into this one Spirit because we are one Body.

"For the body is not one member, but many" (1 Corinthians 12:14). Just as the Word tells us, we have different expressions and manifestations. In the mind of man, we always try to turn differences into division, whether it is different sexes, different colors of skin, or different occupations. Anything that is different becomes a source of separation and division. We live in different nations, and that bothers people to the point that nation goes to war against nation. Division is a human reaction, but it is not the Spirit's reaction. It is God who makes us different. The Spirit Himself divides Himself among us, imparting different gifts, anointings, and ministries. God is not afraid of difference. In the heart of God, difference is not division, because He already knows that we are one in Him. "But now there are many members, but one body" (1 Corinthians 12:20). I love our differences! Maybe our organizations will never be the same, but those are only our housings within the Body. I am not my organization; I am a member of the Body of Christ.

Today, let's not celebrate Palm Sunday as a historical event that took place thousands of years ago. Let's celebrate a living Palm Sunday in which we recognize the coming of Christ. We exalt God by recognizing how He is bringing Christ's Body into one. He is creating many different manifestations and members, but one Body of Christ. God, give us eyes to see it. We do not want to be those who fall into judgment.

Everyone on this earth needs Christ. We have a commission to speak the Word, to make disciples of all the nations (Matthew 28:19-20). But we will never do that if we cannot recognize each other in the Lord. "Now you are Christ's body, and individually members

---

Matthew 28:19-20 "Go therefore and make disciples of all the nations, baptizing them in the name of the Father and the Son and the Holy Spirit, [20] teaching them to observe all that I commanded you; and lo, I am with you always, even to the end of the age."

of it" (1 Corinthians 12:27). We must think about one another as Christ manifested in the earth today. We are all members of His Body. Questioning this is as ridiculous as questioning who that was who was sitting on the colt, going through the gates of Jerusalem. There is no question. That was the Messiah, the Christ. And we are the Body of Christ. We carry His Lordship today.

Here is another example of our oneness that Paul gave us in Romans 12: "For just as we have many members in one body and all the members do not have the same function, so we, who are many, are one body in Christ, and individually members one of another" (Romans 12:4-5). I am a member of you. We are members of one another's hearts. Let's remember Jesus' prayer in John 17:20-23:

> "I do not ask in behalf of these alone, but for those also who believe in Me through their word; that they may all be one; even as Thou, Father, art in Me, and I in Thee, that they also may be in Us; that the world may believe that Thou didst send Me. And the glory which Thou hast given Me I have given to them; that they may be one, just as We are one; I in them, and Thou in Me, that they may be perfected into one, that the world may know that Thou didst send Me, and didst love them, even as Thou didst love Me."

Jesus prayed to the Father: "The glory which You have given to Me I have given to them; that they may be one, just as We are one." We are not supposed to just get along. Amazingly, we are supposed to be as one as Christ and the Father are one. Jesus gave us His glory so that this can really happen.

In Jesus' prayer to the Father, He tells us how this is to take place. "I in them, and Thou in Me, that they may be perfected into one" (John 17:23). The Church is waiting for the next level of perfection, growth and release into the will of God, but we cannot attain it if we are divided. The power of the Church has been lost in its division. We need the glory and the authority of the Lord to be released. We need the power that Christ has, seated at the right hand of the Father, to move through us in order for us to move the earth as the manifestation of Christ—"that the world may know that Thou didst send Me" (John 17:23).

If we are here to spread the Gospel and to make disciples of all men, then we can only do that because we are one. When the Body of Christ recognizes and honors its oneness, then the world will likewise recognize the Christ. "That they may be perfected into one, that the world may know that Thou didst send Me" (John 17:23). Our greatest desire is that the whole world would recognize that, because of His love, the Father sent His Son Jesus into the earth to go to the cross, to die for us, and to experience judgment in our stead. When the Body of Christ is one, the world will "know that Thou didst send Me." Don't you think that makes it worth becoming one? The world's knowledge of the Lord comes as we believe that we are one, as we are perfected into a unit. That means that as we come together in oneness, gathering, worshiping, and discovering our oneness, we are releasing a tidal wave of the knowledge of the Lord upon the earth.

The prophecy was that the knowledge of the Lord would cover the earth as the waters cover the sea (Isaiah 11:9). Today we can initiate the force of that tidal wave by standing on the truth that we are one. If Jesus prayed to the Father that we be one, sometime, at some moment in history, that oneness will be a reality. Perhaps you worry that the division runs too deep, that it has been gaining ground for hundreds of years. No matter how long it has existed, our response should be to open our hearts today as Jesus is coming through the gates and say, "Blessed is He who comes in the name of the Lord."

Isaiah 11:9 They will not hurt or destroy in all My holy mountain, for the earth will be full of the knowledge of the Lord as the waters cover the sea.

Today, we can be one and change the way the Church has lived and functioned for thousands of years. We can release a tidal wave of faith that will sweep the whole world until all will know that the Father sent His Son. Let's be driven that this same truth will be turned loose in our perception. Jerusalem represented all of the religious order, all the resistance of that age; but as we celebrate Palm Sunday today, we open our gates and receive Jesus as He comes in His many-membered Body. We say, "Blessed is He who comes in the name of the Lord!"

Chapter 23

Only As One Can We Take the Kingdom

March 31, 2013
Igreja A Palavra Viva, Mount Zion, Niteroi, Brazil

During this annual gathering of churches for the celebration of the Feast of Passover, the series of messages focusing on the leaders of the Body of Christ continued.

I want to paint a picture for you in this message. This is something that came by the Holy Spirit. It will help you to see the uniqueness of this time we are in as the Body of Christ. We may never be at this point again, and it is very significant. What we are experiencing now follows the same pattern found in the Scriptures about Israel. Everything regarding God's interactions with Israel in the Old Testament is an illustration of what God wants to do with the Body of Christ today. Israel is a type of the Body of Christ. The name Israel, referring to the chosen nation, actually came from Jacob, whose name had been changed to Israel (Genesis 32:28). We call them the children of Israel because they are the descendants of the twelve individuals who were recognized as the sons of Israel. In Genesis chapter 49, before Jacob passed away, he laid his hands

---

Genesis 32:28 And he said, "Your name shall no longer be Jacob, but Israel; for you have striven with God and with men and have prevailed."

on each one of his twelve sons and spoke a prophecy by the Holy Spirit over each one. The prophecies that Israel made by the Holy Spirit declared who each son was in personality and destiny. That impartation rested upon his children, their children, and their children's children, down through history.

When we read in the Scriptures about God working with Israel, throughout their history He always worked distinctly with the sons of Israel, within those twelve tribes. However, it is easy to lose that picture when the sons of Israel were in Egypt for 400 years. In their bondage, they lost their function as the distinct tribes of Israel. According to the prophecies of Jacob, they were to move as the sons of Israel in a very real way. Each family, each tribe, having an anointing, was to carry an impartation of who and what they were. Yet that identity and function seemed to be lost under their slavery in Egypt.

Ultimately, the children of Israel were delivered out of Egypt, as the observance of Passover recalls every year; and at that time they could immediately identify with their families again. Their identity as the twelve tribes of Israel came back, the individuality of who they were. In the wilderness, the sons of Israel were once again recognizable as they camped by families and tribes. You can see it in the description of how they were separated by families and camped around the tabernacle in the wilderness. "Now the LORD spoke to Moses and to Aaron, saying, 'The sons of Israel shall camp, each by his own standard, with the banners of their fathers' households; they shall camp around the tent of meeting at a distance'" (Numbers 2:1-2). So we see, emerging out of the bondage and the judgments of Egypt, the revelation of the children of Israel both as a nation and as individual families. We can see that the Body of Christ is an example of this same thing. Let's read about this in 1 Corinthians chapter 12:

> But one and the same Spirit works all these things, distributing to each one individually just as He wills.

> For even as the body is one and yet has many members, and all the members of the body, though they are many, are one body, so also is Christ. For by one Spirit we were all baptized into one body, whether Jews or Greeks, whether slaves or free, and we were all made to drink of one Spirit. For the body is not one member, but many. (1 Corinthians 12:11-14)

By the Spirit, there is a distribution of anointings, gifts, ministries, and personalities that God brings forth in the Church. Can you see the similarity to the experience of the children of Israel? By the Holy Spirit, Jacob laid hands on each one of his sons, prophesying and distributing gifts, responsibilities, and personalities. I want you to see how permanent that was. Those distinctions of families in Israel never left them; they were never done away with. Their bondage in Egypt was satan's attempt to destroy them and take away their identity, because their identity was prophetic. If you want to destroy the people of God, take away their Word from God. Without a vision, the people are in disorder (Proverbs 29:18).

The understanding of what God is doing today is right there in the Hebrew Scriptures. When God delivered the children of Israel, He restored the personality of the Word of God over every tribe, over every family, and that identification became established. Once they had come out of the wilderness and crossed the Jordan River, Joshua sat them all down on the plains of Jericho. In obedience, all of the males were physically circumcised. God also circumcised them in their hearts. When they celebrated the Passover there, the tribes were all blended together as one people, Israel. The Captain of the

---

Proverbs 29:18 Where there is no vision, the people are unrestrained, but happy is he who keeps the law.

Lord's hosts appeared to them, to lead them into taking the land of Canaan (Joshua 5:2-3, 9-10, 13-14).

It is very significant that the Israelites did not possess the land as individual families. They had to come together as a nation in oneness. Without that oneness, there would have been no force behind what they were doing. They had to exercise a tremendous carefulness to preserve that oneness. One example of this occurred before they crossed the River Jordan. The Israelites had taken land in battle on the wilderness side of the Jordan which was perfect for livestock. Understanding the battle that was about to ensue on the other side of the Jordan, the tribes of Reuben and Gad and half of the tribe of Manasseh came to Moses and requested that land for their inheritance. Rather than go into battle beyond the Jordan, these tribes wanted to settle on this good land and move into their inheritance right away (Numbers 32:1-5).

Joshua 5:2-3 At that time the Lord said to Joshua, "Make for yourself flint knives and circumcise again the sons of Israel the second time." ³ So Joshua made himself flint knives and circumcised the sons of Israel at Gibeath-haaraloth.

Joshua 5:9-10 Then the Lord said to Joshua, "Today I have rolled away the reproach of Egypt from you." So the name of that place is called Gilgal to this day. ¹⁰ While the sons of Israel camped at Gilgal, they observed the Passover on the evening of the fourteenth day of the month on the desert plains of Jericho.

Joshua 5:13-14 Now it came about when Joshua was by Jericho, that he lifted up his eyes and looked, and behold, a man was standing opposite him with his sword drawn in his hand, and Joshua went to him and said to him, "Are you for us or for our adversaries?" ¹⁴ And he said, "No, rather I indeed come now as captain of the host of the Lord." And Joshua fell on his face to the earth, and bowed down, and said to him, "What has my lord to say to his servant?"

Numbers 32:1-5 Now the sons of Reuben and the sons of Gad had an exceedingly large number of livestock. So when they saw the land of Jazer and the land of Gilead, that it was indeed a place suitable for livestock, ² the sons of Gad and the sons of Reuben came and spoke to Moses and to Eleazar the priest and to the leaders of the congregation, saying, ³ "Ataroth, Dibon, Jazer, Nimrah, Heshbon, Elealeh, Sebam, Nebo and Beon, ⁴ the land which the Lord conquered before the congregation of Israel, is a land for livestock; and your servants have livestock." ⁵ And they said, "If we have found favor in your sight, let this land be given to your servants as a possession; do not take us across the Jordan."

Boy, did that create a problem! Moses became very angry, and he questioned whether they were trying to divide Israel (Numbers 32:6-7). He understood that the only way Israel could take the land was as one man. Forty years earlier, Moses had sent out one representative from each of the tribes to spy out the land of Canaan that had been promised to them by the Father. When the spies returned, Joshua and Caleb alone said, "Let's go take the land; it is ours." The others said, "I don't think we can do this" (Numbers 32:8-9). Moses could not allow the tribes of Joshua and Caleb to take their inheritance alone. Therefore, **all** Israel was made to wait forty years in the wilderness and return to the River Jordan with a commitment to possess their inheritance as one man. Now, with the request of the tribes of Reuben, Gad, and half of Manasseh, it appeared to Moses as if history were repeating itself. But Moses knew that they could only take the land as one. They had to be one nation, one Israel, one man before God. So Moses required all of the tribes to go in together to possess the land.

To us, the taking of the land of Canaan is representative of possessing the Kingdom of God. There is no way to possess the Kingdom of God without the Body of Christ being one. At the time of the Passover beyond the Jordan at Gilgal, the Israelites were all together as one people. They were all circumcised together. After they celebrated the Passover, the Captain of the Lord's hosts appeared to them as one. So the tribes of Reuben, Gad, and half of Manasseh, had to make an agreement with Moses. In essence, they said, "We will leave our wives, children, and livestock safely on this land; but we, the

---

Numbers 32:6-7 But Moses said to the sons of Gad and to the sons of Reuben, "Shall your brothers go to war while you yourselves sit here? ⁷ Now why are you discouraging the sons of Israel from crossing over into the land which the Lord has given them?"

Numbers 32:8-9 "This is what your fathers did when I sent them from Kadesh-barnea to see the land. ⁹ For when they went up to the valley of Eshcol and saw the land, they discouraged the sons of Israel so that they did not go into the land which the Lord had given them."

men of war, will arm ourselves and go in absolute oneness with the rest of Israel. We will fight to the last man until every one of the families of Israel possesses its inheritance, and then we will come back to our inheritance" (Numbers 32:16-18). The Scripture says, "The first shall be last" (Matthew 20:16). Reuben, Gad, and the half-tribe of Manasseh got their inheritance first, but they were the last ones of the tribes of Israel to come back and possess that inheritance (Numbers 32:33). That was because they had agreed with the rest of Israel to enter Canaan as one man. The only way we can take the Kingdom of God, the only way that we can possess our inheritance, is to be one man with the Lordship of Jesus Christ leading us.

If you look at maps of the land of Canaan after the Israelites possessed it, you will see something interesting. Once they took the land, they divided it up by families. They lived in the land of Israel as twelve separate tribes. They took the land as one man, but they dwelt in it according to the Word of God over them as families. Let's apply this to the present. It may disturb us at times that God is practically forcing us to be one as the Body of Christ. After all, most of our differences have to do with the gifts, ministries, or Words from the Lord that created us to begin with. Every church or fellowship has a distinct and different anointing and function. But God has a purpose for us to become one man.

Numbers 32:16-18 Then they came near to him and said, "We will build here sheepfolds for our livestock and cities for our little ones; [17] but we ourselves will be armed ready to go before the sons of Israel, until we have brought them to their place, while our little ones live in the fortified cities because of the inhabitants of the land. [18] We will not return to our homes until every one of the sons of Israel has possessed his inheritance."

Matthew 20:16 "Thus the last shall be first, and the first last."

Numbers 32:33 So Moses gave to them, to the sons of Gad and to the sons of Reuben and to the half-tribe of Joseph's son Manasseh, the kingdom of Sihon, king of the Amorites and the kingdom of Og, the king of Bashan, the land with its cities with their territories, the cities of the surrounding land.

The whole Body of Christ is diverse, yet we still fight the perception that our differences are divisions. They are not divisions; they are unique aspects of His Spirit. What we perceive as differences may exist well into the Kingdom of God as diverse functions of the Body of Christ. The children of Israel lived divided by families in the wilderness, but they came together as one man under the Captain of the Lord's hosts. As long as they were one man, they were enabled to take the land. But once they took the land, they settled back into their families.

The unique attributes of every aspect of Christ's Body are distributed to us as gifts and blessings of the Holy Spirit. These attributes may have a purpose in the future that is far beyond what we understand now; we will need them to function in the Kingdom of God. Now, on a human level, they may seem to give license to division. But they are created by one and the same Spirit, distributed to each as God has willed (1 Corinthians 12:11). No matter how diverse we are in the Body of Christ, for this time in which we live, we must become one in our hearts.

This is a crucial moment in the ages; it is like the turning point at Gilgal. The Body of Christ must be one; we must come together to take the land. The divisions in the Body will never allow us to have enough force and capacity to take the land. But as one man, we will have the leadership and enabling of God to possess the Kingdom. This may be what Jesus meant when He said, "In My Father's house are many dwelling places" (John 14:2). Jesus then prayed for us to be one that the world may know that the Father sent Him.

Now we have the picture of what happened with Israel in that important Passover. When Israel came and dwelt in the land, every family was moving together, both as one nation and as the separate

---

1 Corinthians 12:11   But one and the same Spirit works all these things, distributing to each one individually just as He wills.

families that God had created. What God is trying to do with the Body of Christ today is so much simpler than we have imagined. As a result of Israel's obedience at Gilgal, they had an experience very much like facing the resurrected Christ. They fell on their faces, submitted their hearts to be one, and followed Him as the Captain of the Lord's hosts. They followed Him into battle and took the land of Canaan, as was promised. God did not allow each tribe to divide up the land that they would come across. He did something in their spirits; He required them to help one another possess their inheritance.

In this hour, God is requiring of His people that we be committed to the possession of the Kingdom in this same spirit. We have to possess one another's fulfillment. We must be that committed to one another, without necessarily knowing what each of us will inherit out of our efforts. Look at us today; there are many families in the Body of Christ. We have Protestants, Catholics, Pentecostals, and so many more. But it is not enough for each group to be a single family or tribe. I do not think God will ever give us our inheritance individually. I know we may have unique promises, but we are interested in the fulfillments of what God has promised us. We will never possess our own inheritance if we are only dedicated to possessing our little corner of the Kingdom. It will only happen when the whole Body of Christ comes together and is driven to obtain the inheritance for their brothers. Our hearts must burn to see the success of each other's ministries, and seek to possess the inheritance for each different expression of His Body. The Kingdom of God must be possessed as one. As the Kingdom develops, we may settle in it with many dwelling places. More than we understand, the Kingdom may come to look like that ancient land of Israel. We will see different people in diverse places with unique functions, making their living in a multitude of ways, expressing the Spirit with various characteristics.

It is time to possess the land, just as Israel did. We must open our eyes to see the Captain of the Lord's hosts. Our response must be to fall on our faces, let Him circumcise our hearts, and commit our spirits to become one as we follow Him. This is the Lordship of Jesus Christ. He has risen from the dead, and He is in charge. We may be establishing many of our brothers in their own inheritances before we receive our own, and yet our hearts will be just as driven! There will be great times of spiritual warfare, but the Body of Christ will prevail as one. Only as one can we take the Kingdom.

Chapter 24

Making Disciples of the Nations

July 3, 2013
Shiloh Church, Kalona, Iowa

At the Shiloh School of Prophets, an annual, international conference, this message was recorded as a radio broadcast for Vatican Radio, to be aired during World Youth Day in Rio de Janeiro, Brazil.

It is our great joy to be involved with the 2013 World Youth Day in Rio de Janeiro, Brazil. We were invited by a dear brother in the Vatican who works very diligently to create relationships and oneness throughout the whole Body of Christ. This has been a tremendous experience for us. We have been praying and believing for years that we would see a great oneness manifest within the whole Body of Christ; and so our opportunity to be involved with World Youth Day is a great blessing and a great honor, not only for us and our apostolic ministry in Brazil, but also for the whole of The Living Word Fellowship throughout the United States, Brazil, and other parts of the world.

Some people would say, "What are Protestants doing getting involved with World Youth Day, which is a Catholic event?" A statement from a catechesis by Pope Francis explains why.

> Divisions among us, but also divisions among communities: evangelical Christians, orthodox Christians, Catholic Christians, but why divided?[13]

That is a great question. Why divided? Paul asked a similar question: "Is Christ divided?" (1 Corinthians 1:13, KJV). We all know that Christ is not divided. He is the singular head of one Body, and that Body is not divided. Therefore, we realize that we are all one in Christ. In his catechesis, Pope Francis continued:

> We must try to bring about unity. Let me tell you something, today, before leaving home, I spent 40 minutes more or less, half an hour, with an evangelistic pastor. And we prayed together, seeking unity.
>
> But we Catholics must pray with each other and other Christians. Pray that the Lord gift us [with] unity.[14]

I love Pope Francis. I believe that he is a fulfillment of the prophecy, "I will give you shepherds after My own heart" (Jeremiah 3:15). I want all of us to be one with him, and one with his efforts. His vision for oneness is the same as our vision for oneness. His drive for unity in the Body of Christ is also our drive for unity. The motto chosen for the 2013 World Youth Day is "Go and make disciples of all nations" (Matthew 28:19). Think about the vision contained within

---

1 Corinthians 1:13, KJV   Is Christ divided? was Paul crucified for you? or were ye baptized in the name of Paul?

Jeremiah 3:15   "Then I will give you shepherds after My own heart, who will feed you on knowledge and understanding."

Matthew 28:19   "Go therefore and make disciples of all the nations, baptizing them in the name of the Father and the Son and the Holy Spirit."

[13.] Deacon Keith Fournier, "The Prayer of Jesus – May They Be One: Francis Is Another Pope of Christian Unity," *Catholic Online*, June 24, 2013, http://www.catholic.org/news/international/europe/story.php?id=51440 (accessed September 4, 2014).

[14.] Ibid.

that motto. That vision to make disciples of all nations is impossible to fulfill without oneness. Pope Francis, as a worldwide voice for the unity of the Body of Christ, is helping to lead us into this oneness.

The heart of Jesus for all of us is that we be one. In His prayer to the Father He said, "And for their sakes I sanctify Myself, that they themselves also may be sanctified in truth" (John 17:19). Jesus wants us to be sanctified in truth. His sacrifice on the cross opened the door for us to be sanctified along with Him. Then He said, "I do not ask in behalf of these alone," speaking of those who were listening to Him at that moment, "but for those also who believe in Me through their word" (John 17:20). The Body of Christ that exists today is the result of faith through the words of the apostles, spoken to us in the Gospels (Romans 10:17). What else did Jesus pray? "That they may all be one; even as Thou, Father, art in Me, and I in Thee, that they also may be in Us; that the world may believe that Thou didst send Me" (John 17:21). Jesus said that the world will believe when we are one. How then can we accomplish this command to make disciples of all the nations without being one? It is time for the Body of Christ to be one.

Pope Francis is a great voice speaking today to the global Body of Christ that it is time to be one. He has also been speaking about the Holy Spirit. I believe this is the other great piece of the puzzle. To make disciples of all the nations, we must be one, and we must be clothed with power from the Holy Spirit (Luke 24:49). Pope Francis said:

> The Holy Spirit upsets us because it moves us, it makes us walk, it pushes the Church forward. [We wish] to calm down the Holy Spirit, we want to tame it and this is wrong.

Romans 10:17 So faith comes from hearing, and hearing by the word of Christ.

Luke 24:49 "And behold, I am sending forth the promise of My Father upon you; but you are to stay in the city until you are clothed with power from on high."

That's because the Holy Spirit is the strength of God; it's what gives us the strength to go forward.[15]

Look at Acts the first chapter. After the resurrection, Christ appeared to the disciples. He was teaching them, directing them about what they were to do. They were the first ones to receive this command from Jesus to go and make disciples of all the nations. But remember what He told them, and consider why He did so. Jesus said, "You are not ready. Go wait in Jerusalem until you are endued with power from on high by the Holy Spirit" (Acts 1:4, 8).

I agree with what the Pope is saying. We can no longer resist how the Holy Spirit would lead us and guide us. It is significant that young people from all over the world gathered together in Brazil to reach into a greater experience in the Holy Spirit. We need to see a tremendous outpouring of oneness and power of the Holy Spirit upon the youth of this world. They must be ready to move with the Pope in oneness and in the power of the Holy Spirit, and be a force of faith behind his drive for unity in the Church. We also unify ourselves and become a force of faith behind the heart and drive of Pope Francis to see the fulfillment of this vision. It is time for the fulfillment of this great commission, and this is how we will accomplish it. I believe that World Youth Day 2013 is the beginning of a fire of faith that will consume the nations.

One of the key commands from the Lord is to make disciples, to see the world receive Jesus Christ. When we see that as our goal,

---

Acts 1:4 And gathering them together, He commanded them not to leave Jerusalem, but to wait for what the Father had promised, "Which," He said, "you heard of from Me."

Acts 1:8 "But you shall receive power when the Holy Spirit has come upon you; and you shall be My witnesses both in Jerusalem, and in all Judea and Samaria, and even to the remotest part of the earth."

[15] News.va, "Pope: 2nd Vatican Council, Work of Holy Spirit but Some Want to Turn Back the Clock," *Vatican Radio*, April 16, 2013, http://www.news.va/en/news/pope-2nd-vatican-council-work-of-holy-spirit-but-s (accessed September 4, 2014).

then the question becomes, how valid are the little issues that keep us separated from one another in the Body of Christ? None of our doctrines or practices can be bigger, or more important to us, than this singular vision to see Christ preached in all the nations. With that vision and drive in our hearts, we should open our hearts to receive our brothers and sisters in the Catholic Church and throughout the Body of Christ. It is going to happen. Jesus asked the Father for this oneness. Do you think the Father will honor the prayer of His Son? If there has ever been a prayer that has been uttered that God plans to answer, it is this prayer from His Son: "Father, let them be one, as You and I are one." Then comes the promise: when we are one, the world will believe.

Drop the idea that we are here for projects, plans, or our own fellowship or ministry. Our heart is that the world may believe that "God so loved the world, that He gave His only begotten Son." Whosoever believes in Him shall be saved (John 3:16). The Body of Christ is to be the instrument through which the world believes. Therefore, we must be dedicated to oneness, to seek together the outpourings of the Holy Spirit upon His people. That is the kind of faith we take for this time in which we live. We do not need group meetings where people just hear another sermon. Let us see gatherings where people have a meeting with God. Remember what happened on the Day of Pentecost. Greater works than these shall we do (John 14:12). Today, through the oneness of the Body of Christ, we again are looking for a great outpouring of the Holy Spirit that will reach the entire earth.

John 3:16 "For God so loved the world, that He gave His only begotten Son, that whoever believes in Him should not perish, but have eternal life."

John 14:12 "Truly, truly, I say to you, he who believes in Me, the works that I do shall he do also; and greater works than these shall he do; because I go to the Father."

Chapter 25

In Oneness and Filled With the Spirit

July 18, 2013
Padre Miguel, Rio de Janeiro, Brazil

This message was spoken at a pre-World Youth Day event, where expectant young Catholic believers from all over the world filled an auditorium to worship together and hear a Word from God.

A Catholic brother recently asked me, "Do you believe that Catholics are saved?" I thought, "What a strange question." Of course they are saved. They believe in the same Savior that all Christians believe in. There is not one sacrificial blood for Catholics and another sacrificial blood for Protestants. There is the one blood of Jesus Christ that was shed at the cross for all of us. Believers of any background can partake of the sacrifice of our Lord Jesus Christ, His body and His blood that was given for us. His sacrifice is for the forgiveness of our sins and for the creation of one body of people. There is not Catholic and Protestant and Orthodox; those divisions come out of the imaginations of men.

Paul asked the question, "Is Christ divided?" (1 Corinthians 1:13, KJV). No, Christ is not divided. There is "one Lord, one faith, one

---

1 Corinthians 1:13, KJV Is Christ divided? was Paul crucified for you? or were ye baptized in the name of Paul?

baptism" (Ephesians 4:5). When we realize and receive that truth, we can come together and celebrate the oneness of our Lord Jesus Christ. He is one, and so we are one. There is no division in the Body of Christ (1 Corinthians 12:12). We are all part of the same family, members of one another (Romans 12:5). We may be from different denominations and groups, but when we come together and hear a Word from the Lord spoken, we realize that we can all be changed and impacted by the Word as it comes through many diverse vessels. This is how oneness works within the Body of Christ. Oneness is not something we have to try to create; we already are one in Christ. In the Spirit, there is already no division. As we begin to see and understand that oneness is the reality in Christ, we become aware of the absolute need for it in our lives.

During World Youth Day 2013, Pope Francis is challenging young people with a great purpose: to make disciples of all the nations (Matthew 28:19). This is a tremendous challenge and responsibility for all of us. It should grip our hearts to recognize that for 2,000 years, the Church has been trying to get the world to believe. Why is it then that we still do not see the world believing? If it had worked the way it was supposed to, then we would not be hearing this admonition to go and make disciples of all the nations. What is the missing ingredient? In reality, there are two missing ingredients, the first and foremost of which is our oneness. Jesus' heart for our oneness can be seen in John chapter 17, when He prayed to the Father. His intentions for us are so clear. What a tremendous relationship He is conveying. It is a relationship that is beyond

---

1 Corinthians 12:12 For even as the body is one and yet has many members, and all the members of the body, though they are many, are one body, so also is Christ.

Romans 12:5 So we, who are many, are one body in Christ, and individually members one of another.

Matthew 28:19 "Go therefore and make disciples of all the nations, baptizing them in the name of the Father and the Son and the Holy Spirit."

any human understanding, and yet it is completely available for us in Him.

When Jesus prayed, "That they may be one," He was talking about us (John 17:22). In the same way that He and the Father are one, He wants us to be one. "I in them, and Thou in Me, that they may be perfected into one" (John 17:23). That means that our perfection comes in our oneness. Then what happens? "That the world may know that Thou didst send Me, and didst love them, even as Thou didst love Me" (John 17:23). Once that oneness is visible in us, it will allow the world to see and know that the Father, by His love, truly sent Jesus into the world. The drive to make disciples of the nations begins with our oneness. As we become one, we can go into our communities, our cities, our nations, and people can know that Jesus walked this earth, died for their sins, and shed His blood for all so that they may believe and be saved. If we are one, what we speak will come alive. We can make disciples of all the nations; now is the time for it. The making of disciples is not a Protestant commission, a Catholic commission, or an Orthodox commission. It was the commission that Jesus gave to His disciples, and we are those disciples.

The second missing ingredient is the power of the Holy Spirit. It is our equipping to make disciples of all nations. Consider what Jesus did after He was crucified, buried, and resurrected. He appeared to His disciples, and many others, over a period of forty days (Acts 1:3). According to Paul, Jesus appeared in His resurrection body and

---

John 17:22 "And the glory which Thou hast given Me I have given to them; that they may be one, just as We are one."

Acts 1:3 To these He also presented Himself alive, after His suffering, by many convincing proofs, appearing to them over a period of forty days, and speaking of the things concerning the kingdom of God.

spoke to over 500 brethren at one time (1 Corinthians 15:6). During those forty days, He taught His disciples, those who were following Him, how to make disciples of the nations. Think about what they must have heard from Him at that time. Imagine being there for forty days with the resurrected Jesus teaching and training you! The disciples were probably so inspired that they were ready, right then and there, to make disciples of the nations. Yet Jesus did something very interesting. He told them that they must not go out yet. Now, if I was there as one of those disciples, after being with the Lord for three and a half years, and then receiving forty days of training from the resurrected Christ, I would be thinking, "What else do I need to understand? What else do I need to have?" Jesus said, "Here is what you're going to do. Go to Jerusalem and wait until you're endued with power from on high" (Acts 1:4, 8).

Even though the disciples had been given so much, they were not ready yet. In the same way, when we gather together today it is to receive something greater than revelation, greater than understanding or teaching. We want what the disciples received, according to the second chapter of Acts. Why had Jesus told them to wait, and what were they waiting for? They had to wait for the Holy Spirit to pour out the power of Christ upon them. Only when they were filled with the Spirit would they be ready. On the Day of Pentecost, there were 120 disciples who had gone to wait in that upper room (Acts 1:15). There were 120 upon whom the Holy Spirit

---

1 Corinthians 15:6 After that He appeared to more than five hundred brethren at one time, most of whom remain until now, but some have fallen asleep.

Acts 1:4 And gathering them together, He commanded them not to leave Jerusalem, but to wait for what the Father had promised, "Which," He said, "you heard of from Me."

Acts 1:8 "But you shall receive power when the Holy Spirit has come upon you; and you shall be My witnesses both in Jerusalem, and in all Judea and Samaria, and even to the remotest part of the earth."

Acts 1:15 And at this time Peter stood up in the midst of the brethren (a gathering of about one hundred and twenty persons was there together), and said:

fell, and by that power they began to make disciples of all the nations. What happened to those other 380 people that heard the Lord after His resurrection? Why were they not there in the upper room with the 120? Probably many were distracted by other issues. That is not what we want at this time. We do not want to be distracted. We need to face this time in which we live with faith and determination. We are here for a purpose. As disciples, we may know all that we need to know, but none of that works unless we are endued with power from on high.

One of the greatest pictures of this faith and determination, waiting for the outpouring of the Spirit, was Mary, the mother of Jesus. We know that she was faithful with every step, because she was there in that upper room on the Day of Pentecost when the mighty rushing wind came in the outpouring of the Spirit (Acts 1:14). Mary was one of those people speaking in new tongues proclaiming the glory of God. She was a woman of faith, obedient to Christ to wait for that empowering of the Holy Spirit, and then on the Day of Pentecost, she was one of those speaking with cloven tongues of fire (Acts 2:3-4). Mary was also part of that group that moved out from Jerusalem to make disciples of all the nations. In the same way, we can experience a tremendous outpouring of the Holy Spirit.

We see then that two things are necessary to make disciples of all nations; oneness comes first. On the Day of Pentecost, "they were all with one accord in one place" (Acts 2:1, KJV). We come together as one man, one heart, and one faith. Then, we must be endued with power from on high by the Holy Spirit. Jesus taught us that if we ask

---

Acts 1:14 These all with one mind were continually devoting themselves to prayer, along with the women, and Mary the mother of Jesus, and with His brothers.

Acts 2:3-4 And there appeared to them tongues as of fire distributing themselves, and they rested on each one of them. ⁴ And they were all filled with the Holy Spirit and began to speak with other tongues, as the Spirit was giving them utterance.

the Father, He will give us the Holy Spirit (Luke 11:13). Maybe you have heard that the Holy Spirit is not for today, that it is for another dispensation. Some would also discount miracles, healings, and other divine examples of God moving today. When I went to Bible school I had professors, Bible scholars, who taught those doctrines. The truth is that the Holy Spirit is still being given today and is very much available, according to Christ's own Words (John 14:16-17). When I read the Bible, it is very clear that the Scriptures are right and those professors were mistaken.

You can receive the Holy Spirit today in the same way that you receive salvation. To receive salvation, you simply open your heart and ask the Lord Jesus to come in. "If we confess our sins, He is faithful and righteous to forgive us our sins and to cleanse us from all unrighteousness" (1 John 1:9). However you partake of Christ's body and blood, whether in a Protestant Communion service or by celebrating a mass, when you confess your sins you are cleansed by faith. You simply ask Him for it. It is the same way with receiving the Holy Spirit. If you ask, the Father will give you the Holy Spirit. The Holy Spirit is always available. Just by making a decision, we can give our wills to the Lord and ask the Holy Spirit to come into our lives. We can call on the Holy Spirit to take charge whenever we assemble in oneness. Simply ask the Lord, and He will begin to fill you with His Holy Spirit. You will receive power from on high. The Scripture says, "Not by might nor by power, but by My Spirit, says the Lord of hosts" (Zechariah 4:6). The greatest power, the greatest anointing, is that which comes when we are filled with God's Spirit.

Luke 11:13 "If you then, being evil, know how to give good gifts to your children, how much more shall your heavenly Father give the Holy Spirit to those who ask Him?"

John 14:16-17 "And I will ask the Father, and He will give you another Helper, that He may be with you forever; [17] that is the Spirit of truth, whom the world cannot receive, because it does not behold Him or know Him, but you know Him because He abides with you, and will be in you."

If we are going to make disciples of all the nations, then we must be one, and we must move in the power of the Holy Spirit.

Chapter 26

Remember, You Were Included

July 21, 2013
Igreja A Palavra Viva, Mount Zion, Niteroi, Brazil

This was a Communion message spoken to the local church congregation at Mount Zion, with special guests from the Catholic Church in attendance.

After I heard that some Evangelical churches had decided to protest Pope Francis' visit to Brazil for World Youth Day 2013, I was reminded of the account of Peter's visit to Cornelius in Acts chapter 10. This is the story of how we, as Gentiles, were grafted into the family of God (Romans 11:17). The Bible explains clearly that Gentiles were in the world without God, without hope, and without any connection to the promises and the provisions of God (Ephesians 2:11-12). Yet, as this beautiful story of the first Gentiles being included in the Church shows us, God went to great lengths

---

Romans 11:17 But if some of the branches were broken off, and you, being a wild olive, were grafted in among them and became partaker with them of the rich root of the olive tree.

Ephesians 2:11-12 Therefore remember, that formerly you, the Gentiles in the flesh, who are called "Uncircumcision" by the so-called "Circumcision," which is performed in the flesh by human hands— 12 remember that you were at that time separate from Christ, excluded from the commonwealth of Israel, and strangers to the covenants of promise, having no hope and without God in the world.

to include them into His covenant and promises, and to reveal that fact to the early Church.

This story was very real to me as I recognized how these Gentile churches, through their protest, were desiring to exclude other Gentile believers from the things of God. It is heartbreaking. Here is one sect of Gentile believers talking about another sect of Gentile believers saying, "We're the real Christians and you're not. We're worthy. What you're doing is not acceptable." You cannot "ungraft" other believers from the life of Christ or, by virtue of your own opinion, separate them from the family of God. If it were not for the grace of God and the heart of the Jewish people to include us, we as Gentiles would still be separated. Even though it was in the heart of God to include the Gentiles in salvation through the blood of Jesus Christ, it took something more to make it happen. It took more than the cross; it took more than the resurrection to include the Gentiles. There had to be those faithful Jews who opened their hearts. It was not easy for Peter to open his heart. The concept that God would include anyone other than the Jews was a difficult issue for Peter to grasp. God had to speak to him three times, "What I have cleansed, don't you call unclean" (Acts 10:15-16).

Separation and division are so ingrained in the fabric of our being. Think how entrenched it must have been for the Jewish people. What Peter did in entering the house of Cornelius was a sin for him, as a Jew; and yet, by the revelation of God, he overcame his strongly-held conditioning. Not only did Peter accept this truth, but after the events at the house of Cornelius, the whole leadership of the early Church did also. Keep in mind that prior to this, for about fifteen years following the resurrection of Jesus, what was called the *ekklesia* had been only Jews. For fifteen years, the concept of the

---

Acts 10:15-16 And again a voice came to him a second time, "What God has cleansed, no longer consider unholy." [16] And this happened three times; and immediately the object was taken up into the sky.

ekklesia was that the work of the cross was only for God's chosen people, the Jews.

This was a radical concept for the early Church to deal with. Deeply ingrained in not only the Jewish belief system, but in what was then the Christian belief system, was the idea that salvation was exclusive to the Jewish people. It took a tremendous revelation from God to change that. What amazing open hearts the early Jewish disciples had! When I read about this recently, I just wept over the hearts of Peter, James, and the apostles and elders in Jerusalem. Imagine what it was like for them. As they were listening to the story of how the Lord gave Peter the vision, they were shaken at first. But as soon as they heard him out, their hearts opened, and they embraced what God was doing (Acts 15:4-6, 19-20).

In light of this tremendous heritage, it is utterly wrong that Gentile Christians today should protest the acceptance of others who have embraced Jesus Christ as their Savior. It is beyond arrogance; it is demonic deception. I want us to remember what a privilege we have to come together in Communion to take of the body and the blood of the Lord Jesus. We were not always included or welcomed. And it was not only God who welcomed the Gentiles into the promises. Peter and James, along with the other apostles and elders and all of those Jewish believers in the early Church, opened their hearts. They recognized what God was doing, and received the Gentiles into the family of God.

Acts 15:4-6 And when they arrived at Jerusalem, they were received by the church and the apostles and the elders, and they reported all that God had done with them. [5] But certain ones of the sect of the Pharisees who had believed, stood up, saying, "It is necessary to circumcise them, and to direct them to observe the Law of Moses." [6] And the apostles and the elders came together to look into this matter.

Acts 15:19-20 "Therefore it is my judgment that we do not trouble those who are turning to God from among the Gentiles, [20] but that we write to them that they abstain from things contaminated by idols and from fornication and from what is strangled and from blood."

Read what happened when Peter entered the house of Cornelius: "And he said to them, 'You yourselves know how unlawful it is for a man who is a Jew to associate with a foreigner or to visit him; and yet God has shown me that I should not call any man unholy or unclean. That is why I came'" (Acts 10:28-29). Peter freely entered the house of Cornelius because God had made real to him that no man was unclean. Then, while Peter was still speaking, God interrupted his message and poured His Spirit out on the Gentiles (Acts 10:44). They began to speak with other tongues, exalting God (Acts 10:46). The Holy Spirit actually cut Peter's sermon short and confirmed the Word with power. What a confirmation to Peter; suddenly he realized that God had not only included the Gentiles, but they also had access to the power of the Holy Spirit!

In Communion we humble our hearts before God and remember His mercy. When you take Communion, it should be with such thankfulness that God has included you. You do not have to continue in this world cut off from God, separated from His promises and provisions. As you receive the elements, let your heart be open, just as Peter's heart was open, to realize that God has accepted and opened the door for many peoples, many lands, and many diversities. This oneness will only work if God has a human instrument, like Peter, to open the door of love and include those who may feel excluded from the life of God. It is not in God's heart to exclude, nor is He doing the excluding. He looks down and sees all His believers, those who love Him as you love Him. In openness to the Holy Spirit, this revelation can come and flow out to others. We can create the openness to one another by faith. Then it will become a prophetic Communion that will draw others around us

---

Acts 10:44 While Peter was still speaking these words, the Holy Spirit fell upon all those who were listening to the message.

Acts 10:46 For they were hearing them speaking with tongues and exalting God. Then Peter answered.

into His presence—not exclude them. Something can happen to us, and through us, if we open up to this Word.

Lord, Your body was broken to include us, the Gentiles, into Your promises. Let our hearts be broken in order that we may include all those for whom You have made this provision. We embrace Your cross, Your heart of love, and the provision that it brings to us. We remember that we too were included. Now Lord, let that become our heart and may our faith include others.

Chapter 27

Immaturity Is the Direct Result of Division

August 25, 2013
Church of the Living Word, North Hills, California

This message was brought to the local congregation in Los Angeles, following a trip to Brazil that included fellowship with many Protestant and Catholic Church leaders.

Our specific drive, as apostolic ministries, is to see the maturing of the individual believers in the Body of Christ. Our goal is that each believer comes "to the measure of the stature which belongs to the fulness of Christ" (Ephesians 4:13). Once we receive Christ and are saved, then we begin a process of growing in Him. We each go through a personal "cross experience" in which we die to our own ways, taking on the responsibility of a son of God and growing up in all aspects into Christ, who is the head (Galatians 6:14; Ephesians 4:15). As part of the foundations of this fellowship, our founder and spiritual father John Robert Stevens taught us that when we relate to Jesus Christ not only as our Savior but as the Lord over our life, it leads to maturity.

Galatians 6:14 But may it never be that I should boast, except in the cross of our Lord Jesus Christ, through which the world has been crucified to me, and I to the world.

Ephesians 4:15 But speaking the truth in love, we are to grow up in all aspects into Him, who is the head, even Christ.

In our pursuit for oneness in the Body of Christ, it is important to recognize the connection between that drive for oneness and this drive to see the Body of Christ mature. In fact, everything we are doing in making connections with God's people, whether they be Protestant, Catholic, or Jewish, is part of this same drive for maturing the sons of God. In 1 Corinthians 3, we see this link between oneness and maturity:

> And I, brethren, could not speak to you as to spiritual men, but as to men of flesh, as to babes in Christ. I gave you milk to drink, not solid food; for you were not yet able to receive it. Indeed, even now you are not yet able, for you are still fleshly. For since there is jealousy and strife among you, are you not fleshly, and are you not walking like mere men? (1 Corinthians 3:1-3)

Paul was facing a problem in the Corinthian church because of the divisions among them, and the direct result of those divisions was immaturity. Not only were the individual believers immature; the church as a whole was immature. When Paul told the Corinthians that they were still babes in Christ, he was basically saying, "I cannot impart to you what I want to because you are immature."

You can only give children so much, whether it's blessings or gifts or even responsibility. There is only so much you can do with their limited understanding and experience. This same problem exists in the Body of Christ today. Immaturity is one of the biggest problems Christianity has in this age. That includes every congregation, as well as every individual that is a part of those congregations. This immaturity, as Paul clearly identifies in this Scripture, is a direct result of division. Inciting division has been the methodology satan has used for thousands of years to literally block what the Body of Christ is to be. As long as he can keep the Church divided, the believers will remain immature, and thus ineffective.

You don't have to read very many chapters in the Book of Acts before you find disagreement and division occurring among the believers (Acts 6:1). It was because of the division that the apostles established the deacons, allowing the apostles to continue in the ministry of the Word (Acts 6:2-4). Knowing the effects of division on the Body of Christ, I am not completely sure that they were right in that decision. I'm not saying that there shouldn't be deacons, but rather that the issue of division was so important that the apostles should have dealt with it directly. Two thousand years later it is evident how the Church has been ravaged by division. The danger of allowing division to continue is very clear. Once a divisive spirit invades, it permeates the whole Body of Christ. Division, in any form, warrants our attention as leaders in our local fellowships, as well as throughout the Body of Christ.

By virtue of division, the Body of Christ is stunted in immaturity. We should be much farther along than we are. As long as we are immature, it blocks God Himself from being able to give to us. You could say that the answer for the Body of Christ is an outpouring of the Holy Spirit, and that is true. However, the Holy Spirit will only come in an atmosphere of oneness. Go back to the first chapter of Acts. Before Christ ascended to the Father, He gave instruction to the disciples not to run off and begin making disciples, but to go back to Jerusalem. He told them to go and wait in the upper

---

Acts 6:1 Now at this time while the disciples were increasing in number, a complaint arose on the part of the Hellenistic Jews against the native Hebrews, because their widows were being overlooked in the daily serving of food.

Acts 6:2-4 And the twelve summoned the congregation of the disciples and said, "It is not desirable for us to neglect the word of God in order to serve tables. [3] But select from among you, brethren, seven men of good reputation, full of the Spirit and of wisdom, whom we may put in charge of this task. [4] But we will devote ourselves to prayer, and to the ministry of the word."

room together (Acts 1:4-5). What were they waiting for? They were waiting for their oneness to be worked out. And remember, Jesus was not there to work it out for them. They were there by themselves to work it out with one another.

When the disciples emerged from the upper room, "they were all with one accord in one place" (Acts 2:1, KJV). They were one. That oneness was the atmosphere in which God brought the Holy Spirit to rest upon the beginning foundations of the *ekklesia*. So yes, we need the Holy Spirit; but even if we pray persistently for an outpouring of the Spirit, we may not see it happen. God is making it clear that there is something more that we need to do. We need to go back to Jerusalem and get into our own upper rooms. We need to begin to deal with the issues of our oneness. Without oneness, we are protracting our own infancy. The Holy Spirit is given to us to teach us and lead us into all things (John 14:26). The promise is that the Spirit will lead us until we do not need to teach every man his brother, saying, "Know the Lord." We shall all know Him (Jeremiah 31:34). That describes a quality of maturity that should be reflective of every individual believer.

It is our own lack of unity that holds back the real release of the Holy Spirit in power. Do you have salvation? It is limited if you remain a baby. Do you have the Holy Spirit? The Spirit is not as effective if He is restrained from maturing and teaching you. Jesus said to

---

Acts 1:4-5 And gathering them together, He commanded them not to leave Jerusalem, but to wait for what the Father had promised, "Which," He said, "you heard of from Me; ⁵ for John baptized with water, but you shall be baptized with the Holy Spirit not many days from now."

John 14:26 "But the Helper, the Holy Spirit, whom the Father will send in My name, He will teach you all things, and bring to your remembrance all that I said to you."

Jeremiah 31:34 "And they shall not teach again, each man his neighbor and each man his brother, saying, 'Know the Lord,' for they shall all know Me, from the least of them to the greatest of them," declares the Lord, "for I will forgive their iniquity, and their sin I will remember no more."

the disciples, "I have many things to teach you, but you cannot yet receive them" (John 16:12). Even the disciples needed to go through this process of oneness before they were able to receive from Christ Himself. There is a saying, "You can't get there from here!" We will not see an outpouring of the Holy Spirit separate from the drive that we have to come into oneness. Oneness creates the atmosphere for the Holy Spirit to be poured out.

Paul wanted to give the Corinthians spiritual meat, the teaching that would resolve their problems, but he was stuck feeding them milk. As babies, they would not be able to understand what he was saying to them. In the same way, we remain immature through our schisms and division.

Immaturity is the direct result of division, so first we must understand what it means to get rid of division. It does not mean that we need to erase all denominational lines and differences and literally come into one big universal Church. A lot of the division in the Church began with simple differences, diversities of gifts and callings. Those diversities do not necessitate division; yet walls and schisms developed over what should have been recognized as the diversity that God Himself originated. 1 Corinthians 12 gives a picture of the Body of Christ as a physical body made up of many different parts. These diverse parts are all needed for the body to function properly. If you want the physical body to be healthy, you cannot stuff all the parts into a blender to make everything become one. If you tried that, you would not be healthy; you would be dead! The physical body is created in diversity for a purpose. It must have a heart, a liver, a brain, and every other part. A living, functioning, healthy body needs all of these parts working together. The Body of Christ is the same way. If we try to stuff each other into the blenders of our own doctrines until we are all homogenized and our differences

---

John 16:12 "I have many more things to say to you, but you cannot bear them now."

are no longer evident, then Christ's Body will not function. The differences in the Body of Christ may become even more evident in the future, but those differences do not equal division. They are diversity, just as God ordained.

Diversity is not division, and division is not diversity. Just because you have a different gift than your brother, or there are different churches with diverse purposes, does not mean you need to be separate from one another. If you remain separate, then you have merely given in to division rather than seeing the expression of God's diversity. God is going to bring forth a very diverse Body of Christ, yet without division. So as we work at this, do not necessarily expect the lines of distinct beliefs to blur. For example, as we were establishing a relationship with the Catholic Church, we were very careful to keep our own identity. We said, "We are not becoming Catholics; we are going to retain the expression of who and what we are." Each fellowship is very distinct and gifted by the Lord, and must retain that distinctiveness for the real oneness to function. If each individual and each fellowship loses that unique aspect of what God has made them, then they have nothing to give to the whole of Christ's Body in the earth. Those diversities are what each one brings to the table in the Body of Christ. We don't want to lose who we are; we want to share what we are. Others can partake of your gifts, but then do not expect them to become what you are, or to look and act like you as a believer. It is human nature to pressure others to become like you. Instead, we must honor those diversities and be edified by them, while not losing our own callings.

So how is this oneness going to work? It will only work in love. It is a oneness that is drawing us together in love. A quote from our founder helps us understand how prophetically foundational this principle is:

> Because the Corinthians were in this state of sectarianism, Paul could not speak unto them as unto spiritual, but

> only as unto babes. This shows clearly that the purpose of sectarianism is to hold God's people in an infant stage. In sectarianism the infancy of the believer is protracted, and the deeper teachings and real purposes of God do not unfold to those who are prone to follow after men as they did in the Corinthian church. There were about four major divisions in that church. How many divisions are there in the Body of Christ now? The trend of sectarianism has been strong in the modern Church, but that trend is being reversed for us today.[16]

The "today" mentioned here was over fifty years ago. But now we are literally seeing with our eyes these Words beginning to be fulfilled. This prophetic Word was years ahead of its time.

> Anything that truly comes forth from God usually is preceded by an Ishmael manifestation. The false makes its appearance before the true. Today the ecumenical plan says that there must be a gathering together based upon the common doctrines in the Protestant and the Catholic religions. Various branches of Catholicism are making an effort to bridge the gap between themselves and the more liberal Protestant groups, but in reality they are striving toward a great world church which is an antichrist manifestation. Such unity is not based upon a moving of God's Spirit, but is an amalgamation brought about by human initiative and organization. God is not in the picture at all.[17]

---

[16] John Robert Stevens, "Lesson 7: The Second Coming of Christ," *The School of Prophets, Series 13, The Second Coming of Christ* (North Hollywood, CA: The Living Word, 1977), 1-2.

[17] Ibid.

Remember, this message was spoken half a century ago. It is interesting to study how history has confirmed what was spoken. At that time, there was a tremendous drive afoot for unity throughout Christianity. It was largely driven by the Catholics; we must give credit where credit is due. This drive for unity was called the ecumenical movement. However, as John Stevens pointed out, the initial ecumenical movement began on a wrong foundation. It was an attempt to gather all of these vast churches and religions together, and remove from each group's doctrines whatever was offensive or problematic to the others. As Stevens used to say back then, "The problem is, you don't end up with a Holy Bible; you end up with a Bible full of holes." It is no wonder that the ecumenical movement did not accomplish its purpose.

Trying to resolve our conflicts through doctrine will never get us to our goal of unity. This approach is similar to the political correctness we see in the world today. Political correctness seeks to remove everything that is offensive to someone else. That will never work; you will always be offensive to someone. And when you are looking for an offense, you will always find something that will offend you. Political correctness fosters a culture in which people remain in a cycle of division and criticism of one another. This approach of trying to impose agreement, or of eliminating distinctions to create agreement, is doomed to fail.

How then is our current drive for oneness in the Body of Christ different from the ecumenical movement? We are not seeking an administrative, organizational, doctrinal approach to find agreement; we are seeking unity based upon another principle entirely. God is opening a door so that we are literally falling in love with each other. As you fall in love with each other, what happens? Love covers a multitude of sins, and love is not easily offended (1 Peter 4:8; 1 Corinthians 13:5). When you are in love, your perception opens to see things differently; your heart becomes willing to change. Love opens the door for a oneness that reaches beyond the differences that would otherwise cause problems.

This very principle may even be God's answer for the world at large. If you look at other nations and cultures through the lens of political correctness, you do not see racism and division abated; you see it highlighted. Everything that is spoken is interpreted with racial undertones. Look at the conflicts around the world; most of them are brother against brother, or religion against religion. We cannot solve these conflicts with political correctness. People hate each other, and yet they are trying to find some way to come together. There is no way to achieve true understanding and reconciliation in that atmosphere. You have to remove the hatred and mistrust, which you can never do until you love one another. And the only love that will make it possible is the love of God the Father. God is the answer. The only way we can stop this hatred is by literally falling in love with each other. Don't minimize the global importance of how God is moving now within His Body. The Body of Christ, in its oneness, will affect both the spiritual and secular arenas of the world.

This oneness is founded upon falling in love with one another. The scriptural pattern for this is found in Ephesians chapter 4, in which Paul is speaking to the whole Body of Christ:

> I, therefore, the prisoner of the Lord, entreat you to walk in a manner worthy of the calling with which you have been called, with all humility and gentleness, with patience, showing forbearance to one another in love, being diligent

---

1 Peter 4:8 Above all, keep fervent in your love for one another, because love covers a multitude of sins.

1 Corinthians 13:5 Does not act unbecomingly; it does not seek its own, is not provoked, does not take into account a wrong suffered.

> to preserve the unity of the Spirit in the bond of peace.
> (Ephesians 4:1-3)

We must have forbearance **in love**. Do not depend upon forbearance alone; forbearance without love can become nothing more than political correctness. You can't just put up with me; you have to love me. I can't just put up with you; I have to love you. If I love you, putting up with you becomes fairly easy to do.

Satan has been at work in this age to cause the love of many to grow cold (Matthew 24:12). It is seen in the breakdown of the family. Families often cannot put up with each other anymore. So the father leaves, the mother leaves, and in one way or another, the children leave. When there is no love, there is more and more distance from one another. What is emotional or spiritual distance? It is division. You divide yourself from one another. The direct source of that separation from one another is a loss of love. We live in a generation where the loss of love is almost beyond our ability to grasp. Mothers leave their babies in garbage cans, children get bored and decide to shoot someone, and men have gone so far as to use nerve gas on their own brothers in their nation. All of these actions stem from a lack of love. When there is no love, concern for one another fades until you do not even care what happens to the other person.

The apostle Paul taught the early churches how to walk in love. Without real love, there is no humility; you can become testy with each other. Forbearance, gentleness, and patience can also wear out. So how is love maintained? By "being diligent to preserve the unity of the Spirit in the bond of peace" (Ephesians 4:3). When the love flows, there is an ability to maintain unity in the Spirit. However, oneness of spirit does not mean that I will always agree with you. It does not mean my perception will always be just like yours. Yet oneness, born out of fervent love, allows me to be humble, gentle,

---

Matthew 24:12 "And because lawlessness is increased, most people's love will grow cold."

patient, and forbearing. All of these things are now possible. The relationship changes when I fall in love with you; division begins to melt away. In its place there is a closeness, a drive to be a force of faith to one another.

Remember the relationship between oneness and maturity? Staying divided keeps us immature; and as long as we are immature, we do not yet know the greatness of what God has for us. But God is in our coming together, therefore it is becoming a delight. We are seeing the Lord in one another, and that becomes the overriding factor. This is what Paul was explaining to the Ephesians. It is the whole formula for how this oneness happens:

> There is one body and one Spirit, just as also you were called in one hope of your calling; one Lord, one faith, one baptism, one God and Father of all who is over all and through all and in all. But to each one of us grace was given according to the measure of Christ's gift. (Ephesians 4:4-7)

> For the equipping of the saints for the work of service, to the building up of the body of Christ; until we all attain to the unity of the faith, and of the knowledge of the Son of God, to a mature man, to the measure of the stature which belongs to the fulness of Christ. (Ephesians 4:12-13)

Paul is saying that we begin by loving one another, and then we work to preserve the unity, knowing that we are all one Body. If we come into this love, generated by His Spirit, we will see our differences as being needed for the whole. As we become one in spirit, we may still not agree on many things. But as we move together in oneness, we will come into "the knowledge of the Son of God, to a mature man."

Through our immaturity, the Holy Spirit is restrained from teaching us what He wants to teach us. Because we have not been educated by Him, we are still ignorant. This means that much of what we think or do or believe is born out of a level of ignorance maintained by immaturity. And the root of that immaturity is division. We have a cycle: the more division there is, the more immaturity persists; the more immaturity persists, the more division there is. Then when I look at you, I cannot even understand you. The truth is, we are probably both wrong; we are locked up by the same immaturity. Nobody is discerning the whole picture, or even seeing one another correctly.

Jesus said, "No man knows the Father except the Son" (Matthew 11:27). He had a corner on the market; only He knew the Father. But that relationship was not meant to be unattainable; we are reaching for the knowledge of the Father. Who teaches us about the Father? Jesus Christ. Who is the access to the Father? Jesus Christ (John 14:6). Who teaches us the things of Christ? The Holy Spirit (John 16:15). And Christ is manifesting Himself in this age through His Body. Thus, the relationship between us literally becomes the fulcrum point upon which everything rests; if we remain divided, none of it works. But if we begin to come into a oneness of spirit, then the process of maturity can begin.

It is phenomenal how absolutely committed many people are to division and hatred. Something has to come and melt our hearts in the Lord until we take on the love of God. God does not love only Christians. "God so loved the world, that He gave His only

---

Matthew 11:27 "All things have been handed over to Me by My Father; and no one knows the Son, except the Father; nor does anyone know the Father, except the Son, and anyone to whom the Son wills to reveal Him."

John 14:6 Jesus said to him, "I am the way, and the truth, and the life; no one comes to the Father, but through Me."

John 16:15 "All things that the Father has are Mine; therefore I said, that He takes of Mine, and will disclose it to you."

begotten Son" (John 3:16). This is the love that we are beginning to take on; it is the attitude of the Father. This love drives us into the oneness of spirit, and ultimately will bring us to the oneness of faith. The ecumenical movement did not work, because it was striving for oneness of faith rather than oneness of spirit. We need to exercise this love that God is bringing us into. Don't be put off by things you don't agree with; reach in for God's love for one another. Then you will find the Holy Spirit working in a whole new way in your hearts. Immaturity will begin to drop away. The ability to hear from the Holy Spirit—an outpouring of the Spirit—can begin to take place. The Father gave Christ the Holy Spirit without measure (John 3:34). That is what we are looking for. We have the Spirit, but it is in a measure. We are stuck in that place until we eradicate division.

Just beyond that place is the fulfillment of our dreams in our walk with the Lord. Paul saw this coming and knew that we were going to attain it. He wrote, "Now we request you, brethren, with regard to the coming of our Lord Jesus Christ, and our gathering together to Him" (2 Thessalonians 2:1). The word for "gathering together" in the Greek is *episunagoge*. It refers to the synagogue, the gathering place. It also means "a bringing together," or "an assembling." When you add the Greek prefix *epi*, meaning "on," it takes on the aspect of being drawn together, almost being pushed together. One Greek lexicon actually recognizes this as an end-time event that is to happen in accordance with this verse in 2 Thessalonians.[18]

John 3:16 "For God so loved the world, that He gave His only begotten Son, that whoever believes in Him should not perish, but have eternal life."

John 3:34 "For He whom God has sent speaks the words of God; for He gives the Spirit without measure."

[18.] T. Friberg, B. Friberg, and N.F. Miller, *Analytical Lexicon of the Greek New Testament*, vol.4, *Baker's Greek New Testament Library* (Grand Rapids, MI: Baker Books, 2000), 168.

Many people believe we are in the end time. If that is true, then one of the greatest events we should be looking for is the coming together of the Body of Christ. In the following quote, Stevens points out how this comes forth:

> Even with the numerous divisions in modernistic Christianity, as well as in the old traditional denominations, there is a striving to come into a union. The Scriptures speak of something similar. Paul wrote, "I beseech you brethren, by the presence (*Parousia*) of our Lord Jesus Christ, and our gathering together unto Him." The Body of Christ is coming together today, but not by something that man will create. There was a time when people would die over differences of doctrine, but God's people in this hour have advanced in the true moving of the Spirit to a place where they are striving more for the unity of the Spirit than for the unity of doctrine. This does not mean that they can preach false ideas, but they are endeavoring to keep the unity of the Spirit (Ephesians 4:3).
>
> The Scriptures explain that God gave the heavenly gifts of apostles and prophets so that we would all come to the unity of the faith (Ephesians 4:11-13). The unity of the Spirit will exist, however, before the unity of the faith. Long after people have come into a unity in their spirits with one another, they may still have their own peculiar ideas about some things, and what one believes may seem odd to another. Even when there are different ideas concerning the major doctrinal concepts, this does not

---

Ephesians 4:11-13 And He gave some as apostles, and some as prophets, and some as evangelists, and some as pastors and teachers, [12] for the equipping of the saints for the work of service, to the building up of the body of Christ; [13] until we all attain to the unity of the faith, and of the knowledge of the Son of God, to a mature man, to the measure of the stature which belongs to the fulness of Christ.

prevent the people in those groups from coming into the fullness of the Holy Spirit. The moving of the Spirit and the unity of the Spirit exist before the unity of the faith. The outpouring of the Holy Spirit among God's people is bringing forth a unity of the Spirit. This is one of the greatest signs of the end time.[19]

The outpouring is all dependent on this love that melts away the division, that brings about a oneness of spirit. The love allows the Body of Christ to grow up and mature, and the maturity of the Body of Christ fosters the oneness. In our maturity, God is actually able to feed us those things that we need to know, to impart to us what we need to become, and to allow us, as His global Body, to truly function in the power and fullness of the Holy Spirit.

---

[19] Stevens, "Lesson 7: The Second Coming of Christ," 3.

Chapter 28

Creating Oneness in the Body of Christ

October 19, 2013
Church of the Living Word, North Hills, California
New Heart Catholic Community, Engenho Novo, Rio de Janeiro, Brazil
(via video conference)

This message was broadcast from Los Angeles to the New Heart Catholic Community in Engenho Novo, Rio de Janeiro, for the Convergence of Christians Conference, a gathering of Catholic and Protestant leaders.

God has been speaking to us about the oneness of the Body of Christ for many years, and I believe that now is the time when this Word will begin to manifest and have its fulfillment. It is a revelation that has come through prophetic Words over decades in Protestant and Evangelical groups as well as through popes and cardinals, especially from the Second Vatican Council. The prophetic Word of oneness is a legacy in our fellowship, as we read in a message from our spiritual father, John Robert Stevens. This message dates back to 1958 and contains prophecies about these days of the coming together of the Body of Christ. Just as the teachings from Vatican II have shed light on the path to oneness, these prophecies have been a guiding light for us; and they have directed us for almost sixty years to work toward this oneness of the Body. In these prophecies John Stevens said,

> The Spirit of the Lord is constantly speaking unity to the house of the Lord. He is saying, "You shall not walk divided. You are no longer to look at yourself as an individual, but you will look at yourself as part of a Body" (Ephesians 2:19-22). You shall prepare your hearts to walk together….
>
> …What will make this Body a unit of one, except the love of God as He pours out upon you? The Lord said, "For unity comes through perfect love, and will I not pour out My perfect love unto you? Will I not draw you together as one? Will I not unite you in love in your God alone? As I and the Father are one, won't you be one in Me and in each other?" Follow close after your God and learn and seek of Him, for from Him comes the perfect love that shall unite you as one….
>
> …You will open your heart to the Word that God is sending forth in the earth, that God's people will be made one. You will hear it and it will be something in your heart to wonder at, for the mind cannot understand it or reason it out. The Lord your God says that you shall embrace it in your heart, that the Lord's Body is one Body. There is one faith, there is one Lord, there is one baptism (Ephesians 4:4-6); and you will come into this

---

Ephesians 2:19-22 So then you are no longer strangers and aliens, but you are fellow citizens with the saints, and are of God's household, [20] having been built upon the foundation of the apostles and prophets, Christ Jesus Himself being the corner stone, [21] in whom the whole building, being fitted together is growing into a holy temple in the Lord; [22] in whom you also are being built together into a dwelling of God in the Spirit.

Ephesians 4:4-6 There is one body and one Spirit, just as also you were called in one hope of your calling; [5] one Lord, one faith, one baptism, [6] one God and Father of all who is over all and through all and in all.

unity; you will come into this oneness—with the Lord and with one another.[20]

Because we have had the same prophetic vision and burden, we are grateful for the determination of Pope Francis to see Catholics and Protestants come together in fulfillment of the Words that came by the Holy Spirit from the Second Vatican Council. A decree issued in 1964 by the Council states,

> The restoration of unity among all Christians is one of the principal concerns of the Second Vatican Council. Christ the Lord founded one Church and one Church only. However, many Christian communions present themselves to men as the true inheritors of Jesus Christ; all indeed profess to be followers of the Lord but differ in mind and go their different ways, as if Christ Himself were divided (1 Corinthians 1:13). Such division openly contradicts the will of Christ, scandalizes the world, and damages the holy cause of preaching the Gospel to every creature.
>
> But the Lord of Ages wisely and patiently follows out the plan of grace on our behalf, sinners that we are. In recent times more than ever before, He has been rousing divided Christians to remorse over their divisions and to a longing for unity. Everywhere large numbers have felt the impulse of this grace, and among our separated brethren also there increases from day to day the movement, fostered by the grace of the Holy Spirit, for the restoration of unity among all Christians.[21]

---

1 Corinthians 1:13 Has Christ been divided? Paul was not crucified for you, was he? Or were you baptized in the name of Paul?

[20.] John Robert Stevens, "Prophecy May 25, 1958," *This Week, Vol. XIII, No. 4* (North Hollywood, CA: The Living Word, 1982), 1, 4, 6.

[21.] *Decree On Ecumenism: Unitatis Redintegratio* in the Documents of the II Vatican Council, under "Decrees," http://www.vatican.va/archive/hist_councils/ii_vatican_council/index.htm (accessed September 13, 2014).

As we see from these two prophetic statements, the vision for oneness has been a shared burden and drive in Christian fellowships for many years. Today there is a resurgence of this drive, as people from different groups—Protestants, Evangelicals, and Catholics—are making a bold commitment to walk together in oneness. We know that there is a price to be paid. There are many who would criticize our involvement with oneness between Catholics and Protestants, but we are doing the right thing. We join our hearts together as believers to stand firm in the faith and in the Word that God is speaking about the love and oneness of the Body of Christ. We commit ourselves and our ministries and our churches to see this oneness come about, no matter what criticism or persecution may arise. We believe that God will touch the hearts of both Catholics and Protestants as we see this move of oneness come forth.

It is important that we lay a foundation in the Scriptures as we begin to move into oneness so that we are able to stand on the Word of God about what we are doing and be strong in the faith. As Jesus said, we are going to build on the rock of revelation, and because we build on the rock of revelation in the Word of God, the house that we build will be strong (Matthew 16:18; 7:24-25). The oneness that is coming today is founded upon the Scriptures. God is bringing us back to the original experience as an *ekklesia* that we read about in the Book of Acts, being baptized in the Holy Spirit and walking in

---

Matthew 16:18 "And I also say to you that you are Peter, and upon this rock I will build My church; and the gates of Hades shall not overpower it."

Matthew 7:24-25 "Therefore everyone who hears these words of Mine, and acts upon them, may be compared to a wise man, who built his house upon the rock. [25] And the rain descended, and the floods came, and the winds blew, and burst against that house; and yet it did not fall, for it had been founded upon the rock."

love one with another (Acts 2:38, 41-42). We are truly beginning to walk in the new commandment that Jesus gave us, as we read in John 13:34-35: "A new commandment I give to you, that you love one another, even as I have loved you, that you also love one another. By this all men will know that you are My disciples, if you have love for one another."

This is what Christ required of His disciples, and this is the commandment that He is giving us today—that we love one another. In this assembling of Christians, in this convergence of believers, we are not trying to duplicate what existed in the ecumenical movement of the past. At that time, people tried to bring about oneness by attempting to agree on doctrines, beliefs, or creeds. We are approaching this time in a new way. It is not about doctrine; it is about this commandment to love. By His grace, by His Spirit, God is pouring out a love in our hearts, and we are finding a deep sense of love for one another. It is a new thing that God is doing. We read in the Word, "Behold, I will do a new thing; will you be aware?" (Isaiah 43:19). This deep love and connection that we are experiencing between Catholics and Protestants is a new thing.

Jesus did not say for us to be one because of our doctrines. He told us to love one another. He said, "The world will know that you are My disciples because of this love that you have one for another" (John 13:35). All Evangelicals, Protestants, and Catholics

---

Acts 2:38 And Peter said to them, "Repent, and let each of you be baptized in the name of Jesus Christ for the forgiveness of your sins; and you shall receive the gift of the Holy Spirit."

Acts 2:41-42 So then, those who had received his word were baptized; and there were added that day about three thousand souls. [42] And they were continually devoting themselves to the apostles' teaching and to fellowship, to the breaking of bread and to prayer.

Isaiah 43:19 "Behold, I will do something new, now it will spring forth; will you not be aware of it? I will even make a roadway in the wilderness, rivers in the desert."

John 13:35 "By this all men will know that you are My disciples, if you have love for one another."

claim that their burden is for the salvation of unbelievers; yet the simplicity of the world believing Christ's message is not born out of our works, nor is it born out of our doctrines. People will witness the love that we have for one another, and that love will be the testimony. This was the basis of the relationship between Jesus and the Father, which Christ explains in His prayer found in John 17:20-23.

The relationship between Jesus and the Father was not a relationship of doctrine; it was a relationship of love. The Father loved the Son, and the Son loved the Father. It was this love that made them one, and Jesus prayed that we would have the same relationship of oneness.

How will the Church in this current day, with all of its apparent separation and division, ever become one? It will become one as we love one another. The oneness that Jesus prayed for us to have was born out of the relationship of love between Himself and the Father. We do not need to pray for oneness and unity; we simply need to have a love for one another. We need to obey the commandment that Jesus left us. This oneness and love is something that existed in the early days of the Church; it began on the Day of Pentecost and continued with the believers who had been with Jesus (Acts 4:13). They were baptized, not only in the Holy Spirit, but also into this

---

John 17:20-23 "I do not ask in behalf of these alone, but for those also who believe in Me through their word; [21] that they may all be one; even as Thou, Father, art in me, and I in Thee, that they also may be in Us; that the world may believe that Thou didst send Me. [22] And the glory which Thou hast given Me I have given to them; that they may be one, just as We are one; [23] I in them, and Thou in Me, that they may be perfected into one, that the world may know that Thou didst send Me, and didst love them, even as Thou didst love Me."

Acts 4:13 Now as they observed the confidence of Peter and John, and understood that they were uneducated and untrained men, they were marveling, and began to recognize them as having been with Jesus.

love for one another (Romans 5:5). The Church, however, has lost what it had at its beginning. We are believing for a restoration of what Jesus began when He initiated the *ekklesia* of love and oneness in the family of believers.

This oneness was demonstrated in Acts 4:31: "And when they had prayed, the place where they had gathered together was shaken, and they were all filled with the Holy Spirit, and began to speak the word of God with boldness." One of the manifestations of this love relationship was that the disciples were all filled with the Holy Spirit, and we see that happening again today. The infilling of the Holy Spirit is very prevalent in the new Catholic communities. It is coming once again as the strength that we read about in the fourth chapter of Acts. It is what Jesus described when He said, "I have given them My glory that they may be one" (John 17:22). The Holy Spirit is the glory of Jesus Christ poured out upon His family.

> And the congregation of those who believed were of one heart and soul; and not one of them claimed that anything belonging to him was his own; but all things were common property to them. And with great power the apostles were giving witness to the resurrection of the Lord Jesus, and abundant grace was upon them all. (Acts 4:32-33)

This was the atmosphere of the *ekklesia* that existed following Christ's ascension. We must look back on the Church's beginning and understand its significance for us today. We must believe that Christ is restoring the Church as it existed in those days, until it is once again based not on doctrine or on denomination, but based on this commandment of love one for another. At that time, the leaders were moving in power and miracles, and the family was one heart

---

Romans 5:5 And hope does not disappoint, because the love of God has been poured out within our hearts through the Holy Spirit who was given to us.

and one soul. Let it be that way again, Lord, as we come together in love.

Central to this revelation of oneness is the picture of the *ekklesia*, or the Church, as the Body of Christ. In writing to the Corinthians, the apostle Paul compared the Church to the human body. "For even as the body is one and yet has many members, and all the members of the body, though they are many, are one body, so also is Christ" (1 Corinthians 12:12). Today Christ is manifesting in His Body, and even though we have many separations, many different gifts, and many different names, we are one. According to Paul, this is the picture of Christ. "For by one Spirit we were all baptized into one body" (1 Corinthians 12:13). Whatever names we have for our denominations or groups, they cannot take away from this revelation that in Christ we are truly one Body of people. We have been baptized by one Spirit into one Body "whether Jews or Greeks, whether slaves or free, and we were all made to drink of one Spirit. For the body is not one member, but many" (1 Corinthians 12:13-14).

We often allow our differences and our diversities to be perceived as divisions, but that is not how Paul saw it. He said that even though we are many members, we are one Body in Christ. "But now God has placed the members, each one of them, in the body, just as He desired. And if they were all one member, where would the body be? But now there are many members, but one body" (1 Corinthians 12:18-20). As our eyes are opened to one another in love, we will see how beautiful our diversity is. Our differences are beautiful in the eyes of the Father, and they will be beautiful in our eyes also. We will see that we may be many in our differences, but in truth we are only one Body in Christ. As Paul asked, "Is Christ divided?" (1 Corinthians 1:13, KJV). Our answer must be "No! Christ cannot be divided." Christ is one. His Body is one. It may have many members but it is one, and we are going to enjoy our diversity and our differences in our love for one another.

As we fall in love with one another, we will begin to love and appreciate those things that have seemingly divided us in our history. As we continue reading in 1 Corinthians 12, we see that Paul is very clear: no matter what the differences are, there is to be no division in the Body. "But God has so composed the body, giving more abundant honor to that member which lacked, that there should be no division in the body, but that the members should have the same care for one another" (1 Corinthians 12:24-25). This is beginning to happen within the Church across former divisions. We are beginning to love one another, pray for one another, bless one another, and be a part of one another. We are beginning to care for one another in love.

> And if one member suffers, all the members suffer with it; if one member is honored, all the members rejoice with it. Now you are Christ's body, and individually members of it. And God has appointed in the church, first apostles, second prophets, third teachers. (1 Corinthians 12:26-28)

Paul describes the ministries and authorities and order of the Church, but do not forget that it all begins with the Church being a Body. In our focus on all of the titles and types of leadership, we have lost the true focus on the Church being a Body. We know that we have fathers and bishops and pastors and all of these other ministries, but Paul places that secondary to the revelation that we are one Body. Today, as we see the Holy Spirit moving, we must once again come to this revelation that the most important aspect is the oneness of the Body.

I believe that over the course of the history of the Church, this revelation of the Body has been lost. The Body has been devastated because of the lack of love. It is this love that enables the Body of Christ to grow, as Paul explains: "But speaking the truth in love, we are to grow up in all aspects into Him, who is the head, even Christ" (Ephesians 4:15). We are to grow up to be like Christ, for He is the head of the Body. "From whom the whole body, being fitted and held together by that which every joint supplies" (Ephesians 4:16). Without the oneness of all the members, the Body flies apart; and that is what we have seen happen. Each joint is to hold the Body together, but instead, it has gone into division and separation. "According to the proper working of each individual part, causes the growth of the body for the building up of itself in love" (Ephesians 4:16). The only way the Body can grow and mature is with love being the foundation of all we do. That is what causes the proper working of each individual part. Paul makes it clear that each of us is responsible. We are all a part of this Body and we must function properly in it; and our functioning is dependent on following Jesus' simple commandment: love one another.

If the members of the Body are loving one another, if we are holding onto one another, then the Body will grow and mature into the head, which is Christ Jesus our Lord. What a beautiful picture! Yet throughout the history of the Church, this oneness has waned. We have not held to one another, and the Body has separated. We may appear strong, having endured this process of separation and division, but the truth is that we have been devastated. Where do we find the world believing because of our love? Where is the release of salvation to all the earth that comes through our oneness, as Jesus prayed in John 17? Where is the power that existed in those original apostles and other ministries as they moved in oneness and love as a true family? We read about the days when all it took was Peter's shadow falling on the sick as he walked through the street, and people were healed (Acts 5:15). We need Christ's deliverance coming into this world again just as it did in Peter's day. We have a sick world that needs to believe. It needs to know Jesus. It needs to be filled with the Holy Spirit. This will not happen because of our

---

Acts 5:15 To such an extent that they even carried the sick out into the streets, and laid them on cots and pallets, so that when Peter came by, at least his shadow might fall on any one of them.

denominations and our doctrines; it will only happen because of our love and oneness.

The Book of Jude contains a warning about the end times, the days in which we live right now:

> But you, beloved, ought to remember the words that were spoken beforehand by the apostles of our Lord Jesus Christ, that they were saying to you, "In the last time there shall be mockers, following after their own ungodly lusts." These are the ones who cause divisions, worldly-minded, devoid of the Spirit. But you, beloved, building yourselves up on your most holy faith; praying in the Holy Spirit; keep yourselves in the love of God, waiting anxiously for the mercy of our Lord Jesus Christ to eternal life. (Jude 17-21)

In describing what would come, Jude warned that the Body of Christ would experience division; but he also gave us the answer to the problem. He said, "Beloved, pray in the Holy Spirit and love one another." Today we are seeing this answer happening. It is happening in Catholic, Evangelical, and Protestant churches as young people are being encouraged to be filled with the Holy Spirit, to pray in the Holy Spirit, and to love one another. We are witnessing a great outpouring in which God is bringing to us this deep love one for another. This love that God is pouring out will be the healing of the Church. We will become the *ekklesia* that Jesus built on the rock of revelation, a revelation of love for one another.

Chapter 29

A Prophetic Message for the Church Today

October 19, 2013
Church of the Living Word, North Hills, California
New Heart Catholic Community, Engenho Novo, Rio de Janeiro, Brazil
(via video conference)

This message was broadcast from Los Angeles to the New Heart Catholic Community in Engenho Novo, Rio de Janeiro, for the Convergence of Christians Conference, a gathering of Catholic and Protestant leaders.

The Scriptures contain a prophetic message for us as believers in this day and age. It is a message about the restoration of the oneness that the Church had at its beginnings; for it is a oneness that has been lost. Throughout its history, the Christian Church has followed the same pattern that the Hebrew Scriptures depict concerning Israel in its relationship with God. This has nothing at all to do with the concept of replacement theology, which is the teaching that the Christian Church replaces Israel in the fulfillment of God's promises. Christians do not usurp the Jewish people or take over their prophecies and Words. The prophecies of the Hebrew Scriptures are about the Jewish people and they are for the Jewish people. Those prophecies will have a very specific fulfillment over the Jewish people, who are our brothers. However, I also know that there is a corresponding fulfillment and relationship that these prophecies have to Christians and to the Church. In Christ, we were grafted into God's family (Romans 11:17). So, in a sense, it is as though we are like another tribe of Israel, and we are included in all of the Words that God has spoken over Israel.

When we follow the history of the Jewish people, we see a pattern that unfolded in accordance with all that God spoke to them. First, God met Israel at Sinai (Exodus 19:17, 20), and there He made a covenant with Israel to be His people (Exodus 19:5-6). Then, God gave commandments, or ordinances, for them to follow (Exodus 24:3). However, they sinned and failed in following those commandments, and they continued in idolatry despite repeated warnings from God. Therefore, they experienced the consequences that God had warned them about (Deuteronomy 11:16-17). They were removed from the land of Israel and taken into captivity; the Temple was torn down and Israel as a land became a ruin. Israel, as a

---

Romans 11:17 But if some of the branches were broken off, and you, being a wild olive, were grafted in among them and became partaker with them of the rich root of the olive tree.

Exodus 19:17 And Moses brought the people out of the camp to meet God, and they stood at the foot of the mountain.

Exodus 19:20 And the Lord came down on Mount Sinai, to the top of the mountain; and the Lord called Moses to the top of the mountain, and Moses went up.

Exodus 19:5-6 "'Now then, if you will indeed obey My voice and keep My covenant, then you shall be My own possession among all the peoples, for all the earth is Mine; ⁶ and you shall be to Me a kingdom of priests and a holy nation.' These are the words that you shall speak to the sons of Israel."

Exodus 24:3 Then Moses came and recounted to the people all the words of the Lord and all the ordinances; and all the people answered with one voice, and said, "All the words which the Lord has spoken we will do!"

Deuteronomy 11:16-17 "Beware, lest your hearts be deceived and you turn away and serve other gods and worship them. ¹⁷ Or the anger of the Lord will be kindled against you, and He will shut up the heavens so that there will be no rain and the ground will not yield its fruit; and you will perish quickly from the good land which the Lord is giving you."

people, was dispersed throughout the world in a diaspora that exists to this day. We can see in the Scriptures the distinct phases that Israel went through in its relationship with God. God met them. He made His covenant with them. He gave His commandments and His instructions to them. When they failed to faithfully live according to those instructions, there were consequences. These are exactly the same phases that the Church has gone through in its history.

Christ's appearance in the flesh was God meeting the world, just as He had met Israel at Sinai. Christ gave us a new covenant, which is the covenant in His blood (Luke 22:20). This covenant connects us as believers to the promise in Jeremiah 31:31-33, that God will make a new covenant whereby He will write His law on our hearts. This new covenant includes a new commandment from the Lord that we love one another (John 13:34). It was in this meeting with God, in this new covenant, and in this commandment to love one another that the *ekklesia* first began in oneness. However, the Church has sinned and has failed to walk in the commandment given to us by Christ, and we have suffered the consequences. The Church has gone into devastation and division. The power and the witness that we had at the beginning has been lost because we have not walked in the oneness that the Lord commanded.

Luke 22:20 And in the same way He took the cup after they had eaten, saying, "This cup which is poured out for you is the new covenant in My blood."

Jeremiah 31:31-33 "Behold, days are coming," declares the Lord, "when I will make a new covenant with the house of Israel and with the house of Judah, [32] not like the covenant which I made with their fathers in the day I took them by the hand to bring them out of the land of Egypt, My covenant which they broke, although I was a husband to them," declares the Lord. [33] "But this is the covenant which I will make with the house of Israel after those days," declares the Lord, "I will put My law within them, and on their heart I will write it; and I will be their God, and they shall be My people."

John 13:34 "A new commandment I give to you, that you love one another, even as I have loved you, that you also love one another."

The Christian Church, whether Catholic or Protestant, is guilty of failing in this commandment that Christ gave us. We have not loved one another; we have not been one and we have allowed division to continually come in, despite the Lord's command to us. That is our sin, just as idolatry was the sin of Israel in Old Testament times. Therefore, we live with the consequences. Many have heard the teaching from the Book of Revelation describing Babylon as the failed Church (Revelation 18:2). This teaching has often been applied to the Church of the Middle Ages. To me, however, the proof that the Church is still in Babylon is the lack of His presence, the lack of power, the lack of anointing and miracles, and the lack of the blessings of God on the Church. There is a lack of the world believing in Jesus, because they do not see oneness in His believers. We do not have the ability to produce the fulfillment that God wants because we are still in Babylon. If Christians today do not understand the dissatisfaction they feel and what they are yearning for, it is simply that we are weeping by the rivers of Babylon over what has been lost (Psalm 137:1).

What our hearts and spirits are crying for is the restoration of the oneness that will return the Church to its original power. God promised the children of Judah a time of restoration after they were held captive in Babylon (Jeremiah 29:10, 14). During the reign of

---

Revelation 18:2 And he cried out with a mighty voice, saying, "Fallen, fallen is Babylon the great! And she has become a dwelling place of demons and a prison of every unclean spirit, and a prison of every unclean and hateful bird."

Psalm 137:1 By the rivers of Babylon, there we sat down and wept, when we remembered Zion.

Jeremiah 29:10 "For thus says the Lord, 'When seventy years have been completed for Babylon, I will visit you and fulfill My good word to you, to bring you back to this place.'"

Jeremiah 29:14 "'And I will be found by you,' declares the Lord, 'and I will restore your fortunes and will gather you from all the nations and from all the places where I have driven you,' declares the Lord, 'and I will bring you back to the place from where I sent you into exile.'"

Cyrus, they were allowed to return to their land. Jerusalem was restored and the Temple was rebuilt (Ezra 1:2-3). The Church has followed the same pattern as Israel that has led to devastation, captivity, and the diaspora. Now the Lord is restoring the Church just as He restored Israel. Today we see many of the gifts and ministries that were part of the original Church operating in both Catholic and Protestant congregations all over the world. Still, the fact that the Church went into so much chaos and division since the time of the Reformation means that the restoration is incomplete, and we all share in the responsibility for that failure.

We are aware that we live in the devastated Church; however, God is in the process of bringing a restoration by His grace. The Scriptures provide an understanding of the process we are in. One of the greatest prophets of Israel regarding the captivity was Ezekiel. Ezekiel himself was taken into captivity and was part of the second group that went into Babylon, so he knew what he was prophesying about. He experienced it. He lived it. Ezekiel spoke about the devastation, but he also brought tremendous prophecies of hope about the restoration of Israel. Those prophecies also apply to us today. The prophecy in Ezekiel 36 applies to who we are, what we have done and where we are going in our relationships with one another.

God said to Ezekiel, "But I had concern for My holy name, which the house of Israel had profaned among the nations where they went" (Ezekiel 36:21). Israel had profaned the name of God through their idolatry, and that is the reason He took them into Babylon. They did not follow the commandment to love the Lord their God with

---

Ezra 1:2-3 "Thus says Cyrus king of Persia, 'The LORD, the God of heaven, has given me all the kingdoms of the earth, and He has appointed me to build Him a house in Jerusalem, which is in Judah. ³ Whoever there is among you of all His people, may his God be with him! Let him go up to Jerusalem which is in Judah, and rebuild the house of the LORD, the God of Israel; He is the God who is in Jerusalem.'"

all their heart (Deuteronomy 6:5), and so He said, "I am concerned about My name because you as the house of Israel have profaned My name among the nations by the way you live." We need to apply this same admonition to ourselves. In our history as the Church, whether Catholics or Protestants or Evangelicals, we have all been guilty in the eyes of God of violating the simple commandment that Jesus gave to us. We have violated His commandment in the same way that Israel did. In our failure to love one another, we have profaned the name of God among the nations. I believe that God will begin to correct every one of these situations, because the name of God shall no longer be profaned among the nations through our failures.

God continued speaking to Ezekiel:

> "Therefore, say to the house of Israel, 'Thus says the Lord God, "It is not for your sake, O house of Israel, that I am about to act, but for My holy name, which you have profaned among the nations where you went. And I will vindicate the holiness of My great name which has been profaned among the nations, which you have profaned in their midst. Then the nations will know that I am the Lord," declares the Lord God, "when I prove Myself holy among you in their sight."'" (Ezekiel 36:22-23)

The way that God will clear His name today is by proving Himself holy in the Church. He will glorify Himself by what He manifests in His people, as He restores the Body of Christ in this hour. We are in the time when God is getting ready to glorify His name by showing Himself holy among His people. "For I will take you from the nations, gather you from all the lands, and bring you into your own land" (Ezekiel 36:24). That is a beautiful picture of what God is

---

Deuteronomy 6:5 "And you shall love the Lord your God with all your heart and with all your soul and with all your might."

speaking to us today. He is going to gather the Body of Christ from all nations, from all denominations, out of all doctrines, and bring us together to honor the one simple commandment that we love one another. "Then I will sprinkle clean water on you, and you will be clean; I will cleanse you from all your filthiness and from all your idols. Moreover, I will give you a new heart and put a new spirit within you" (Ezekiel 36:25-26). God is once again filling His Body with the Holy Spirit, so that we walk and are moved and driven by His Spirit. "And I will remove the heart of stone from your flesh and give you a heart of flesh" (Ezekiel 36:26).

God is taking away the heart of stone—the ways in which we would not love one another as we should—and He is giving us a heart of flesh, a heart of love for one another.

> "I will put My Spirit within you and cause you to walk in My statutes, and you will be careful to observe My ordinances. And you will live in the land that I gave to your forefathers; so you will be My people, and I will be your God." (Ezekiel 36:27-28)

This prophecy is about the great restoration of the children of Israel. It is about bringing them back out of their sin of idolatry and making them once again a people in whom God is proud, a people in whom He can manifest Himself. This is also what God is doing for the Church. He is removing the sin of division and restoring the love and oneness so that we can reveal the Father's heart to the world.

We read in the next chapter that God gave Ezekiel a great vision. It is still very accurate today as a vision of the Jewish people, and where they are in the plan of God. They too are in a time of restoration. We know that this is their Word and their vision, and it is manifesting for them, but it is also happening for the Body of Christ. Ezekiel had a vision of a valley filled with dry bones, and God caused Ezekiel to pass through all of those bones and said, "Son of man, can these bones live?" (Ezekiel 37:1-3). As we look at the Body of Christ, we see the same picture. It is devastated to the point of being like a valley of dry bones lying in a wilderness, but something is happening in our hearts. God is saying to us, "Can these bones live?" Is it possible that something can change this picture we see today in the Body of Christ?

We may think that we are doing well, but we had better check ourselves. Having lost our love and having disintegrated into division, we have become like a valley of dry bones. Now God is speaking a word and He is challenging us as He challenged Ezekiel: "Can these bones live?" Can we change this picture of what the Body of Christ has become? It may seem impossible to imagine oneness happening among Catholics and Protestants, among all the denominations and schisms, but that is what God is saying. We are becoming one. He is giving us the love that can make us one. When God asked Ezekiel, "Can these bones live?" Ezekiel's answer was probably how we would respond today: "God, only You know." It seems impossible; God only knows if this can work. God's response is,

> "Prophesy over these bones, and say to them, 'O dry bones, hear the word of the Lord.' Thus says the Lord God to these bones, 'Behold, I will cause breath to enter you that you may come to life. And I will put sinews on you, make flesh grow back on you, cover you with skin, and put breath in you that you may come alive; and you will know that I am the Lord.'" So I prophesied as I was commanded; and as I prophesied, there was a noise, and

---

Ezekiel 37:1-3 The hand of the Lord was upon me, and He brought me out by the Spirit of the Lord and set me down in the middle of the valley; and it was full of bones. ² And He caused me to pass among them round about, and behold, there were very many on the surface of the valley; and lo, they were very dry. ³ And He said to me, "Son of man, can these bones live?" And I answered, "O Lord God, Thou knowest."

behold, a rattling; and the bones came together, bone to its bone. And I looked, and behold, sinews were on them, and flesh grew, and skin covered them; but there was no breath in them. Then He said to me, "Prophesy to the breath, prophesy, son of man, and say to the breath, 'Thus says the Lord God, "Come from the four winds, O breath, and breathe on these slain, that they come to life."'" So I prophesied as He commanded me, and the breath came into them, and they came to life, and stood on their feet, an exceedingly great army. (Ezekiel 37:4-10)

Even though the Body of Christ has become dry, disconnected bones lying in a valley, the Lord is challenging us to prophesy to these bones and command them to come together. This is what the Spirit is speaking through the Pope, through bishops and fathers in the Catholic Church, and through Protestant pastors and ministries who are following the Lord's command to bring about this oneness. Those of you who have this great vision of love and oneness in your heart, you are the Ezekiel company that God is speaking to today. This may seem impossible, but God is saying to prophesy a release to the Holy Spirit, the breath of God, to come now upon the dry bones of the Body of Christ. We prophesy another outpouring of the Holy Spirit of God upon the dry bones of Christ's Body. We say, "Come alive!" Let the bones come together bone to bone, and let flesh be placed on them. Let our hearts come together heart to heart until we are one mighty people, until we are filled with the Holy Spirit, and the Body of Christ once again stands in the earth as an exceedingly great army.

That was what happened through Ezekiel's prophecy. The restoration was brought forth. It did not just happen on its own. Those of us who are believing for oneness may seem like a small remnant, and there may be much criticism against us, but it is not about us. This is about the command of the Lord. Ezekiel prophesied the Word that the Lord commanded. Today, as the Body of Christ comes together in love, we obey Jesus' commandment to love one another. It is by this love and concern for one another that we rise up like Ezekiel did in his day. I am sure there were many who criticized him. After being in Babylon and seeing the Temple destroyed, they might have said, "You are crazy. This could never happen." Maybe some felt it wasn't right, just as many today feel that it is wrong for Protestants and Catholics to come together. We do not have to argue. We just have to prophesy as Ezekiel did.

We come together to speak the Word of the Lord, to prophesy to the bones and command them to come together. We prophesy, "Holy Spirit, fill Your Body until it rises up and stands on its feet as a great army in this hour, in all of our nations." We need His Body, the great army of God, filled with the Holy Spirit as a testimony and a witness that Christ has come and brought for us salvation and hope. Father, just as Ezekiel did, we proclaim life to Your Body. More than just Christians meeting together, we come together as those bones, connecting heart to heart. Let our hearts be open and melted together in oneness. We proclaim the beginning of a tremendous force of oneness. We agree together to take the responsibility to be the Ezekiels in this day—in our society, in our cities, and in our towns—to prophesy life, to prophesy love, and to prophesy oneness in the Body of Christ. We declare that this prophetic Word will stand as a guiding light for us as we move forward. God has given us a Word of who we are and how we are to move, and we release it today in the name of the Lord.

Chapter 30

The Lord Our God Is One

May 25, 2014
Grace Chapel of Honolulu, Honolulu, Oahu, Hawaii

In preparation for the Feast of Pentecost, this message was spoken to the local congregation.

In the days just preceding the Feast of Pentecost, following the crucifixion of Christ and His ascension to the right hand of the Father, 120 of His disciples were in the upper room intensely seeking God. They did this as one, in preparation for the great outpouring of the Holy Spirit. We also are looking to be in one accord, in one place, seeking God with all of our hearts, and looking for a great outpouring of His Spirit. Pentecost, of course, is one of the main biblical feasts, and we find the instruction for it in Exodus 34:22. This is called *Shavu'ot* by the Jews. The celebration of *Shavu'ot*, or Pentecost, by the Jewish people has an emphasis on the giving of the Law. While you cannot find anything in the Scriptures that explicitly connects the Feast of Pentecost to the giving of the Law, the Jewish tradition is that this was the time God gave the Law to Israel at Mount Sinai. Why would they celebrate Pentecost as the time when God gave the Law to Israel if that cannot be backed up

---

Exodus 34:22 "And you shall celebrate the Feast of Weeks, that is, the first fruits of the wheat harvest, and the Feast of Ingathering at the turn of the year."

in the Scriptures? There is a connection that is very important for us, because the giving of the Law ties very much into Pentecost as we know it from the New Testament. When Christians think about Pentecost, we think about the birth of the Church, the giving of the Holy Spirit, and the oneness that was on the disciples at that time. In fact, oneness is deeply connected to Pentecost and has become very much a focus for that Feast. So then, how does Pentecost apply to the giving of the Law? To understand this in the context of the oneness that we celebrate at Pentecost, we need to read from Deuteronomy the 6th chapter.

> "Now this is the commandment, the statutes and the judgments which the Lord your God has commanded me to teach you, that you might do them in the land where you are going over to possess it, so that you and your son and your grandson might fear the Lord your God, to keep all His statutes and His commandments, which I command you, all the days of your life, and that your days may be prolonged. O Israel, you should listen and be careful to do it, that it may be well with you and that you may multiply greatly, just as the Lord, the God of your fathers, has promised you, in a land flowing with milk and honey." (Deuteronomy 6:1-3)

Here at the end of their wanderings, Moses again rehearses for the people the commandments that God gave, just as he had done on different occasions in the wilderness. As Christians, our mind immediately goes to the Ten Commandments. That is what we think of when we say, "the Law." However, the giving of the Law was not just about the Ten Commandments. There are actually 613 *mitzvot*, or commands, in the Law. Considering the difficulty we have in obeying the Ten Commandments, maybe it's wise that we don't try to follow 613 commandments! But regardless, the Scriptures are not limited to the Ten Commandments; they contain the whole of the

Law that God gave to Moses. Here in this Scripture is a beautiful example of Moses saying, "This is the commandment. What I am telling you right now is the statute. This is the Law that the Lord gave me to teach to you."

When Moses began to rehearse to Israel the commandments, telling them how important it was to listen and keep them, he began with this statement: "Hear, O Israel! The Lord is our God, the Lord is one!" (Deuteronomy 6:4). In Hebrew this is, "*Shema, Yisraeil! Adonai Eloheinu, Adonai echad!*" This is probably the prayer voiced most often in all of Judaism. The Jewish people pray this when they wake up every morning, and it is supposed to be the last prayer they pray before they die. It is called the *Shema*, meaning "to listen and obey," or "do what you are hearing." Moses was saying, "Listen and do." What is it that we are to listen to and do? "The Lord is our God, the Lord is one!" When you think about it, that does not really sound like a commandment, nor does it sound like something you can do. And yet it was presented by Moses as the first commandment, statute, and law. Moses continued, saying,

> "And you shall love the Lord your God with all your heart and with all your soul and with all your might. And these words, which I am commanding you today, shall be on your heart; and you shall teach them diligently to your sons and shall talk of them when you sit in your house and when you walk by the way and when you lie down and when you rise up." (Deuteronomy 6:5-7)

Moses emphasized this commandment as the very first: God is one, and we are to love Him with all our heart, soul, and might. Now, it is interesting that the Jewish people connect the Feast of Pentecost to the giving of the Law, because the Law proclaims that God is one. In the Jewish tradition regarding the giving of the Law, the oneness of God and our loving Him are associated with the Feast of Pentecost. This is a beautiful picture that is repeated in the New Testament. In

Mark chapter 12 we read how one of the scribes asked Jesus, "What commandment is the foremost of all?" (Mark 12:28). Notice that he asked, "What is the foremost commandment?" He did not say, "Choose one of the Ten Commandments that is the greatest." In Jesus' day, they talked about all of the commandments, all of the Law of Moses. The scribe was asking, "What is the foremost thing that God told Israel out of all the commandments?"

> Jesus answered, "The foremost is, 'Hear, O Israel! The Lord our God is one Lord; and you shall love the Lord your God with all your heart, and with all your soul, and with all your mind, and with all your strength.' The second is this, 'You shall love your neighbor as yourself.' There is no other commandment greater than these." (Mark 12:29-31)

When Jesus was asked, "What is the foremost commandment?" He replied with this same prayer of the Jewish people: "*Shema, Yisraeil! Adonai Eloheinu, Adonai echad!*" He said, "The foremost commandment is that God is one." Then He took it a step further and said, "Not only will I give you the first, most important commandment, God is one, but I will also give you the second greatest commandment: love your neighbor as yourself."

You cannot have any greater confirmation than out of the mouth of Jesus. With all the things that He could have chosen out of the Law, Jesus chose the commandment that God is one and that we are to love Him with all of our heart. There are two major personality traits, or identifying aspects, of God that are given in the Bible. The first is that God is one. If you want to know who God is, the first thing you have to understand is that God is one. The other aspect is

---

Mark 12:28 And one of the scribes came and heard them arguing, and recognizing that He had answered them well, asked Him, "What commandment is the foremost of all?"

that God is love (1 John 4:8). Both of these things don't really seem like commandments, because they speak about who and what God is. Moses said to the people, "If you do these commandments, you will prosper. And here is the first commandment that God gave me to teach you: God is one." What do you do with that? How do you obey the commandment, "God is one"? In the New Testament we find a similar challenge: "God is love." However, that is something we can do. We can reach into that love. This foremost commandment, spoken by Moses and Jesus, draws both aspects of God's nature and puts them together. God is one, and you shall love God with all your heart, with all your soul, and with all your might. Why? Because God is love. The aspect that God is one, which seems impossible for us to do, is united with this other aspect that God is love, which is possible for us to perform. This means that we can walk in oneness.

We know that when the 120 were gathered in the upper room seeking God, they were of one mind (Acts 1:14). We also read that on the Day of Pentecost they were all together in one place (Acts 2:1, KJV). Young's Literal Translation reads, "They were all with one accord at the same place." The meaning in the Greek is a little deeper than simply being in the same geographic location. We can plainly see that the foundation of the Church grew out of the oneness that was achieved by those 120 in the upper room in the days preceding Pentecost. They were walking in the foremost commandment; they were being one.

---

1 John 4:8 The one who does not love does not know God, for God is love.

Acts 1:14 These all with one mind were continually devoting themselves to prayer, along with the women, and Mary the mother of Jesus, and with His brothers.

Acts 2:1, KJV And when the day of Pentecost was fully come, they were all with one accord in one place.

Remember what Jesus told them: "You shall be My witnesses" (Acts 1:8). In another account, He told them to remain in Jerusalem until they were endued with power from on high, enabling them to be witnesses (Luke 24:48-49). We are to be witnesses also, but what are we to be witnesses of? How can the Church possibly be the witness of Christ if we are not a witness of oneness? The thinking of the Church tends to separate oneness from the cross and the resurrection. Christians think, "We are to be witnesses that Jesus died on the cross and was resurrected." Then we wonder why people have such an incomplete picture of what God is really doing. Jesus said, "I and the Father are one" (John 10:30). Everything that happened on the cross and in the resurrection of Jesus happened because Jesus understood the *Shema*. He was one with the Father. Therefore, Jesus was enabled to go to the cross and literally be God's sacrifice for our sins. Without the oneness He had with the Father, the cross would not work, and there would be no resurrection. Oneness is what being a witness of Christ is all about. We are to be the witnesses of the oneness of God, the oneness of Christ, and the oneness of the Holy Spirit. We are also to be the witnesses of Their oneness with us. Without that, we are missing the main point of the story.

The oneness that God wants for us can be traced in the Scriptures all the way back to the beginning. It may not be as explicitly stated as we would like it to be, but it is there. As we saw, according to Jewish tradition, the Feast of Pentecost was first observed with the giving of the Law, and the Law reveals that God is one. By the time we come to the Pentecost after the resurrection of Christ, this feast

---

Acts 1:8 "But you shall receive power when the Holy Spirit has come upon you; and you shall be My witnesses both in Jerusalem, and in all Judea and Samaria, and even to the remotest part of the earth."

Luke 24:48-49 "You are witnesses of these things. [49] And behold, I am sending forth the promise of My Father upon you; but you are to stay in the city until you are clothed with power from on high."

is definitely all about the oneness of God's people. In between those two events, during the Babylonian captivity, Ezekiel prophesied that the Lord would take the tribe of Judah and the tribes of Israel in His hand and make them one (Ezekiel 37:19). So it is evident from this prophecy that the purpose of God is to end up in oneness with His people. However, the Scripture that makes this fact abundantly clear is found in the Book of Genesis:

> And the man gave names to all the cattle, and to the birds of the sky, and to every beast of the field, but for Adam there was not found a helper suitable for him. So the Lord God caused a deep sleep to fall upon the man, and he slept; then He took one of his ribs, and closed up the flesh at that place. And the Lord God fashioned into a woman the rib which He had taken from the man, and brought her to the man. And the man said, "This is now bone of my bones, and flesh of my flesh; she shall be called Woman, because she was taken out of Man." For this cause a man shall leave his father and his mother, and shall cleave to his wife; and they shall become one flesh. And the man and his wife were both naked and were not ashamed. (Genesis 2:20-25)

Adam and Eve were not ashamed, because they were one flesh. No matter how you interpret the biblical account, the creation of mankind is about oneness. People are divided over whether to take this literally or view it as a poetic story about our creation. Either way, it has the same message: when God created humanity, He took two separate beings and made them one. Some say, "This story is sexist, because God took the rib out of the man to make the woman." But God also told the man to leave his father and mother and cleave

---

Ezekiel 37:19 "Say to them, 'Thus says the Lord God, "Behold, I will take the stick of Joseph, which is in the hand of Ephraim, and the tribes of Israel, his companions; and I will put them with it, with the stick of Judah, and make them one stick, and they will be one in My hand."'"

to his wife. In a relationship based on true oneness, no one gives or takes more than the other. In true oneness, all of the struggle over differences goes away. That is part of why we, as humans, have such a hard time coming into a real oneness. Remember, oneness is not a doctrine. It is not something that we can achieve through our own striving. What is oneness? It is God. If we say that God is love, then we also have to say that God is one. When we talk about oneness, we are not saying, "Let's work really hard to get oneness between us." Oneness does not happen because a husband and wife say, "Let's really try to be one with each other." No, it only happens by coming into the nature of God. It is about a transformation into the personality of God. When you truly have oneness, you literally become like God. We know that this is what happens with love. If we would become love, we would become what God is (1 John 4:16-17).

If we go back a little further in the Book of Genesis, we find another aspect of the creation story. "Then God said, 'Let Us make man in Our image'" (Genesis 1:26). Isn't that interesting? God, who is one, said, "Let **Us** make man in **Our** image." If you study the grammar of the Hebrew text, that is exactly how this verse reads. I know of no English translation that translates it any differently. The Hebrew word for "make" is plural. If the author intended to convey more than one God, the sentence would read, "Let Us make man in Our **images**." Instead, "make" is plural and "image" is singular: "Let Us (who are one God) make man in Our image." This understanding of oneness does not take away from the sovereignty of God. The Jews have trouble with Christians regarding this point. Because we believe in God the Father, a deified Jesus, as well as the Holy Spirit, we are considered idolaters, worshiping three gods. The argument we are making in this message is that if you understand oneness,

---

1 John 4:16-17 And we have come to know and have believed the love which God has for us. God is love, and the one who abides in love abides in God, and God abides in him. [17] By this, love is perfected with us, that we may have confidence in the day of judgment; because as He is, so also are we in this world.

then you are worshiping the one God. There is only one God. He is *echad*—one. God is one, and yet He referred to Himself in the plural in the making of man.

As humans, this destiny of oneness was given to us at the very moment of our creation. We are to be one. In being one, what happens? We actually reflect the personality of God. God will always be spirit (John 4:24). But in the physical realm, who of all His creation can reflect and express who and what God is? Angels cannot do that because they are also spirit (Hebrews 1:7, KJV). Only man can do it, and we will only accomplish that as we become one. When we are one, we will reflect who and what God is on this earth, in the physical realm. God made us for that very purpose.

> Then God said, "Let Us make man in Our image, according to Our likeness; and let them rule over the fish of the sea and over the birds of the sky and over the cattle and over all the earth, and over every creeping thing that creeps on the earth." And God created man in His own image, in the image of God He created him; male and female He created them. (Genesis 1:26-27)

God said, "I am one. That is who I am; that is what I am. Let Me create man in My own image." Then what does He do? He creates two different genders. Sometimes trying to understand what God is doing makes you want to pull your hair out, but He is showing us something. He wants us to see that in all His expression through the Holy Spirit and through His Son, He is one. When He created us, He created male and female, two different and distinct individuals, in His image, which is one.

John 4:24 "God is spirit, and those who worship Him must worship in spirit and truth."

Hebrews 1:7, KJV And of the angels he saith, Who maketh his angels spirits, and his ministers a flame of fire.

We can say the same thing about the Body of Christ; it is one (1 Corinthians 12:12). We, as the Body, are one because we were created in oneness. At the birth of the Church on the Day of Pentecost, that was absolutely expressed. The Church was created in the image of the oneness of God the Father and Jesus Christ His Son. There will be a time in our humanity when oneness prevails, and there will be a time when the Church becomes the expression of the oneness of God in the earth. Not being one is more than a sin; it is an absolute rejection of God Himself and His nature. The literal meaning of the word "sin" means to miss the mark, to go astray. More than going astray, rejecting oneness is refusing to become like God, refusing to live and be what He is. We have to get out of this mode of rejecting God's oneness in our personal lives, in our families, and in the Body of Christ. Since we know that on the Day of Pentecost the Church was born in oneness, we must recognize that the Church's present-day rejection of oneness has crept in through our hardness of heart.

In 1 John chapter 4, we are commanded to love one another. This love is born out of the realization that God is love. Again, this is about the very nature of God and how we should be the reflection of His nature.

> Beloved, let us love one another, for love is from God; and everyone who loves is born of God and knows God. The one who does not love does not know God, for God is love. By this the love of God was manifested in us, that God has sent His only begotten Son into the world so that we might live through Him. In this is love, not that we loved God, but that He loved us and sent His Son to be the propitiation for our sins. Beloved, if God so loved us, we also ought to love one another. No one has beheld God at

---

1 Corinthians 12:12 For even as the body is one and yet has many members, and all the members of the body, though they are many, are one body, so also is Christ.

> any time; if we love one another, God abides in us, and His love is perfected in us. By this we know that we abide in Him and He in us, because He has given us of His Spirit. (1 John 4:7-13)

In this epistle, John is saying, "Whatever God is in His nature, we should be that too." If God is love, then we should be determined to be as God is. We should be driven to be filled with love, and express that love one to another. If we achieve that, then we are in God, and God is in us, because we have become like Him. This transcends the concept of commandments, which are orders that we must comply with. Instead, this is talking about becoming the very nature of God. Paul also writes about love in chapter 13 of 1 Corinthians. If we know that God is love, we should understand what it means if we do not have love.

> If I speak with the tongues of men and of angels, but do not have love, I have become a noisy gong or a clanging cymbal. And if I have the gift of prophecy, and know all mysteries and all knowledge; and if I have all faith, so as to remove mountains, but do not have love, I am nothing. And if I give all my possessions to feed the poor, and if I deliver my body to be burned, but do not have love, it profits me nothing. (1 Corinthians 13:1-3)

To know all mysteries and all knowledge, to have all faith—those are things we would do anything to possess. However, without love they would profit us nothing. Why? Because without love there is no likeness of God in us. So what good are those things? This is an important message for the Church right now. We can do all kinds of works. We can have all kinds of spiritual gifts. We can teach the Scriptures, and know the mysteries; but if we do not come into God's love, then, as Paul warned, we are nothing. Remember, we did not love God first. He first loved us; therefore we must draw His love (1 John 4:19). We want to be filled with what God is. We want to be filled with His very nature, personality, and being.

What is God's personality? It is love and it is oneness. In this passage, Paul gives a beautiful illustration of a principle that is difficult to understand in the Hebrew Scriptures because we do not think of oneness as something to do. But we can see oneness very clearly expressed when we talk about love. God is love; therefore we need to be the love of God manifested in the earth to people. How will they see that God is love unless we, as His people, become the expression of that love? We will do that only by becoming one. Maybe that doesn't seem as important to us as love, but we know a house divided against itself will not stand (Matthew 12:25). What we see happening in the world, in the destruction of mankind through wars and killing, all comes from a lack of oneness, as well as from a lack of love. If you are one with someone, you are not going to persecute them, kill them, or go to war with them.

Satan continually works to divide people and nations. The rhetoric in the world seems to be more and more divisive. What we hear people say about one another are statements that divide us along the lines of race, culture, and gender. Everything is designed to set one person against another. That is satan's purpose. You might ask, "Where is God in all of this?" He is not in any part of division at all! He cannot be, because He is one. You will not get anything from God except oneness. God will only be one, and He will only promote oneness. Wherever we find division, we will find that which refuses to come into the nature of God. If someone was refusing to love, we would be upset about that. But what about someone who is refusing to be one? I believe that holds the same weight—and penalty. The answer for this world is the Body of Christ, but the problem with the Body

---

1 John 4:19 We love, because He first loved us.

Matthew 12:25 And knowing their thoughts He said to them, "Any kingdom divided against itself is laid waste; and any city or house divided against itself shall not stand."

of Christ is that we are not one. When we become one, the world will believe that the Father sent Christ into the earth (John 17:21). That is the testimony that will convince people. Why? Because both love and oneness are impossible to achieve on the human level.

We were created in the likeness of God's oneness, but we have lost that. What we must do as Christians, as disciples of Christ, is hold ourselves into the upper room until we become of one mind together. That is something we can focus on; that is something we can pray about. We can prophesy this level of oneness into existence for ourselves individually, for our families, and for our communities. We can believe to see the release of this oneness that God is looking for. The two greatest commandments come together in Christ—the oneness and the love, which are the attributes of the Father.

Lord, bring us into this oneness. Bring us into Your likeness. Make us one. In the beginning, You created us in Your own image. Do it again, Lord! Make us anew in Your likeness. We may be separate as individuals, but You created male and female and made them one. Though we seem to be diverse and disconnected individuals, weld us into one. Make us Your representatives in the earth, in Jesus' name.

John 17:21 "That they may all be one; even as Thou, Father, art in Me, and I in Thee, that they also may be in Us; that the world may believe that Thou didst send Me."

Chapter 31

The Bride of Christ

June 8, 2014
Grace Chapel of Honolulu, Honolulu, Oahu, Hawaii

Soon after the Feast of Pentecost, this message was spoken to the local congregation.

The term "bride of Christ" is a very commonly used term, but do we really know where it comes from, what it means, and why it is significant to us? While the specific phrase "bride of Christ" is not a biblical term, it is very definitely drawn out of the Scriptures through other terminologies, and conveyed through different words. In order to understand its importance to us, we need to look in the Scriptures to see where this idea of the bride of Christ comes from. Is it even valid to talk about there being a bride of Christ? Then, once we learn that it is an important concept, we need to ask, "Who is it referring to, and how does it apply to us in this day?" To begin, let's read from Revelation the 19th chapter:

> "Let us rejoice and be glad and give the glory to Him, for the marriage of the Lamb has come and His bride has made herself ready." And it was given to her to clothe herself in fine linen, bright and clean; for the fine linen is the righteous acts of the saints. And he said to me, "Write, 'Blessed are those who are invited to the marriage supper of the Lamb.'" (Revelation 19:7-9)

Again, the exact terminology "bride of Christ" is not in this Scripture, but it is obviously about a bride for the Lamb, and we know that the Lamb is Christ. In this allegory of a wedding feast, it is significant that the bride clothes herself in "fine linen, bright and clean; for the fine linen is the righteous acts of the saints."

Revelation chapter 21 also contains the word "bride," but in a different context:

> And I saw the holy city, new Jerusalem, coming down out of heaven from God, made ready as a bride adorned for her husband. And I heard a loud voice from the throne, saying, "Behold, the tabernacle of God is among men, and He shall dwell among them, and they shall be His people, and God Himself shall be among them." (Revelation 21:2-3)

Here we have the same idea of a bride who has clothed herself for her husband, but the imagery of the wife is depicted as being Jerusalem coming down out of heaven. Another passage from this chapter gives us the same picture:

> And one of the seven angels who had the seven bowls full of the seven last plagues, came and spoke with me, saying, "Come here, I shall show you the bride, the wife of the Lamb." And he carried me away in the Spirit to a great and high mountain, and showed me the holy city, Jerusalem, coming down out of heaven from God. (Revelation 21:9-10)

We have in our minds that we, the Church, are the bride of Christ; so what does it mean here that Jerusalem is the bride? Don't worry; the imagery of the new Jerusalem coming down out of heaven as a bride adorned for her husband does refer to the Church. Let's read from an article about this in the Anchor Bible Dictionary:

> Although the specific phrase "bride of Christ" does not appear in the NT [New Testament], the concept is found in several NT works as a description of the Church. Paul describes the Corinthian believers as having been betrothed to Christ and presented as a bride to her husband (2 Cor 11:2; cf. Rom 7:1-6). In Eph 5:21-33 the relationship between husband and wife is explained in terms of the relationship that exists between Christ and the Church. The author of Revelation applies the metaphor of the bride of the Lamb (Christ), not only to the Church (19:7), but also to the new Jerusalem, the heavenly city, which is the eschatological manifestation of the people of God (21:2, 9). The source for this imagery is found in the OT [Old Testament] where the relationship between Israel and God is often spoken of in marital terms (Isa 54:1-6; Jer 31:32; Ezek 16:8; Hos 2).[22]

This commentary confirms that the bride, the wife of the Lamb, is the new Jerusalem, and is speaking metaphorically of the Church, or God's people. The Book of Isaiah also uses the illustration of a husband-and-wife relationship to express the relationship that God is looking for between Himself and His people. I am not sure that the human example of marriage we have today is necessarily what God had in mind, but there is something very deep in the relationship between the Father and His people that He is trying to portray. We should feel the impact of this, because God is looking for a relationship with us.

> "For the LORD has called you, like a wife forsaken and grieved in spirit, even like a wife of one's youth when she is rejected," says your God. "For a brief moment I forsook you, but with great compassion I will gather you. In an

---

[22.] Mitchell G. Reddish, "Bride of Christ," in *The Anchor Bible Dictionary*, vol. 1, Gary A. Herion, David F. Graf, and John David Pleins, eds. (New York: Doubleday, 1992), 782.

> outburst of anger I hid My face from you for a moment; but with everlasting lovingkindness I will have compassion on you," says the LORD your Redeemer. (Isaiah 54:6-8)

"The Lord has called you like a wife." That is very clear, isn't it? You cannot dispute what is meant by that Scripture. This picture of Israel's relationship to God as that of a wife is expressed throughout the Hebrew Scriptures. That is the closeness, the intimacy, and the love that He is looking for. Yet it is a stormy relationship. Israel rejects Him, and so He gets angry; at times He puts them aside (Jeremiah 3:1-3). But God's promise is, "I will call you back. I will gather you into this husband-and-wife relationship with Me, and it will be an everlasting relationship." The redemption that God brings to His people is one of everlasting love and compassion. What a beautiful picture!

> "Behold, days are coming," declares the LORD, "when I will make a new covenant with the house of Israel and with the house of Judah, not like the covenant which I made with their fathers in the day I took them by the hand to bring them out of the land of Egypt, My covenant which they broke, although I was a husband to them," declares the LORD. (Jeremiah 31:31-32)

This is a very important passage of Scripture to us as Christians because these verses lead into verse 33, which is about the new

---

Jeremiah 3:1-3 God says, "If a husband divorces his wife, and she goes from him, and belongs to another man, will he still return to her? Will not that land be completely polluted? But you are a harlot with many lovers; yet you turn to Me," declares the LORD. [2] "Lift up your eyes to the bare heights and see; where have you not been violated? By the roads you have sat for them like an Arab in the desert, and you have polluted a land with your harlotry and with your wickedness. [3] Therefore the showers have been withheld, and there has been no spring rain. Yet you had a harlot's forehead; you refused to be ashamed."

Jeremiah 31:33 "But this is the covenant which I will make with the house of Isreal after those days," declares the LORD, "I will put My law within them, and on their heart I will write it; and I will be their God, and they shall be My people."

covenant. This new covenant that we see fulfilled for us in Christ is also likened to the relationship of a wife to her husband. God said, "I was a husband to them, but they broke that covenant of marriage with Me." Again, the Scriptures express this very powerful thought that God is looking for a marital relationship with His people, and with Israel as a nation. The same imagery is found in Ezekiel chapter 16. Using very graphic language about the birth process, this chapter contains an allegory in which God recounts the story of Israel as a nation, from the moment of its birth down through the various phases of its history. When Israel was being born, God said, "You were thrown out into the field; nobody wanted you. But I came and put My cloak over you" (Ezekiel 16:5, 8). This is a beautiful picture of the fact that God is looking to have a marriage relationship with His people. The Lord came and covered Israel with His cloak, which symbolizes marriage. That is also what happened in the story of Ruth. Boaz covered her, which meant that he was going to marry her (Ruth 3:8-9).

Another great Scripture about this marriage relationship is in Hosea chapter 2: "'And it will come about in that day,' declares the LORD, 'that you will call Me Ishi and will no longer call Me Baali'" (Hosea 2:16). To understand the meaning of these Hebrew words, *Ishi* and *Baali*, think of what Jesus said on the cross: "My God, why

---

Ezekiel 16:5 "No eye looked with pity on you to do any of these things for you, to have compassion on you. Rather you were thrown out into the open field, for you were abhorred on the day you were born."

Ezekiel 16:8 "Then I passed by you and saw you, and behold, you were at the time for love; so I spread My skirt over you and covered your nakedness. I also swore to you and entered into a covenant with you so that you became Mine," declares the Lord GOD.

Ruth 3:8-9 And it happened in the middle of the night that the man was startled and bent forward; and behold, a woman was lying at his feet. ⁹ And he said, "Who are you?" And she answered, "I am Ruth your maid. So spread your covering over your maid, for you are a close relative."

have You forsaken Me?" (Matthew 27:46). The Hebrew word for "my God" is *Eli*. The "i" ending on the word *El*, which means "God," makes it "my God." The same ending is used with the Hebrew word *Ishi*. *Ish* means "husband," and therefore *Ishi* means "my husband." It will come about in that day that we will call Him "my Husband." What a day of fulfillment! We will no longer call Him *Baali*. *Baal* was the name of an ancient god. The name *Baal* means "lord," and he lords it over people. By worshiping him, people make him their lord. But we will not have *Baal* as our lord anymore, lording it over us. Now God will be to us "my Husband." What a beautiful picture that is!

We have read from these Hebrew Scriptures to answer the question, "Is the concept of the bride of Christ really biblical?" But why go only to the Old Testament to verify a New Testament concept? Most of the writing in the New Testament about the husband-and-wife relationship comes from Paul, but Paul was a Pharisee of Pharisees, trained in the Hebrew Scriptures (Philippians 3:5). As we have seen, this idea of the husband-and-wife relationship with regard to the Father and His people is very prominent in the Old Testament Scriptures, and so this concept must have been very deep in Paul's thinking. After his conversion experience with Jesus, Paul applied this concept to the realization that the Gentiles were included and had also become God's people (Acts 13:46-47). Therefore they, too, became part of this vision that God will marry His people. In Paul's

---

Matthew 27:46 And about the ninth hour Jesus cried out with a loud voice, saying, "Eli, Eli, lama sabachthani?" that is, "My God, My God, why hast Thou forsaken Me?"

Philippians 3:5 Circumcised the eighth day, of the nation of Israel, of the tribe of Benjamin, a Hebrew of Hebrews; as to the Law, a Pharisee.

Acts 13:46-47 And Paul and Barnabas spoke out boldly and said, "It was necessary that the word of God should be spoken to you first; since you repudiate it, and judge yourselves unworthy of eternal life, behold, we are turning to the Gentiles. ⁴⁷ For thus the Lord has commanded us, 'I have placed You as a light for the Gentiles, that You should bring salvation to the end of the earth.'"

mind, that meant both Israel and the *ekklesia*, or the Church. In Jesus' parable of the wise and foolish virgins, there is more than one wise virgin, so the idea of multiple fulfillments is very real (Matthew 25:1-2). This husband-and-wife relationship continues very much into the New Testament, where the relationship is seen as being directly with Jesus.

> Or do you not know, brethren (for I am speaking to those who know the law), that the law has jurisdiction over a person as long as he lives? For the married woman is bound by law to her husband while he is living; but if her husband dies, she is released from the law concerning the husband. So then if, while her husband is living, she is joined to another man, she shall be called an adulteress; but if her husband dies, she is free from the law, so that she is not an adulteress, though she is joined to another man. Therefore, my brethren, you also were made to die to the Law through the body of Christ, that you might be joined to another, to Him who was raised from the dead, that we might bear fruit for God. (Romans 7:1-4)

When Jesus died, you died to the Law. Therefore, you are free to be remarried. All of the bonds that you made in your previous life with people or anything else, were all broken by the death of Jesus. Therefore, "you might be joined to another, to Him who was raised from the dead [meaning Jesus] that we might bear fruit for God." Paul is saying, "You are to be married. Christ broke your past bonds. He freed you from everything else. Now you will be joined to Christ in this marriage relationship." This is another beautiful picture that brings alive to us what God is looking for. We find this same concept in 2 Corinthians: "For I am jealous for you with a godly jealousy; for

---

Matthew 25:1-2 "Then the kingdom of heaven will be comparable to ten virgins, who took their lamps, and went out to meet the bridegroom. ² And five of them were foolish, and five were prudent."

I betrothed you to one husband, that to Christ I might present you as a pure virgin" (2 Corinthians 11:2). Paul was telling the Corinthians, who were stumbling at the time, "Here is what I, Paul, am doing. I want to present you to Christ at that great marriage supper of the Lamb." This was Paul's motivation in ministering as an apostle to the Church. All of his energy had this one goal, that he was betrothing the Church to Christ. That was his drive, his ministry, and his destiny. In Ephesians chapter 5, he makes this very plain:

> And be subject to one another in the fear of Christ. Wives, be subject to your own husbands, as to the Lord. For the husband is the head of the wife, as Christ also is the head of the church, He Himself being the Savior of the body. But as the church is subject to Christ, so also the wives ought to be to their husbands in everything. Husbands, love your wives, just as Christ also loved the church and gave Himself up for her; that He might sanctify her, having cleansed her by the washing of water with the word, that He might present to Himself the church in all her glory, having no spot or wrinkle or any such thing; but that she should be holy and blameless. (Ephesians 5:21-27)

Paul begins by writing about husbands and wives, then shifts into the concept that Christ is working to present us to Himself in this same marriage relationship. This Scripture also speaks of cleansing and washing. It was a pure virgin that Paul was looking for, "having no spot or wrinkle or any such thing; but that she should be holy and blameless." This work that God is doing in us is all about being presented to Him as a pure bride. We tend to forget that as we go through the dealings of the Lord. We ask, "Why are all these things happening in my life?" It is the preparation to be His bride; it is our purification and our sanctification. In our minds, we have this wonderful image of being the bride of Christ and the beautiful marriage ceremony that we are waiting for. But then we have to deal with the realization that our Husband has some qualifications. He has to choose us, and He has to accept us. As we read in the Book of Revelation, the bride makes herself ready. We must allow this process to take place in our lives that sanctifies us and gets rid of the spots and wrinkles until we are blameless before the Lord.

Why is this revelation so important for us today? How does it relate to the oneness of the Body of Christ? If the Body of Christ is to be His bride, then the qualification is that we be without spot or wrinkle or any such thing. Therefore, we have to recognize that the divisions in Christ's Body are a sin. If we truly believe that Christ's return to the earth is the marriage of the Lamb when He comes for His bride, then we must not fool ourselves—our divisions could be one of the greatest reasons why Christ's return would be delayed. A wedding has to be delayed until the preparations are finalized. If Christ's bride must be a virgin without spot or wrinkle, then how can He come for the Church today with all of its divisions, schisms, and hatred of one another? That does not qualify us to be His bride. That is why God is speaking to us that there must be oneness and love in the Body of Christ.

Oneness does not mean that we all become one big homogeneous organization, but the root of the division, which is hatred, has to go. God's love must take over. The Scriptures make this very clear. Revelation chapter 19, where we read about the marriage supper of the Lamb, begins with rejoicing because of the judgment that comes on the great harlot, Babylon (Revelation 19:1-2). What is Babylon, the great harlot? Every church or denomination has concluded what Babylon is, and it is always somebody else's church

---

Revelation 19:1-2 After these things I heard, as it were, a loud voice of a great multitude in heaven, saying, "Hallelujah! Salvation and glory and power belong to our God; ² BECAUSE HIS JUDGMENTS ARE TRUE AND RIGHTEOUS; for He has judged the great harlot who was corrupting the earth with her immorality, and HE HAS AVENGED THE BLOOD OF HIS BOND-SERVANTS ON HER."

or denomination. Nonetheless, the marriage described in the Book of Revelation is first triggered by the judgment on the impure, unfaithful church. This is speaking directly of the concept in Jesus' parable of the ten virgins. In this parable, Jesus tells of five wise and five foolish virgins (Matthew 25:3-13). These virgins represent God's people, whether they are individuals, churches, or other groups. In this parable, Jesus does not describe the Church as a singular, but as a multi-faceted entity, having different levels of faithfulness to the Lord. The five foolish virgins missed the bridegroom's return because they were not prepared. There will be many groups who begin to come together at Christ's coming, but there will also be those who miss it and are rejected.

When we talk about oneness, we are talking about the unity of those who are seeking to really have a walk with God. The bride of Christ will not just consist of whoever wants to call themselves the bride. It will be those who act like the bride, making themselves ready, crying out for purity and sanctification, who want to get rid of every spot and wrinkle. God is speaking to us, as the global Body of Christ, that one of the ways we can make ourselves ready is by getting rid of division. There are several Scriptures that deal with this. In 2 Thessalonians chapter 2, there is a prophetic statement

---

Matthew 25:3-13 "For when the foolish took their lamps, they took no oil with them, [4] but the prudent took oil in flasks along with their lamps. [5] Now while the bridegroom was delaying, they all got drowsy and began to sleep. [6] But at midnight there was a shout, 'Behold, the bridegroom! Come out to meet him.' [7] Then all those virgins rose, and trimmed their lamps. [8] And the foolish said to the prudent, 'Give us some of your oil, for our lamps are going out.' [9] But the prudent answered, saying, 'No, there will not be enough for us and you too; go instead to the dealers and buy some for yourselves.' [10] And while they were going away to make the purchase, the bridegroom came, and those who were ready went in with him to the wedding feast; and the door was shut. [11] And later the other virgins also came, saying, 'Lord, lord, open up for us.' [12] But he answered and said, 'Truly I say to you, I do not know you.' [13] Be on the alert then, for you do not know the day nor the hour."

that, at some point, there will be oneness in the Church:

> Now we request you, brethren, with regard to the coming of our Lord Jesus Christ, and our gathering together to Him, that you may not be quickly shaken from your composure or be disturbed either by a spirit or a message or a letter as if from us, to the effect that the day of the Lord has come. Let no one in any way deceive you, for it will not come unless the apostasy comes first, and the man of lawlessness is revealed, the son of destruction, who opposes and exalts himself above every so-called god or object of worship, so that he takes his seat in the temple of God, displaying himself as being God. (2 Thessalonians 2:1-4)

> For the mystery of lawlessness is already at work; only he who now restrains will do so until he is taken out of the way. And then that lawless one will be revealed whom the Lord will slay with the breath of His mouth and bring to an end by the appearance of His coming; that is, the one whose coming is in accord with the activity of Satan, with all power and signs and false wonders, and with all the deception of wickedness. (2 Thessalonians 2:7-10)

> But we should always give thanks to God for you, brethren beloved by the Lord, because God has chosen you from the beginning for salvation through sanctification by the Spirit and faith in the truth. And it was for this He called you through our gospel, that you may gain the glory of our Lord Jesus Christ. So then, brethren, stand firm and hold to the traditions which you were taught, whether by word of mouth or by letter from us. Now may our Lord Jesus Christ Himself and God our Father, who has loved us and given us eternal comfort and good hope by grace, comfort and strengthen your hearts in every good work and word. (2 Thessalonians 2:13-17)

This passage is also expressing the idea of a wedding, of the Body of Christ becoming one, and coming to Him as a bride to her husband. Again, we read that, prior to the return of Christ and our coming together to Him, a judgment takes place on that which is apostate. God desires to get His bride out of apostasy, and part of that apostasy is division. We know that Christ's coming will manifest judgment on the great harlot, Babylon. We have to drop all of our conclusions of who that harlot is, because God is putting His finger on all of us. He is saying, "You may be Babylon unless you change, so stop pointing your finger over there. Get the beam out of your own eye" (Matthew 7:3). We all have some homework to do if we are to be a pure bride without spot or wrinkle.

In 2 Corinthians chapter 7, Paul puts the responsibility on us: "Therefore, having these promises, beloved, let us cleanse ourselves from all defilement of flesh and spirit, perfecting holiness in the fear of God" (2 Corinthians 7:1). We have to cleanse ourselves; we have to perfect ourselves in this process. The Lord's disciples had to experience this also. Before Jesus ascended, He commissioned the disciples, saying, "Go into all the world and preach the gospel to all creation" (Mark 16:15). But then He stopped them and said, "Don't go yet. Wait in Jerusalem until you are endued with power from on high" (Luke 24:49). Jesus forced them to first come into oneness and be baptized in the Holy Spirit. The Holy Spirit and oneness are crucial to being the bride of Christ, to accomplish what God wants to do through us as the Body of Christ at this time. Before Jesus went to the cross, He prayed to the Father:

> "I do not ask Thee to take them out of the world, but to keep them from the evil one. They are not of the world,

---

Matthew 7:3 "And why do you look at the speck that is in your brother's eye, but do not notice the log that is in your own eye?"

Luke 24:49 "And behold, I am sending forth the promise of My Father upon you; but you are to stay in the city until you are clothed with power from on high."

> even as I am not of the world. Sanctify them in the truth; Thy word is truth. As Thou didst send Me into the world, I also have sent them into the world. And for their sakes I sanctify Myself, that they themselves also may be sanctified in truth." (John 17:15-19)

Jesus knew that He was going to ascend to the right hand of the Father. He knew it when He commissioned the disciples, and He prayed, "I do not ask Thee to take them out of the world, but to keep them from the evil one. Sanctify them in the truth." This is a clear picture of the beautiful bride of Christ. Jesus was not asking to take the disciples out of the world with Him, because first they had to be sanctified. And He was not only talking about the disciples, because He said, "I do not ask in behalf of these alone, but for those also who believe in Me through their word" (John 17:20). He was talking about us, because we have believed in Christ through their words. He continued His prayer, "That they may all be one; even as Thou, Father, art in Me, and I in Thee, that they also may be in Us; that the world may believe that Thou didst send Me" (John 17:21). It is not enough for Jesus to commission us to go witness to the world. There's no efficacy in that alone. What counts is if the world believes what we are saying, and that is dependent on our oneness. Oneness and being filled with the Holy Spirit are what make our testimony work. You cannot separate Christ's commission that we speak the Gospel to the whole world from His prayer that we be one.

In Christ's prayer, He gave us a key. He said, "And the glory which Thou hast given to Me I have given to them; that they may be one, just as We are one" (John 17:22). It is God's glory resting upon the Body of Christ that allows us to move into this oneness. We should be crying out for the glory of God to return to the house of the Lord, because the glory is what makes us one. We need something; we will not be able to work this up on our own. To become one, we need to have the glory of the Lord, the glory that Christ has given to His bride. "I in them, and Thou in Me, that they may be perfected into one, that the world may know that Thou didst send Me, and didst love them, even as Thou didst love Me" (John 17:23). Can you really accept what this is saying? You have to believe that God literally loves you as much as, and the same as, He loves Jesus; and that Jesus has sent you exactly the same way that the Father sent Him. Those are two things that require a little bit of mind-expanding. But this was Christ's prayer for us, and I believe that God will make it work. Every time you get discouraged and say, "How will this bride, the Body of Christ, ever become one?" just read this prayer and say, "God would never deny His Son's request; therefore, there will be a bride of Christ." It will be without spot or wrinkle or any such thing, because the Father will make it happen. He will bring the glory which Christ imparted to us, and that glory will make us one.

We started out this message by asking, "Is there a bride of Christ? Is it a true concept? Is it scriptural?" We are ending by saying that **we** must be the bride of Christ. We must be God's people who have prepared ourselves, and have put on the linen, clean and white, without spot or wrinkle. Jesus prayed for this and the Father will fulfill it. But in fulfilling it, He will not pretend that it is done. He will have an actual fulfillment, which means that we, as the global bride of Christ, must become the pure virgin that the Scriptures speak of. Let's face it; we will either be one of the wise virgins or one of the foolish virgins. We must seek to become the wise virgins.

> For you were called to freedom, brethren; only do not turn your freedom into an opportunity for the flesh, but through love serve one another. For the whole Law is fulfilled in one word, in the statement, "You shall love your neighbor as yourself." But if you bite and devour one another, take care lest you be consumed by one another. But I say, walk by the Spirit, and you will not carry out the desire of the flesh. For the flesh sets its desire against the Spirit, and

the Spirit against the flesh; for these are in opposition to one another, so that you may not do the things that you please. But if you are led by the Spirit, you are not under the Law. Now the deeds of the flesh are evident, which are: immorality, impurity, sensuality, idolatry, sorcery, enmities, strife, jealousy, outbursts of anger, disputes, dissensions, factions, envying, drunkenness, carousing, and things like these, of which I forewarn you just as I have forewarned you that those who practice such things shall not inherit the kingdom of God. But the fruit of the Spirit is love, joy, peace, patience, kindness, goodness, faithfulness, gentleness, self-control; against such things there is no law. Now those who belong to Christ Jesus have crucified the flesh with its passions and desires. If we live by the Spirit, let us also walk by the Spirit. Let us not become boastful, challenging one another, envying one another. (Galatians 5:13-26)

Look at all of the aspects of the flesh that deal directly with division: "enmities, strife, jealousy, outbursts of anger, disputes, dissensions, factions, envying." These are the elements that divide us. An interesting word that applies to this division is "enmities." Enmity means "mutual hatred or ill will…deep-seated dislike or ill will. Enmity suggests absolute hatred which may be open or concealed, an unspoken enmity."[23]

Enmity means pure hatred. That accurately describes the way many in Christianity relate toward other churches and denominations. This is certainly the relationship that Protestants have had toward Catholics for a long time. Most denominations in Christianity began as a church split. What is often the root of a church split? There is some type of enmity. There is some type of strife, anger,

---

[23] *Merriam-Webster's Collegiate Dictionary*, 11th ed., s.v. "Enmity."

dispute, dissension, faction, or envying. Unfortunately, many things in the Church today that we call differences are not really differences created by the Holy Spirit. I believe in the differences and diversity that the Holy Spirit brings (1 Corinthians 12:4-6). There should be many different groups and churches, but their differences should be based on the diversity of the Holy Spirit's gifts, ministries, and various functions. Born out of the diversity of the Holy Spirit, we should all be able to be one. However, as we look out on the landscape of the Church today, most of the divisions and separations we see arise out of the fruit and deeds of the flesh. They are born out of enmity, strife, jealousy, outbursts, disputes, and dissensions.

We are looking for something different. Love, joy, peace, patience, kindness, goodness, faithfulness, gentleness, and self-control—those are the qualities that God wants in the bride of Christ. You can feel the marriage anointing in what Paul was writing to the Galatians. Christ is saying to His bride, "Those who belong to Me, those who will marry Me, have crucified the flesh with its passions and desires." You cannot minimize Jesus' requirement that the disciples be one and be filled with the Holy Spirit before they began to witness. That is what we need in this day also. That is what this great bride of Christ needs. We need to be filled with the Spirit and move in the oneness that Christ proclaimed. We are called to be the bride of Christ; we are to marry Him at His return. What a beautiful calling! What a fantastic door that God has opened for us! It is a tremendous destiny. But we exclude ourselves from being Christ's bride when we get caught up in division and strife. He is not excluding us; we are excluding ourselves. The Body of Christ has to stop pointing the finger at one another. We have to stop the division. We have to come before the Lord and put on those robes of white

---

1 Corinthians 12:4-6 Now there are varieties of gifts, but the same Spirit. [5] And there are varieties of ministries, and the same Lord. [6] And there are varieties of effects, but the same God who works all things in all persons.

linen, the beautiful works of the saints, which represent the oneness that we are coming into.

When I would get in trouble as a child, my parents would say, "You can't control other people, but you can control yourself. Don't blame your problems on somebody else. You're responsible for your thoughts, your actions, and what you are doing." That is a good place for all of us to start. We cannot excuse our division by saying, "Everyone else is divided." God is not going to buy that. We must accept the responsibility that we can control our own thoughts, actions, words, and deeds. Is there a bride of Christ? Yes. The good news is that every one of us has the opportunity to accept this election as His bride. Our hearts should be joyful, yet live in the repentance necessary to become the bride of Christ. Lord, we open our hearts to be Your bride. We want to marry You.

Chapter 32

Our Oneness – The Measure of His Glory

August 3, 2014
Church of the Living Word, North Hills, California

In this message to the local church congregation in Los Angeles, the Lord illuminated John 17:22, providing a capstone for this book. "And the glory which Thou hast given Me I have given to them; that they may be one, just as We are one."

When we look around at the landscape of Christianity today we see so much division, both globally and locally. How do we become one? Out of this burden to see a real change, we have been discussing the principles of oneness, and how to effectively apply those principles. I want to continue that discussion by examining something that really grabbed my attention out of John chapter 17. I believe it is going to help us a great deal in our faith for oneness.

In His prayer to the Father, Jesus said, "And the glory which Thou hast given Me I have given to them; that they may be one, just as We are one" (John 17:22). Here Jesus expresses the very unique idea that the glory of Christ is given to enable us to come into oneness. We all know that we are to be one, but we grapple with how to actually achieve it, so it is no small thing that Jesus would say, "I gave them My glory to enable them to come into oneness." We need to understand and exercise what Jesus is talking about.

"Glory" is a term that we are all familiar with. It is used in many ways about many different things. But we want to understand the main concepts about the term "glory" as expressed in the Bible. To really understand what the glory of God is all about, we need to look into the Hebrew meanings of the term. We will use a lexicon titled *Dictionary of Biblical Languages With Semantic Domains: Hebrew (Old Testament)*.[24] The Hebrew word for glory is *kā·bôd* (pronounced KA-'VOD). We will go over ten basic meanings of that word out of this lexicon. A lexicon is simply a dictionary containing definitions for words in another language. As with any dictionary, a word can have multiple definitions. It is important to recognize that the concept of glory has a very broad application in the Bible and can mean many things, depending on how it is used or in what specific Scripture it is used.

The first definition of *kā·bôd* is "splendor." Number two is "honor" or "respect, i.e., the attribution of high status to a person." Glory could be the status you give to a person, such as glorifying someone as a king. The third definition is "wealth"; in other words, "what is valued and abundant." Number four is "manifestation of power." Number five is "glorious presence," expressing the idea of something that is magnificent and awe-inspiring. Number six is "reward, i.e., giving of a gift." That seems almost out of place with what we usually think of as glory. Number seven is "vast wealth, wealth of riches, very extensive wealth and possessions." In the eighth definition, glory can actually be the identifier of a person. Many Scriptures regarding the glory are about seeing the Lord Himself. In other words, the glory is the Lord. The ninth definition is "the Glory," which is used occasionally as a title for God. Most of the time "glory" is not capitalized, but it is when it used as a direct name for God in the Bible. In definition number ten, glory can mean "ruler,

---

[24.] James Swanson, *Dictionary of Biblical Languages With Semantic Domains: Hebrew (Old Testament)*, electronic ed. (Oak Harbor: Logos Research Systems, Inc., 1997), s.v. "kā·bôd."

men of high rank, or ones who govern." This definition of glory is very much a human expression. The Bible often applies the word "glory" to things in nature. 1 Corinthians chapter 15 says,

> There are also heavenly bodies and earthly bodies, but the glory of the heavenly is one, and the glory of the earthly is another. There is one glory of the sun, and another glory of the moon, and another glory of the stars; for star differs from star in glory. (1 Corinthians 15:40-41)

Everything in creation has its own glory. These definitions of the word "glory" show that it has many different meanings and uses throughout the Scriptures. But our focus is on what Jesus meant when He said, "I have given them My glory, to enable them to be one." What is the glory Jesus spoke of, and how can we see it expressed in our lives? Jesus said the glory literally does something. He gave us His glory that we might become one, so in His glory there must be an enabling for us to change and become something different.

> "And the glory which Thou hast given Me I have given to them; that they may be one, just as We are one; I in them, and Thou in Me, that they may be perfected into one, that the world may know that Thou didst send Me, and didst love them, even as Thou didst love Me. Father, I desire that they also, whom Thou hast given Me, be with Me where I am, in order that they may behold My glory, which Thou hast given Me; for Thou didst love Me before the foundation of the world." (John 17:22-24)

Beyond giving us His glory that we might become one, Christ also prayed that we could literally behold the same level of glory that He had with the Father before the foundation of the world. He prayed that we would be where He is, beholding the Father's glory.

We see this same idea expressed in 2 Corinthians chapter 3: "Having therefore such a hope, we use great boldness in our speech, and are not as Moses, who used to put a veil over his face that the sons of Israel might not look intently at the end of what was fading away" (2 Corinthians 3:12-13). We know that when Moses went up to the mountain, he cried out to God, "Show me Your glory!" (Exodus 33:18). I believe that what Moses was asking was, "Let me see You," and the Lord answered him in that context. He said, "No man can see Me and live, but I can cause My glory to pass by you" (Exodus 33:20-22). Moses did not see the fullness of God, but he saw some of God's glory and was literally transformed by it. When he came down from the mountain, his face shone (Exodus 34:29-30). Isn't this what happened to Jesus on the Mount of Transfiguration? He was transfigured and His face shone as the sun as He looked upon the glory of the Father that also was surrounding Moses and Elijah (Matthew 17:1-3).

If Jesus Himself was transformed by glory, don't you think it will have an effect on us as well? As people who really love the Lord and are trying to walk with God, we look for change. We look for change in our spirits, change in our souls, and change in our physical

---

Exodus 33:18 Then Moses said, "I pray Thee, show me Thy glory!"

Exodus 33:20-22 But He said, "You cannot see My face, for no man can see Me and live!" [21] Then the LORD said, "Behold, there is a place by Me, and you shall stand there on the rock; [22] and it will come about, while My glory is passing by, that I will put you in the cleft of the rock and cover you with My hand until I have passed by."

Exodus 34:29-30 And it came about when Moses was coming down from Mount Sinai (and the two tablets of the testimony were in Moses' hand as he was coming down from the mountain), that Moses did not know that the skin of his face shone because of his speaking with Him. [30] So when Aaron and all the sons of Israel saw Moses, behold, the skin of his face shone, and they were afraid to come near him.

Matthew 17:1-3 And six days later Jesus took with Him Peter and James and John his brother, and brought them up to a high mountain by themselves. [2] And He was transfigured before them; and His face shone like the sun, and His garments became as white as light. [3] And behold, Moses and Elijah appeared to them, talking with Him.

bodies. Beholding the glory of the Lord will become the vehicle for our change, transformation, and transfiguration, just as it was for Jesus. Paul continues on with this idea of the glory and says that it truly is the instrument of our change:

> Now the Lord is the Spirit; and where the Spirit of the Lord is, there is liberty. But we all, with unveiled face beholding as in a mirror the glory of the Lord, are being transformed into the same image from glory to glory, just as from the Lord, the Spirit. (2 Corinthians 3:17-18)

You can search through the Scriptures, as I have done for a long time, asking, "Lord, I want to change. How do I change?" This verse provides the most clear, concise, and specific method of change that you will find anywhere in the Bible. While you behold the glory of the Lord, you are changed from glory to glory. The change may not be instant or complete, but while you are beholding the glory of the Lord, you are changed into the same image of that glory you are beholding. In this Scripture, we define glory as meaning God, or Christ. This means we are changing into the very image of Their glory; we are becoming as Christ is. That is the transformation. It may be a process, and we don't know how long it will take, but process can be wonderful compared to not changing at all! Do you feel like you've been stuck in the same place for a long time? How do you get out of it? Find the way to behold the glory of the Lord until you're changed.

In some ways this may seem different than what we read about in John chapter 17, but it really is not. When we talk about oneness, we are talking about the very personality of God. One of the greatest prayers of the Hebrew people is *Shema, Yisraeil! Adonai Eloheinu, Adonai echad*! "Hear, O Israel! The Lord is our God, the Lord is one!" (Deuteronomy 6:4). This is called a commandment; but how do you perform a commandment that simply states that God is one (Deuteronomy 6:1)? You must behold the Lord. You cannot try to perform this commandment; you must behold Him until you become the Glory that you behold. The first and greatest thing we must do is see that the nature of God is one. We all understand how important it is that the Body of Christ moves into oneness. And we know that we should be striving with everything within us to become absolutely one. Why? It is not because it is convenient, or because it will solve arguments or disputes among us. It is because the very nature of God is one.

God is also love (1 John 4:8, 16). When Jesus was asked, "What is the foremost commandment of all?" He took the Old Testament expression "God is one" and the New Testament expression "God is love" and brought them together into one declaration: "THE LORD OUR GOD IS ONE LORD; AND YOU SHALL LOVE THE LORD YOUR GOD WITH ALL YOUR HEART, AND...YOU SHALL LOVE YOUR NEIGHBOR AS YOURSELF" (Mark 12:29-31). Jesus was saying that we must become like God; we become His nature. That is what He meant when He prayed, "I have given them My glory, that they may be one." He defined what oneness is. He did not say, "I want them to be one." He said, "The glory which Thou hast given Me I have given to them; that they may be one, just as We are one" (John 17:22). It is not just any oneness. It is the oneness that Christ had with the Father. It is the oneness that is the very nature of God. Jesus was speaking about a tremendously deep transformation. As we read in 2 Corinthians 3:18, we change from glory to glory into the same

---

Deuteronomy 6:1 "Now this is the commandment, the statutes and the judgments which the LORD your God has commanded me to teach you, that you might do them in the land where you are going over to possess it."

1 John 4:8 The one who does not love does not know God, for God is love.

1 John 4:16 And we have come to know and have believed the love which God has for us. God is love, and the one who abides in love abides in God, and God abides in him.

image. What is the image? The image is the glory of the Lord. This change is a change into His likeness.

Why is it essential that the Church becomes one? Because only as we are one do we represent the Father, the Son, and the Holy Spirit to the world. It is the very nature of God Himself that is being etched upon our hearts progressively, step by step, from glory to glory, until we become one. When we are one, we are in the likeness of God. Jesus said, "If you had seen Me, you would have seen the Father also" (John 14:7). Why? Because He was one with the Father. There was no difference between Jesus and the Father. Do you see where this oneness is leading us? It is not a doctrine. It has a purpose even greater than restoring the power of the Holy Spirit to the Church. It encompasses the very purpose of God. Jesus came to reconcile us to the Father, so that we would come into the very nature of the Father. Do we really see in our minds how great His purpose is? I think it is something that we do not yet grasp.

In the Hebrew Scriptures, when we read about a sanctuary, tent of meeting, or place where God comes and speaks to His people, we usually find one attending manifestation: God's glory. In the wilderness, the people built the tabernacle under Moses' direction. "Then the cloud covered the tent of meeting, and the glory of the LORD filled the tabernacle" (Exodus 40:34). The glory of God always rested on the tabernacle in the wilderness, and His glory was again manifested at the dedication of Solomon's Temple. After the Temple was constructed, as soon as the priests came in from the holy place, "the cloud filled the house of the LORD, so that the priests could not stand to minister because of the cloud, for the glory of the LORD filled the house of the LORD" (1 Kings 8:10-11).

John 14:7 "If you had known Me, you would have known My Father also; from now on you know Him, and have seen Him."

This idea of God's glory filling the tabernacle, sanctuary, or place of His dwelling, continues into the New Testament Scriptures, which describe us as being built together into the temple of God (Ephesians 2:21-22). "Do you not know that you are a temple of God, and that the Spirit of God dwells in you?" (1 Corinthians 3:16). God is creating His people into the place of His dwelling so that we will be filled with His glory. As His Spirit dwells in us, the glory of the Lord will no longer be limited to a temple or a dwelling. Read Numbers 14:20-21: "So the LORD said, 'I have pardoned them according to your word; but indeed, as I live, all the earth will be filled with the glory of the LORD.'" We are looking for a time when the entire earth will be filled with God's presence so that all can behold Him. And the more that all are able to behold Him, the more they will be changed from glory to glory into His likeness. So we understand that the heart of God is for His glory to expand from a temple into something that fills the whole world.

As we continue our study of the glory of the Lord, we find something tragic taking place. The time when the glory of the Lord filled the Temple, as it did in the days of Solomon, did not last. When the people of Israel sinned and did not walk with God, they were taken away into captivity in Babylon. During that time the glory of God left the Temple. Ezekiel's vision in chapters 10 and 11 is very picturesque in its depiction of how it happened. It was a slow process. God's presence did not just disappear. Slowly but surely, it began to leave the Temple. Ezekiel saw it happen in stages. First the glory of the Lord rose from the Temple and stood above the cherubim. Then the cherubim began to move, carrying the glory,

---

Ephesians 2:21-22 In whom the whole building, being fitted together is growing into a holy temple in the Lord; [22] in whom you also are being built together into a dwelling of God in the Spirit.

and stood over the east gate (Ezekiel 10:18-19). It stayed there for a while, then left the Temple, and left Jerusalem, and moved to a mountain east of the city (Ezekiel 11:22-23). We know that moving to the east out of the doors of the Temple takes you to the Mount of Olives. The glory rested there for a time, and then departed completely and Israel was left without the presence of God. Later we read another vision of the glory in Ezekiel: "Then he led me to the gate, the gate facing toward the east; and behold, the glory of the God of Israel was coming from the way of the east. And His voice was like the sound of many waters; and the earth shone with His glory" (Ezekiel 43:1-2). The gate mentioned by Ezekiel is called the Golden Gate. This gate was sealed by Suleiman in the 16th century. According to Jewish tradition, he did this to block the Messiah's entry into Jerusalem and the Temple.

The prophecies of Ezekiel are prophecies of the departure and the return of the glory of the Lord. I believe that those prophecies are not just about what happened to Israel, but also about what has happened, and will happen, to the Church. In its beginning, the Church experienced the glory of the Lord. The people, who were God's temple in that day, were filled with His glory. This was not the tabernacle of Moses in the wilderness, or the Temple of Solomon, but it was the 120 who were in the upper room on the Day of Pentecost. The Holy Spirit came, and the glory of the Lord rested on them in tongues of fire and flashes of sound, like the sound of many

---

Ezekiel 10:18-19 Then the glory of the LORD departed from the threshold of the temple and stood over the cherubim. [19] When the cherubim departed, they lifted their wings and rose up from the earth in my sight with the wheels beside them; and they stood still at the entrance of the east gate of the LORD's house. And the glory of the God of Israel hovered over them.

Ezekiel 11:22-23 Then the cherubim lifted up their wings with the wheels beside them, and the glory of the God of Israel hovered over them. [23] And the glory of the LORD went up from the midst of the city, and stood over the mountain which is east of the city.

waters described in Ezekiel (Acts 2:2-3). A great glory rested upon the Church at its beginning.

As we read those early chapters of the Book of Acts, we see that everything that took place transpired because they were a people living in the midst of the glory. They were a people filled with the glory of the Lord, and that glory was transformational. There was a dramatic difference in the disciples' abilities and capacities after the Day of Pentecost. They were transformed from glory to glory into the very image of Christ. As the Church began and thousands were being added day by day, the glory of the Lord continued to rest upon them when they came together and worshipped (Acts 2:46-47). The glory of the Lord filled them, and the glory of the Lord was manifested to the world around them. People said of them, "These that have turned the world upside down have come here also" (Acts 17:6). Just Peter's shadow falling on someone standing in the street would be the occasion of a healing and a miracle (Acts 5:15). So much happened, and it was not only through the apostles; it was through the congregation also. As they all prayed—in one voice and one accord—the place where they stood was shaken and they all

---

Acts 2:2-3 And suddenly there came from heaven a noise like a violent, rushing wind, and it filled the whole house where they were sitting. [3] And there appeared to them tongues as of fire distributing themselves, and they rested on each one of them.

Acts 2:46-47 And day by day continuing with one mind in the temple, and breaking bread from house to house, they were taking their meals together with gladness and sincerity of heart, [47] praising God, and having favor with all the people. And the Lord was adding to their number day by day those who were being saved.

Acts 17:6 And when they did not find them, they began dragging Jason and some brethren before the city authorities, shouting, "These men who have upset the world have come here also."

Acts 5:15 To such an extent that they even carried the sick out into the streets, and laid them on cots and pallets, so that when Peter came by, at least his shadow might fall on any one of them.

began to speak the Word of God with boldness (Acts 4:31). They all became the vessels of God to speak His Word and to manifest His presence. There was a glory that rested on the early Church that was as real, or even more real, than the glory that rested on Solomon's Temple, or that rested on Moses when he came down from the mountain, or that remained on the tent of meeting in the wilderness. The Church had a true glory, the glory of Christ that rested upon them and made them one.

The Book of Acts relates how the disciples were all one, and none of them considered that anything was their own, but they had all things in common (Acts 2:44-45). Some people say, "That was a commune. It was Communism." They are missing the point. It was oneness. They did not hold anything they owned to themselves because they were one. Oneness existed in the early Church. Why? Because Jesus gave His glory to the Church, that we would be enabled to be one. We therefore have to ask the question, "Has the Church literally experienced the departure of the glory of God just as Israel did?" Maybe you react to that question and think, "That's a horrible accusation!" But if we are honest, based on the state of oneness in the Body of Christ, we would have to say that something has been lost.

If the glory of the Lord is given in order that we may be one, then what is the measure of the presence of Christ, or the presence of the Father in our midst? **Our oneness is the measure**. If the glory was given for that purpose, then let's not fool ourselves and say, "Oh, we have such a fantastic presence of the Lord! We came to the service

---

Acts 4:31 And when they had prayed, the place where they had gathered together was shaken, and they were all filled with the Holy Spirit, and began to speak the word of God with boldness.

Acts 2:44-45 And all those who had believed were together, and had all things in common; [45] and they began selling their property and possessions, and were sharing them with all, as anyone might have need.

this morning and the glory was there!" "How do you know the glory was there?" "There were signs of it. There was a cloud. There were other manifestations." Remember the definitions of "glory" in the Scriptures. The cloud is not the glory of the Lord. There is only one true measurement of His glory, and that is oneness. If you are saying that you had the presence of the Lord, then tell me about the oneness that came to pass. Tell me about the transformation. We can be in a service and say, "Wow, the presence of God was so thick! The glory of the Lord was manifested!" Then show me the change that took place. If there is glory, there will be change. If the glory of the Lord is in our midst, we will be transformed.

If the glory of the Lord transformed Jesus Christ, then it will transform us. If there is no oneness, we really do not have the glory, or the presence of the Lord, that we should have. We have lost something. You may say, "We haven't lost all of it!" Praise God for that. But I would say we have lost quite a bit. To me, it is a heartbreak. We are trying to reach the Body of Christ with a burden to become one, but what is really the issue? Is it that we are not one, or that we have lost the presence of Christ in our midst? Is the lack of oneness saying something bigger than just the fact that there are schisms and divisions? Is it saying that Jesus has left and nobody really noticed? That is what happened in Ezekiel's day. Slowly, progressively, the presence of God left.

Let's have a positive faith. If the prophecy of the glory departing has been fulfilled, then let's believe that we are closer to His return. Let's believe that we are in the time when the prophecy is fulfilled that the presence of God begins to return from the east. It begins to shine. It begins to ring out like the sound of many waters, many nations of the earth coming together. Let there be something in our hearts that rises up and believes that no matter what we have lost, it is not the end of the story. Our hearts are set on a day of restoration. Do we need to repent? Yes. Do we need to break our hearts before the

Lord? Yes. Do we need to cry out to God? We do. We need to cry out for our own congregations and for the global Body of Christ.

In the Book of Matthew we read,

> And Jesus came up and spoke to them, saying, "All authority has been given to Me in heaven and on earth. Go therefore and make disciples of all the nations, baptizing them in the name of the Father and the Son and the Holy Spirit, teaching them to observe all that I commanded you; and lo, I am with you always, even to the end of the age." (Matthew 28:18-20)

Jesus promised that we could have His presence with us. The phrase "I am with you always" is better translated from the Greek as, "I am with you every day. I am with you from day to day." That is more expressive. There does not have to be a single day in which we are without the presence of Christ in our lives. That is what He promised. He is saying, "Today you can have My glory. Today you can have My presence. I am with you today, the next day, and every day until the end of the age." There is no reason for us not to experience His wonderful presence every day. Jesus said, "Wherever two or three gather, I'm in their midst" (Matthew 18:20). That needs to be our experience, not a doctrine. It needs to be something that we realize we must initiate. Let's bring Jesus back to the Church. Let's have His presence return in our personal lives, in the lives of our families, and in the lives of our churches. Let's see something spark a real change in the entire Body of Christ.

Jesus said, "I give you My glory." If that glory has departed, I believe we can bring it back. We have the prophecy that tells us we can bring it back. We know how to repent. We know how to seek God

---

Matthew 18:20 "For where two or three have gathered together in My name, there I am in their midst."

until something changes. We can reach in and see the glory of God, the very presence of the Lord, fill our services until every time we come together there is a change from glory to glory, until we are all changed and brought into His presence. We have a gauge that we can check every day: our oneness. Are we becoming more one? John Stevens, the founder of our churches, expressed this same idea in a book titled *Bonded Together*:

> We are going to see the glory. Let me explain how it will take place. In John 17:22, Jesus said, "The glory which Thou hast given unto Me, I have given unto them that they all may be one." When you see the unity [or the oneness], you are seeing the evidence of the glory [or the presence of the Lord]. Whether you see the glory visibly or not, the unity that is here is the evidence of it. I would rather see the unity in the Body and know that this is the sign of true glory, than to see a cloud that has not yet reached the people because the unity has not yet been worked in them. We know the glory is with us because we are really moving into a oneness.[25]

The oneness of the Body of Christ will be the sign of His return. I believe that Jesus will return in that way before He is visibly seen and establishes His Kingdom. Let's not forget that oneness is His personality. It is His nature. The nature of God will begin to fill our hearts and we will be one. In that oneness we will know that the presence of Christ, the presence of the Father, and the presence of the Holy Spirit are with us and in us (John 14:17).

John 14:17 "That is the Spirit of truth, whom the world cannot receive, because it does not behold Him or know Him, but you know Him because He abides with you, and will be in you."

[25.] John Robert Stevens, "Together," in *Bonded Together*, (North Hollywood, CA: The Living Word, 1974), 89-90.

The Lord has exposed us with this Word. This shows us the truth about where we are. I don't like the fact that we do not see the sign of His glory. Lord, we contend for that day. We have lost so much, but we are not crying over the fact that we have lost oneness. We are not crying over the fact that we struggle with unity. We weep because we have lost Your presence. Let this Word work deeply in our spirits. Lord Jesus, we humble our hearts and ask for the fulfillment of the great prophecy of Ezekiel. Let the presence of the Father return to Your house. We hunger for Your presence and all that it brings—the transformation of our lives, our spirits, and the transformation of our physical bodies. We cry, "Come into our midst, Lord Jesus." We ask you, as Solomon did, to make this your dwelling place, Lord. If we have sinned and we return to You and humble our hearts, you have promised that your glory will return (2 Chronicles 7:14). Lord, we ask that Your glory, Your presence, return now to Your house. We ask it in Jesus' name. Amen.

---

2 Chronicles 7:14   "And My people who are called by My name humble themselves and pray, and seek My face and turn from their wicked ways, then I will hear from heaven, will forgive their sin, and will heal their land."

Endorsements

Mahesh and Bonnie Chavda,
Chavda Ministries International

Is Christ Divided? trumpets what is surely the most important and timely prophetic voice of the hour. The Body of Christ is standing on the brink of historic reformation and hope is risen out of Christ's undivided heart. Our Great Shepherd is beckoning His sheep to "Come together" and return to the fold as one. In *Is Christ Divided?* Gary Hargrave sees "God is bringing us back to the original experience as an *ekklesia* that we read about in the Book of Acts (2:38, 41-42)…the new commandment that Jesus gave us."

Western civilization is at a crossroads. We must not miss this window. The great power and abundant grace the church of the first Pentecost demonstrated was witnessed and experienced in order that the devastated world of their day might believe and receive the Gospel. As *Is Christ Divided?* reminds us, those who believe are destined to be of one heart and one soul…not one claiming that anything belonging to him—including doctrine and history—is his own, but rather, holding all things in community with one another (Acts 4:32). As Gary says, in this convergence of believers we are not "trying to duplicate what existed in the ecumenical movement of the past. ...We are approaching this time in a new way. ...It is about this commandment to love...that love will be the testimony." In this and only this word of Christ shall a stunned world find its heart and hope. By this blessed command we would see a release of salvation as Jesus prayed (John 17), with resulting apostolic grace falling to heal and deliver (Acts 5:15).

We each have an obligation and responsibility to honor our inheritance so freely shared in the redemption meal Jesus provides. May God's previously profaned name be cleared among the nations as He, for His own sake, shows Himself holy amidst a unified Body. The future of the world is at stake. As nations blaze with scorching fires of virulent cultural and ethnic prejudice and pride, the Spirit poured out on One Body of Christ can quench the Destroyer's fire.

Gary and Marilyn Hargrave and the apostolic community they continue to create have heaven's heart and ear. Bonnie and I are witnesses to the unique supernatural grace and gift Christ has given His Body in and through the Hargraves and the international Living Word Fellowship community. Theirs is truly the voice of an apostle, complete with attesting miracles confirming this word, freely and gracefully offered in *Is Christ Divided?*

For the sake of Christ, in memory of the faithful and martyrs, in faithfulness to our children, in keeping the desire and commission of Jesus, let us listen and do! We stand in the midst of Ezekiel's prophetic vision. Let bone come together with bone that there may be sinew, flesh, and breath, God's great army rising. *Is Christ Divided?* is your compass from the valley of division into the Father's Desire. Let us prepare our hearts and embrace His gift. *Is Christ Divided?* courageously and gracefully shows us the way home.

❖ ❖ ❖

Professor Matteo Calisi, Representative of Pope Francis for Christian unity and oneness, President and Founder of the Community of Jesus, in Bari, Italy

---

The Holy Spirit challenges us Christians to pursue the unity of the Church according to Jesus' desire and prayer "that they all may be one, Father, so that the world may believe" (John 17:21), and to remove the scandal of division in the Church.

Gary Hargrave's book is a daring call to overcome all misunderstandings and difficulties to reach Christians' unity. I thank him for having had this courage inspired by the Holy Spirit, which will be greatly edifying for many readers.

Today there are almost two billion Christians in the world thanks to the missionary expansion of the Church. Zealous missionaries have dedicated their lives to evangelize the world.

Unfortunately, despite the most honest intentions, our ecclesial divisions have arrived together with the missions. The Christian church has very quickly appeared divided before the world, and it is Christians' fault if the world has not been completely evangelized yet. The world has not believed in the Gospel when the Christian church has presented itself in various denominations and theologies.

We must admit that in many parts of the world the relationship among our churches is characterized by conflict much more than cooperation, by animosity much more than love, by suspicion much more than trust, by propaganda and ignorance much more than respect for truth.

The Christian nations, like the European ones that once were evangelized, are no longer giving honor and glory to the Lord, and Christians' division is one of the fundamental reasons. The sin wraps up the nations because Christians do not show love one to another, and the world will never believe in the Gospel we preach if we are divided among ourselves.

If the world has not known Jesus yet after two thousand years, the first commitment that should come from us Christians is, therefore, the sincere repentance for not having been faithful to the mission of the Gospel of our beloved Lord and Messiah.

The sin of division in the Church, to which many Christians appear even resigned, is so grave and diabolic. It's like a lethal gas that numbs the Christian community, a poison that "kills" the mission of the Church.

Christians' division is a sin that must be recognized and confessed with sincere repentance, because it has endangered the holiest cause of the Church, which is the evangelization.

As Catholics and Evangelicals, we are called to pray and cooperate with all Christians to fulfill Jesus' prayer in John 17, confessing our sins against the unity that Christ wants for all His disciples "so that the world may believe."

But at the same time, we must deeply trust that the prayer of Jesus to the Father will not go unheard. Jesus' prayer is infallible! This is a challenge the Spirit asks us to face, and that we must take on with courage. Amen!

Shlomo Hizak, President and Founder,
AMI Jerusalem Center for Biblical Studies and Research,
expert on Christian-Jewish relations

I am thankful to my God for your attitude of a Christian friend of Israel. Down through the centuries few Christians have been interested in discovering common roots of Jewish and Christian beliefs. Even fewer were interested in actively building positive relationships and understanding. Undoubtedly, your book underlines the need of building rather than confronting each other. Today more than ever we need the Biblical message of reconciliation.

❖ ❖ ❖

Cardinal Orani João Tempesta, O.Cist.,
Archbishop of Rio de Janeiro, Brazil

The pursuit of oneness is the great appeal of Jesus, which He addresses to the Father in prayer for us: "And not for them only do I pray, but for them also who through their word shall believe in me; That they all may be one, as thou, Father, in me, and I in thee; that they also may be one in us; that the world may believe that thou hast sent me" (John 17:20-21, DRB[*]).

The wonderful assurance that in God there is a dynamic of mutual self-giving in love, infuses in us the confidence that we are called to participate in this divine life, as we were created for this. God loves us with the same infinite love that unites Father and Son within the Holy Trinity.

---

[*] Douay-Rheims Bible

When we take possession of this truth, our life transforms itself radically as that same Love, poured forth into our hearts by the Holy Spirit who is given to us (Romans 5:5), sprouts from us to be taken to others. This is the testimony we need to give in our time, which challenges us on the true discipleship of Christ: "If God hath so loved us; we also ought to love one another" (1 John 4:11, DRB).

Every effort dedicated to this ideal of the Lord is welcome. I congratulate Gary Hargrave's work, which calls Christians to form one flock in the midst of a world divided by economic, political, and religious ideologies, testifying that only love is able to touch and unite the hearts.

❖   ❖   ❖

Bill Hart, Senior Pastor at
Cathedral of Praise in Austin, Texas

It's been forty years since I first met Gary and Marilyn Hargrave. Today my wife and I consider them as our dearest friends. There is no one more qualified to speak to the Church about unity than Gary. I have always admired how even when faced with rejection, trials and conflict his love and message of unity never waver. We are entering into the most exciting time in the history of the Church. Soon the world will see Christ manifesting through His sons. This book reveals the great power and destiny of a Church united. Understanding how unity is first of Spirit and then of Faith clarifies to the believer how unity can be more than a dream but a reality.

❖   ❖   ❖

Father Antonio José Afonso da Costa,
Doctor in Pastoral-Systematic Theology and
Systematic Theology Professor of the Pontifical
Catholic University in Rio de Janeiro, Brazil

> "Dialogue does not extend exclusively to matters of doctrine but engages the whole person; it is also a dialogue of love."
> –Pope John Paul II

About three years ago, the Lord gave me the joy of encountering a part of my "family" that I had never met before. We were generated in the same Blood, share the same origin, live in the same breath and dream, but still we did not know each other!

I am a Roman Catholic Priest in the city of Rio de Janeiro, in Brazil. About three years ago, God's ways led me to "Mount Zion," home to "The Living Word" in our region. There is no better way to describe the feeling I experienced when I arrived there than to say that I discovered brothers that I had not yet known. I was able to identify in those people, so loving and thirsty for God, something that I was also carrying within me. We could no longer walk apart! We started our journey from different points of departure, but we could no longer be separate from each other; we walk in the same direction, towards the target of "the fullness of life in Christ."

When I received the invitation to endorse Gary Hargrave's new book, *Is Christ Divided?* I felt very honored. I know that "loyalty" is an essential word in expressing the relationships between the members of "The Living Word." They believe in the power of lasting relationships and cultivate mutual respect and understanding. Therefore, I also know that this invitation was not just a formality; it was an expression of commitment in the sharing of a journey. And I, in my turn, could do nothing other than accept this request and show that "the commitment was accepted."

I wished to include, at the very beginning, a quote from Pope John Paul II's 1995 encyclical letter "Ut Unum Sint," that he wrote to address Catholics worldwide. In this document, which talks about the search for full and visible oneness among all who confess the Lord Jesus Christ, he states that, "At the Second Vatican Council, the Catholic Church committed herself irrevocably to following the path of the ecumenical venture, thus heeding the Spirit of the Lord, who teaches people to interpret carefully the 'signs of the times.'" I think Gary and all of the communities of "The Living Word" have been able to read and understand these signs, answering generously to the cry of the Spirit of God for our times.

We know in our constant sharing of an outcry and life, that us Roman Catholics, and the brothers of "The Living Word," have many distinct ecclesiological concepts. However, from the outset, we have found that this does not prevent us from walking together, learning from each other, and loving each other with "sincere affection." Therefore, both the Catholic and the Protestant Christian should not expect that the book you have in your hands is a summary of recent theological debates between experts. Surely, this is important, and has been carried out, but what Gary presents to us is not a theory about the oneness among Christians or a "magic theological equation," but a proposal for obedience to the will of the Lord Jesus who calls us today! What can we do now about our oneness? I find it striking how Gary was able to express, with loyalty to his origin and the many brothers within the Christian Reformation that hear him as a lucid and prophetic voice, a human and supernatural sensitivity regarding the urgent purpose of oneness among Christians. And I was moved, as a Catholic, with his concern to both learn and appreciate what he regarded as important contributions, from the Catholic side, to his understanding about the topic. This is oneness experienced, in motion!

I conclude where we began: the search for oneness is not limited around doctrinal problems. Oneness surrounds us entirely, as people, such that our dialogue is a dialogue of love. Otherwise, this search for oneness will have no lasting impact on the movement of God for our times. Gary and the members of "The Living Word" are challenging each of us, us as Catholics but also all Christians who desire to be faithful to the Commandment of the Lord, to face our quest for oneness as a path of continuous conversion of heart. It is there, in this place inside us, that it begins and where it should end, in a greater surrender to the loving Lord, our work for oneness.

❖ ❖ ❖

Daniel Gwertzman, AMI Jerusalem Center for Biblical Studies and Research, training church leaders in Christian-Jewish relations

---

I was very impressed after reading "A Case for Unity Between Christianity and Judaism" from your book *Is Christ Divided?* We each express ourselves in different ways. However, you have expressed a true love of Israel as being at the roots of your faith. Rather than rejecting the Jewish people and their faith, you show acceptance and a desire to learn how to bless so that you will be blessed.

I particularly liked your sentence: "We need to stop trying to evangelize our Jewish brothers; rather, we need to love and create a relationship with them." You are right; the need is to seek the Lord outside the wall of doctrines. According to the Late Professor David Flusser, at the time of the Second Temple there were twenty-four different Jewish sects. Despite this they all prayed in the Temple in Jerusalem. One of the greatest barriers to understanding is indeed Christian eschatological beliefs.

One must look to the rock one was hewn from. One must not divide Jerusalem, but rather come to seek unity in Jerusalem.

> Rejoice ye with Jerusalem, and be glad with her, all ye that love her: rejoice for joy with her, all ye that mourn for her: That ye may suck, and be satisfied with the breasts of her consolations; that ye may milk out, and be delighted with the abundance of her glory. For thus saith the Lord, Behold, I will extend peace to her like a river, and the glory of the Gentiles like a flowing stream: then shall ye suck, ye shall be borne upon her sides, and be dandled upon her knees. (Isaiah 66:10-12, KJV)

This vision of unity, blessing, and grace for all mankind can only be realized when the Gentiles no longer seek to replace the Jews. This is indeed an idea which is also found in the New Testament.

"Ye worship ye know not what: we know what we worship: for salvation is of the Jews." (John 4:22, KJV)

You have done a great work for the Lord in promoting unity in a time of division. May your words enter the hearts of all people.

"So then faith cometh by hearing, and hearing by the word of God." (Romans 10:17, KJV)

*Father Claudio Santana, Parish Priest
of Mary Mother of God Catholic Church,
in Rio de Janeiro, Brazil*

We know that since the birth of the modern Ecumenical movement, more than a century ago, there has always been a clear awareness of the fact that the lack of oneness among Christians impedes a more effective proclamation of the Gospel, as this lack endangers our credibility.

We also have to realize that by the Holy Spirit, which was poured out in the Upper Room and in the hearts of the faithful, this oneness was accomplished in a unique way between diverse races, peoples, and tongues (Acts 2). Paul tells us, "For in one Spirit were we all baptized into one body, whether Jews or Gentiles, whether bond or free [and I add, Catholics or Protestants]; and in one Spirit we have all been made to drink" (1 Corinthians 12:13, DRB).

Before you is an absolutely original, proposed reading concerning the theme of Oneness of the Body of Christ.

I recommend this work; for whoever comes to know Gary through this sweet and light reading will identify the heart of a man who hears God and is driven to build up other believers! Such is Gary's heart! He reveals, in a very clear way, through each written word, the concern to heed the urgency of the Gospel: Be one.

In this book, you will find a balanced view of a biblical-theological trajectory on the Oneness of the Body of Christ. I can affirm: this trajectory is a feature exclusive to this work. A revelation guided by two readings: the Protestant Thought, from the legacy left by the founder of the "The Living Word" churches, John Robert Stevens, and also the Magisterium of the Catholic Church in its documents, principally making reference to the Second Vatican Council.

We know that the Work of Oneness is a Work of the Holy Spirit. We cannot accomplish this Work within ourselves. In your hands is an excellent tool for the seeking of God's will, for in our contemporary world, all of society is hungry to see ourselves as followers of the Risen Christ, authentic and true. This is the purpose of this work! It was made "that the world may believe."

❖ ❖ ❖

About the Author

Gary Hargrave, along with his wife, Marilyn, are the fathering ministries of The Living Word Fellowship, an international group of church communities that are patterned after the early Church as it is described in the New Testament. Though he travels frequently in his ministry, Honolulu is the city Gary calls home. Having been raised in Hawaii, he has a deep love for the Hawaiian people and culture.

In the early years of his ministry, Gary received training and impartation from his spiritual father and mentor, John Robert Stevens. Gary, in turn, is now a spiritual father and mentor to many. Gary works alongside the love of his life, Marilyn, and keeps the family spirit at the center of everything he does. Gary is the founder and chancellor of Shiloh University, an accredited online Bible college and seminary, with its campus located in Kalona, Iowa.

As a prophetic voice to this generation, Gary has a passion for promoting the maturity of the individual believer, and he is driven to see the oneness of the worldwide Body of Christ. Gary works closely with many leaders in the Protestant, Catholic, and Jewish communities.

To find other publications by Gary Hargrave, go to www.livingwordpublications.com.